—— AND THE ——
RAIN CAME
TUMBLING
DOWN

THROUGH CANCER'S FLOOD
ON SOLID GROUND

KAREN KREHBIEL

Quantum
Discovery
A LITERARY AGENCY

Library of Congress Control Number: 2025904281

ISBN
979-8-89641-060-7 (Paperback)
979-8-89641-061-4 (eBook)
979-8-89641-059-1 (Hardcover)

TABLE OF CONTENTS

Acknowledgments xi

Foreword...xiii

Prologue...xv

Our Journey Begins...1

Home to Heal 8

Radiation and Chemotherapy..30

Gone Hunting..53

End of Radiation..73

Neutrophil Counts 80

Headed Home...96

Chemo: Round 1...123

Chemo: Round 2...135

Chemo: Round 3...147

MD Anderson Cancer Center 165

Seizures after Necrosis Surgery 183

Year 2...196

Our Second Christmas at Mercy..225

Physical Therapy...240

Home Health 250

Maple Lawn Manor...264

Gall Bladder Trouble 276

Seizures, Ventilator, and New Growth...................................282

Hospice 294

Transition from Earthly to Eternal 319

Things I Remember 321

Brittany Remembers: The Funeral.................................321

Hope on the Horizon 323

Endnotes 329

"Karen's spiritual insights made me bawl like a baby more than once."

—Ron Hays, Director of Farm Programming
Radio Oklahoma Network

"Jeff battled brain cancer with courage, dignity and at times- a bit of humor."

—Ron Hays, Director of Farm Programming
Radio Oklahoma Network

"And the Rain Came Tumbling Down, Through Cancer's Flood on Solid Ground' allowed me the opportunity to keep up with the cancer battle of Jeff Krehbiel, and provided encouragement to evaluate my own faith and appreciate the blessings in my own life."

—Oklahoma State Senator Ron Justice

"And the Rain Came Tumbling Down' is a living example of keeping your faith in God even in the midst of a trial."

—Alan Seibel, Associate Pastor, Oakwood Christian
Church, Enid, Oklahoma

"An incredible story and encouragement to others"

—Alan Seibel, Associate Pastor, Oakwood Christian
Church, Enid, Oklahoma

"An example of faith that has changed lives- the extent of which will only be realized in eternity."

—Terry Detrick, President, American
Farmers and Ranchers

"And the Rain Came Tumbling Down", by author Karen Krehbiel demonstrates first-hand the example of the "Perfect Peace" found only in Jesus Christ.'

—Terry Detrick, President, American

Farmers and Ranchers

"And the Rain Came Tumbling Down' is full of eloquent and beautiful messages that encourage and lift my heart."

—Lauren Binder, PA, Hydro, OK

ACKNOWLEDGMENTS

We would like to thank the untold number of individuals in the health care industry who cared for Jeff during his battle with cancer. Your career choices alone reflect your desire to help others through tough times.

Our special appreciation goes to Lauren Binder, PA, and the entire staff of Dr. Stutzman. Your genuine compassion for our family is a blessing beyond measure.

To the board members Jeff served with at the time of his diagnosis, you picked up the slack when Jeff's participation was limited. Thank you for allowing him to remain a part of your groups during his illness.

We continue to be humbled by our vast family in Christ who consistently petition Heaven's throne on our behalf. You are the physical arms, feet, and hands that continue to express our Heavenly Father's love to us.

For the indescribable peace that continues to encompass our lives, for the fulfilled promise that we never walk alone, for the guarantee of eternal life to those who trust in Him, for any influence our story may have to encourage others and spread the gospel of Jesus Christ—to God be all ultimate praise.

FOREWORD

Jeffery Allen Krehbiel was born September 9, 1963, to Wayne and Fern Krehbiel. On July 21, 1990, Jeff married Karen Sue Burkhalter. Their daughter, Brittany Vale, was born in September of 1995.

In September 2009, Jeff was diagnosed with glioblastoma, a very invasive form of brain cancer. For two years, Jeff, Karen, and Brittany fought side-by-side through many doctors' visits, radiation sessions, and the chemotherapy. This is their story.

During the early weeks of Jeff's illness, he would quite often post his own comments. You will smile, even laugh at times, at Jeff's wit. But you may also weep as you read his comments when you realize Jeff didn't win his battle with glioblastoma.

The title *And the Rain Came Tumbling Down* was chosen because of Karen's reference to the song "The Wise Man" in her post on August 16, 2011, during the final weeks of Jeff's illness.

When you reach the end of this book, you will be reminded that this journey doesn't really end after a two-year struggle with cancer. No! Those who know Jesus Christ in the free pardon of sin will be forever reunited in His eternal kingdom. The book ends with the exclamation "to be continued eternally."

—Glen E. Burkhalter

PROLOGUE

Karen Krehbiel

Over the last weekend of August 2009, our family moved from the home we had rented for nineteen years to within a mile of Jeff's childhood home. Looking back, there is no doubt God prepared this home for Jeff's time of illness. Jeff wasn't feeling well when we moved, so he let our hired men do most of the work.

The following Monday, Jeff woke with a headache. For the next ten days, signs we dismissed as flu symptoms became more apparent. Jeff was throwing up sporadically, sleeping more as the days went by, and continuing to have headaches.

On Tuesday, September 8, we closed on our home. Jeff was unable to keep a clear thought reading the documents. Wednesday was Jeff's forty-sixth birthday. He was still sick and sleeping almost around the clock. I would wake him up to make him eat and take some liquids because I was concerned he was getting dehydrated, but we still believed he just had flu.

Thursday afternoon, the tenth, I phoned to make a doctor's appointment for Jeff. Our family doctor's office in Weatherford was closed, so I called a physician's assistant in Hydro whom Jeff had seen several times. She was able to see Jeff the next morning! In retrospect, I believe these events were signs of God's hand implementing His plan for Jeff's care.

OUR JOURNEY BEGINS

09/20/09 (Sunday), 11:18PM-Karen

After dismissing Jeff's symptoms as flu for a week and a half, we scheduled a doctor's appointment for Friday, September 11. When reviewing his symptoms with the PA (physician's assistant), I mentioned that just that morning, Jeff chose the wrong word forming a comment about which town we were going to run some errands in after his appointment. Somehow, the circumstances of that comment prompted a CT scan that we later found out revealed the tumor. Having tests run on a Friday often means waiting over the weekend to receive the results. An appointment was made for us to review the CT results with the PA in her office on Monday morning.

Friday evening brought an increase in symptoms and additional trouble formulating answers to questions, but we were still uncertain as to what the CT results were.

Saturday, the twelfth, Jeff slept all day. Saturday evening's symptoms were even more extreme, with trouble choosing correct words. Our daughter, Brittany, finally convinced him that we needed to visit the ER. That visit was our first consult about his CT scan. The tumor was 4 cm in diameter and was on his left temple. The ER doctor recommended keeping the Monday appointment at which time the PA could schedule an appointment with a neurologist.

Monday, the 14th, we kept the appointment at the PA's office. When we arrived, we were overwhelmed with their kindness. The PA had already scheduled an MRI for Wednesday, the sixteenth, and an appointment with the neurosurgeon for Thursday, the seventeenth.

On Wednesday, after returning home from the MRI, I called the neurosurgeon's office for directions. When I gave the receptionist my name, she told me someone in their office was on the other line trying to call me. They had a cancellation and could see Jeff that afternoon.

When we met with the neurosurgeon, he recommended scheduling surgery as soon as possible. It was set for Monday, the 21st. He gave Jeff a prescription for a steroid to reduce the swelling in his brain and indicated that the RX would relieve the symptoms, which it has. Jeff's had several really good days. He was able to go to the football game on Friday and to Sunday school and church this morning. The symptoms are still apparent, but milder, for which I'm thankful.

Please keep our family in your prayers tomorrow as Jeff undergoes surgery. Once the pathology report is available, his treatment plan will be more definite.

We are trusting God to help us place each step we take on this new journey *"a lamp unto our feet, and a light unto our path"* (Psalms 119:105, KJV).

His Peace will sustain us in these days ahead.
Thanks for taking the time to "checkonjeff[1]."

Brittany Remembers:
Talking It Over With Dad

On Saturday evening, September 12, 2009, we took Dad to the emergency room at Weatherford. He had been picking the wrong words consistently that night and we were very concerned. As we drove Dad had a headache and was frustrated with the radio, so we turned it off.

The doctors pulled up Dad's CT scan and reports from Friday. That night we found out Dad had a tumor. The ER doctor said we should keep the doctor's appointment we had scheduled for Monday. There was very little they could do, so we went home.

As we got into the car and Mom started the engine, an amazing thing happened. The radio we had turned off before we got out of the car was on. It continues to amaze me how God comforted me with the song that began to play. The opening chords to "Live Like You Were Dying" by Tim McGraw came through the speakers. "He said, 'I was in my early forties, with a lot of life before me, when a moment came that stopped me on a dime.'" I was so devastated that night. When we got home, I ran upstairs and closed my door behind me. I wasn't ready to lose my dad.

I hadn't been in my room long when Dad knocked on my door. He pulled me into a hug and sat me down on the stairs beside him. I will never forget what he said to me that night. "Brittany, we are a family. We love each other so much, and we will make it through this. No matter what happens, we will see each other again. This isn't the end." Even with all the confusing sentences he had said that night, he had the clearness of mind to comfort me. I was, and still am, blessed by the words I heard him say. To this day, I can still hear his voice from that night.

09/21/09 (Monday), 1:19PM-Karen

Jeff came through surgery good. The surgeon removed as much of the tumor as he could. With this type of cancer, radiation and chemo will be standard treatment. The surgeon indicated that the cancer has most likely infiltrated the good brain tissue even on the other side of the brain, thus causing the need for the radiation and chemo to combat the cancer on a microscopic level.

Once the surgery was over, the surgeon checked Jeff for speech and movement. All seem to be well. Please continue to pray. Thank you for taking the time to checkonjeff.

09/21/09 (Monday), 7:41PM-Karen

Jeff's in ICU this evening and able to visit with a few visitors. Earlier, in recovery, he passed all the squeeze-and-poke testing as well as the name, location, and birthday info quiz. The surgeon is pleased with his status. A CT scan is planned for tomorrow morning to get an updated image of the surgery site. After reviewing the CT scan, they'll decide if he needs to stay another day in the ICU or if he can move to a regular room. I'm humbled by the number of calls, e-mails, and prayer chains. Thanks so much. God will guide us through this time.

But my God shall supply all your need according to his riches in glory by Christ Jesus.

Philippians 4:19 (KJV)

09/22/09, (Tuesday), 8:47AM-Karen

Jeff's brother stayed with him in neuro ICU last night. I was able to get some much-needed rest at my niece's home in Yukon. I'm grateful for a good night's sleep.

Jeff's sitting up some this morning and initiating conversations. Just last night, he seemed to limit his speaking to responses. In the night, he was taken for a CT scan and was wheeled out for an MRI at 8:30 AM. The surgeon is still pleased with his status but wants to keep Jeff in ICU another day. The surgeon indicated at our first appointment that two days in ICU would be expected, but that could vary.

Jeff cleaned his breakfast plate this morning. He probably lost seventeen pounds prior to surgery. Signs of a returning appetite are another blessing.

Everyone who knows Jeff will be glad to know his humor was not located in the area affected by the tumor. He still has his wit, as we are witnessing in his interaction with the staff.

Thank you for your support and, especially, your prayers. There have been so many contacts—calls, e-mails and cards to checkonjeff and encourage us.

09/22/09 (Tuesday), 2:42PM-Karen

Jeff's sitting in a chair! They have removed some of the tubes and the blood circulation leg massagers (not the technical term, I'm sure). He had some visitors and now has taken over the recliner. That position with remote in hand is bound to be comfortable. We're seeing improvement in the clarity of his thinking. He's on pain meds for the headache that comes and goes. He's sleeping quite a bit, especially after each pain pill.

Thanks for checking on us. Keep up the prayers.

09/22/09 (Tuesday), 10:59PM-Karen

Jeff was awake and alert most of the day. We had several visitors and lots of e-mail and posts. Thanks for taking time to read the updates. Jeff's surgeon, Dr. Reynolds, came by about seven this evening and discussed today's MRI with us. It shows a rim of cancer at the back of the original tumor site. This was discussed as a probable outcome of the surgery given the cancer type Jeff has. Dr. Reynolds will contact our oncologist tomorrow morning, and we may meet that specialist as early as tomorrow. Dr. Reynolds expects the radiation and chemo treatment to start in a couple of weeks. The two weeks are needed to allow the surgery site to heal before the radiation and chemo. Starting them too early would slow or stop rapid cell growth, which would include the surgery healing that is good for rapid cell growth. Jeff has another MRI scheduled for 4:00 AM. Dr. Reynolds will be able to review that MRI prior to transferring Jeff to a regular room. Thanks for reading the posts, and keep praying. We know *"all things work together for good to them that love God to them who are the called according to his purpose"* (Romans 8:28, KJV).

09/23/09 (Wednesday), 8:13AM-Karen

Dr. Reynolds gave orders to move Jeff to a regular room today. The drain has been removed from the surgery site. His IV has been stopped. Thanks for your concern, and especially, thanks for your prayers.

09/23/09 (Wednesday), 9:00AM-Karen

Jeff just took pain meds again. The last pain med was at noon yesterday. We didn't realize it had been so long. Another praise, and I had to share...

09/23/09 (Wednesday), 6:44PM-Karen

At ten forty-five this morning, Jeff was moved to intermediate care. About six thirty this evening, he was moved again to a regular room. Dr. Reynolds has spoken of a possibility of going home Thursday evening or Friday. He's sitting up and visiting and has been in good spirits again today. He was able to get a shower this afternoon that really felt good to him. He's had quite a few visitors and enjoyed each of them.

The pathology report confirms the cancer was glioblastoma. We haven't met with the oncologist yet. Keep us in your prayers.

09/24/09 (Thursday), 12:14AM-Karen

We met with our oncologist, Dr. Michael Keefer, this evening in Jeff's hospital room. He discussed Jeff's treatment plan with us. He confirmed Dr. Reynolds's plan to wait until Jeff heals from surgery (about two weeks) and then start radiation and chemo together. I believe he said radiation would be five days a week for five weeks (he may have said six days a week for six weeks). The chemo would continue for whatever time period was necessary based on periodic MRI scans. He said right now he plans Temodar,

which is available in a pill format and Avastin which is available in IV format and would need to be administered biweekly. He's seeing this combination produce good results. Keep praying that through the Holy Spirit working in us, God will show us where to place each step in our journey and grant us His Peace.

> The fruit of the Spirit is love, joy, peace, patience, kindness, goodness, faithfulness, gentleness and self-control, against such things there is no law.
>
> Galatians 5:22–23 (NIV)

As I type the list of the fruit of the Spirit, I notice a few others of which I could use a generous helping. Keep praying for us.

09/24/09 (Thursday), 9:29AM-Karen

Going home! Dr. Reynolds came by about seven and has released Jeff to go home. The hospital brought the release papers, and they have been signed. We are waiting on transport. Then we are headed out. He has a few meds he'll need from the pharmacy, and then we will be home. Keep up the prayer, and we will keep you updated on the appointments as we learn of them.

> But my God shall supply all your need according to his riches in glory by Christ Jesus.

Philippians 4:19 (KJV)

HOME TO HEAL

09/24/09 (Thursday), 8:02PM-Karen

Jeff's home, in his own recliner and settling in. He has been very active today—walking around, visiting, and even in his office by choice for a little while. We were on our way home this morning when a lady from radiology therapy called to schedule an appointment for next Tuesday. We are supposed to contact Dr. Reynolds, the neurosurgeon tomorrow to schedule an appointment to take the stitches out next week. All along they have said Jeff would have to heal a couple of weeks, and then we would start the radiation and chemo. Assuming we count from the surgery date, Jeff may start those treatments in a week or so. His incision looks very clean and a little like baseball stitching. Dr. Reynolds kept the incision inside his hairline, so eventually, the scar won't show.

We also learned Jeff's oncologist doesn't take new patients, and we were very blessed to be accepted… God continues to provide.

Thanks for the prayers. We know God's providing answers daily.

09/25/09 (Friday), 9:54PM-Karen

Jeff got up this morning and cooked bacon and eggs; walked around outside for a while; and then worked in the office some. He's getting stronger each day. He has an appointment

with radiation therapy on Tuesday and gets his stitches out on Thursday, the first.

Thanks for your prayers.

The peace of God, which passeth all understanding, shall keep your hearts and your minds through Christ Jesus.

Philippians 4:7 (KJV)

Karen Remembers:
Outward Signs of Inward Changes

Jeff earned a bachelor's degree in animal science from Oklahoma State University, had excellent command of the English language, and easily converted his thoughts to written documents. Anytime either of us wrote anything formal, we would ask each other to proof our writing and make sure the printed document was as close to perfect as possible. This proofing didn't change much, but occasionally, a second set of eyes will catch something the writer overlooked.

As Jeff wrote many of the early updates, he often asked me to proof them. When I realized his errors weren't just typos and misspelled words but a visible sign of damage from either the initial cancer, surgery, chemo, radiation, or necrosis—which is in effect radiation scarring—I intentionally stopped correcting his posts. I realized his mischosen words, misspelled names of people he knew well, wrong tense of verbs, etc., were things I never had to correct before, and they would be a sign to readers of his true medical condition. As such, Jeff's posts have not been altered. Instead, notes of clarification and/or correction have been added within brackets when needed.

09/26/09 (Saturday), 10:06PM-Jeff

This is Jeff, and this is going to be interesting. I haven't posted on this before, but I am going to try. As I try this, you must remember that they did remove part of my brain, so sometimes I forget what I am typing and will make a mess of this.

Things seem to be going pretty good, but I still have trouble with stamina. I feel pretty good and can do what ever I want, but I run out of energy before I run out of things I need to do.

This morning I cooked eggs and bacon again for breakfast and got ready to do somethings around the house. I am needing to do some paper work in the office, but I seem to run out of patience and will power before I get started. Therefore, I wind up not get started, let alone finishing. I do okay telling people what to do but I have a heard time putting it down with the computer. After breakfast I took a little nap; then we got ready to go to Weatherford. We took the paychecks by Dad's house and then went to check on the new dam being build on my pivot place. It really looks pretty good, and hopefully, we can finish it by the middle of next month. We headed to Weatherford and ate lunch and then went to Wal-Mart, United, and Braum's. We got our groceries and stuff and then headed home. I rode around in the cart most of the time and got along pretty good. I forgot to take my pain pills this afternoon. When we got home, I was worn out.

We had boiled shrimp for supper and a baked potato. This evening the girls worked on the television speakers. They finally got the speakers to work, and everything seems to be working properly.

Thanks for your prayers, and we will update again soon.

—Jeff K

Karen Remembers: Priorities

Jeff had brain surgery on Monday, was released from the hospital on Thursday, and was again in church on the following Sunday. Jeff took the spiritual responsibilities of serving as church deacon very seriously. What a wonderful example!

09/28/09 (Monday), 6:10AM-Jeff

Good morning all. Jeff here again, trying to start another day at the office.

I am feeling pretty good this morning, but I figure I will run out of gas before breakfast is finished. Then I can go back to bed, and you all can do all the work for today.

We had a good day yesterday, but when I get out to much, my legs want to go to sleep, and that causes me some pain. When they start hurting, there doesn't seem to be anything I can do to make them stop. So I walk and sit and drag my butt for a while until they get better. This usually takes about 10 minutes but seems like 2 hours. I think this will pass soon. I just need to be patient and give them a little time.

I don't know if I have overused them or underused them, but I have ticked them off.

I had a good visit yesterday with an old friend of mine that I have not seen in a while named Curt McMurtry. Curt is from the Willow area and now lives in the Fort Worth area. Him and his wife Hiedi was here most of the afternoon, and we had a good visit. I told lies on him, and he told lies on me, but since it was just him and I there at the time, no one really cared. They headed back to Fort Worth this evening.

We should learn a lot this week because they will get the information to us on the plan of attack to combat this cancer. I would ask that you would keep Karen and Brittany in your prayers every day. It is very hard on them to listen to the uncertainty and work the parameters they are delt. Tomorrow someone will find out a lot of what the plan is and where we will be and so forth. I

think it will take place mostly in OKC. We will try to get back on the sight and let you know. Well, it is 6:09, so I better get started with my breakfast duties pretty soon.

—Jeff K.

09/29/09 (Tuesday), 7:04AM-Jeff

Well, today will be a busy day. We go to OKC and meet with all the guys with letters behind their name. I will also get a CAT scan with dye in my blood so they can see where my intelligence actually lies. It should be an all-day process from what I understand. We also have to get some stuff for the house because we are behind getting it ready for the work that we need to start doing here. We have the offices set up, but we are not fully moved in yet, and I can only work a little while. Then I have to go take a nap. We have a big day, and I hope I don't run out of gas before we get started.

Thanks again for your prayers and words of encouragement. I had a good night last night, and I think I slept the most I have slept since the surgery. I went to bed at 11:00 and slept until 5:30 this morning. I am pretty sure that is the most since my surgery.

I plan on posting this evening or having Karen do it. When we find out what our options are. We may be to tired, and I may have to weight until the morning to do it.

Have a great day, and the Lord is King.

—JK

09/30/09 (Wednesday), 7:37AM-Jeff

First of all, Karen and I would like to say thank you for all your prayers yesterday because it was a tough day for us. This cancer is going to be very difficult to compete against, but we are up to the challenge, and from here, we are going to relay on the Lord and the doctors to do most of the work. Please continue to keep us in your thoughts and prayers for the future to see what it holds.

Now for the good stuff. The surgery was very successful for this type of cancer. They are waiting for the injury to heal so they can start the radiaton [radiation] on my head. The first thing they did was tell us about the procedure. They put me on a table similair [similar] to an MRI and made a mask of my face. This mask has dots on it that they will line up the radiation marks on, and then I will go to OKC every day, 5 days a week, for 7 weeks, and they will apply the radiation. After the first week or so, they will also start chemotheropy [chemotherapy] on the cancer, but they don't want to start it until after the healing from the surgery is done. We will learn more about the chemo when we meet with the oncologist. The doctor we met with yesterday was a radiation oncologist only. They claim that I will be able to take myself to the hospital for the therapy and do my own driving, basically do what ever I want to do. There will be days that are better than others, but I have not had any siezures [seizures], so I am legal to drive, and I am already on medicine that will keep me from having any siezures.

My legs seem to be my biggest trouble now. I asked them about my troubles there, and they seemed to think I have a potasium [potassium] problem. That the potasium is low in my blood and it is causing my legs to cramp up. I can't tell any difference this morning, but I ate 2 bananas yesterday and another one this morning. While they were trying to get the IV hooked up for my blood test yesterday, they were having a little trouble finding a blood vain. Four attempts later, they got it hooked up and took a potasium blood test. I didn't see the results yet from that test, but I think I will go to where they are sowing wheat to get me a little 10-20-10^2 for my potasium level. I think the raw stuff will do me about as much good as a banana.

—Jeff

The church youth group is coming to our home for a party this evening. We are looking forward to a fun evening with the kids and their parents.

Again, please keep us in your prayers. We are still in the very early stages of fighting this cancer and need the continued strength and peace that only God provides.

> Some trust in chariots and some in horses, but we trust in the name of the Lord or God. They are brought to their knees and fall, but we rise up and stand firm.

> Psalm 20:7–8 (NIV)

—Jeff and Karen

10/01/09 (Thursday), 6:50AM-Jeff

We had a good time here at the house last night. Brittany invited some friends from school and the youth group from church out for supper and games, and I think they had a good time. I felt good enough in the evening that I cooked the hamburgers and hotdogs for the crew. I think we fed over 20, and I cooked 40 burgers and hotdogs for them. Those guys like Jacob, Raedan, and Andrew can eat like horses, so I just got out of their road.

I had a very good night last night and slept for about 5 hours. This is good for me, I believe, and my legs don't seem to be hurting as much this morning, but the pain may come later. This morning we go to OKC to have my stitches taken out of the side of my head. It has been 10 days since the surgery, so it is time they were removed. I am sure we will also talk about chemotherapy and that type of stuff also. I hope they lay out a plan for me and we get started on the plan soon. I plan to talk to them about my legs and get them working correctly again.

A friend came by and talked to me yesterday and said "Jeff, the Lord has blessed you and you need to accept those blessings." My friend was positively right, and we should focus on the positives.

Focus on the positives today, and the negatives won't be as hard to deal with.

10/02/09 (Friday), 9:53AM-Jeff

Yes, I overslept a little this morning. I didn't sleep long periods of time, but I did get an extra hour or 2 squeezed in. We didn't have anyplace to be today, so I think that helped relieve the need to get up and move around today.

Yesterday we went to meet with the doctor that did the surgery on my head. He took out the stiches, and we talked about the some of the procedures to come in the future. I am basically done with him, but he helped me with the other doctors that I am going to be using. I am set up to meet with the oncologist on October 19 at OKC. He will set up the procedure for some of the drugs that they are using now. We thought that was a little far in the future, but after asking a couple of other doctors, that seemed to be about the right time frame for the tissue in my head to heal and everything. I still believe the radiation will start before that, but we are waiting for a call from them to tell me when that will happen. I think they will call me next week and start the radiation.

My legs still hurt terribly bad most of the time. They seem to be getting worse instead of better. I asked the surgeon, and he thought it was because I wasn't active enough and I needed more exercise, but I am on them about 5 hours a day, and that doesn't seem to help. They also believe it could be a potasium [potassium] deficiency, but when they pulled the tests in OKC, they lost them before they got them ran, so that was a waste of some pretty good Krehbiel blood that took an hour to get. I went to the doctor's office in Hydro yesterday, and Karla pulled another sample. They are going to see if they can come up with a good test and call us back today.

Also, my blood pressure is running about 90 over 62. This seems to be very low, and they thourght this may be causing my legs to hurt. Hopefully, this will get better in the future and I can move on with other things in my everyday rat-killing affair.

Keep my girls in your prayers because their troubles of keeping the business and school work and everything else in line is a major burden for them. I will be all right, but they need your prayers most.

Until tomorrow.

—Jeff K.

10/02/09 (Friday), 10:36AM-Karen

Jeff just got a call from the radiation therapy office. He has an appointment for Monday at 1:00 PM. The time on this first visit may not be his permanent radiation time, but it was scheduled to allow some additional consultation time in conjunction with the initial radiation visit. As I understand it, once they've set his appointment time, it won't vary for the duration of his radiation treatments. As we discussed in earlier posts, he should have five daily appointments—Monday through Friday for seven weeks. We expect Jeff to be able to drive himself to many of these appointments. I'm sure I'll go with him for the first week or so before I'm comfortable putting him on the road by himself.

Please place our travel safety in your prayers as well as Jeff's health.

We continue to receive confirmation from others. God is in control: Jeff's tumor was caught with just one misspoken sentence (who among us hasn't flubbed up a sentence or two now and then?), and he was sent to get a CT scan based on nonstandard procedure (the PA who sent him for the CT scan gives God the credit for her decision). We've had medical personnel ask to pray with us, and had phone calls from people who've never called us before to confirm what doctor we have chosen or, more appropriately, what doctor God has provided. We are certain God's answering our prayer and has a plan. Pray we'll be willing to follow where He leads—even if for now that means a radiation room for Jeff and a waiting room for me.

Thanks for checking on us. We really are humbled by the number of people praying for us.

10/02/09 (Friday), 2:48PM-Karen

Jeff just got another call from the radiation therapy group—Dr. Morrison's office. Dr. Keefer, the overall oncologist wants to start the chemo at the same time Jeff starts radiation. Radiation was scheduled to begin on Monday, but the oncologist's office hasn't ordered/received the new drug Avastin, so radiation is on hold until the Avastin is available to start all treatment at the same time. They should call us back on Monday or Tuesday with a new start date for the radiation and chemo.

Although this puts the radiation off a few days, this may mean Jeff will start chemo earlier than the October 19 appointment as scheduled, which should be a good thing—maybe another blessing from God?

Galatians 5:22–23 (NIV) says, *"The Fruit of the Spirit is love, joy, peace, patience, kindness, goodness, gentleness, faithfulness and self-control."*

When you pray for Jeff's health concerns, please pray also that we will bear "much fruit" (the fruit of the Spirit kind), so we will be a good Christian example for others around us.

Thanks for the prayers, and we will keep you posted.

> This is to my Father's glory, that you bear much fruit, showing yourselves to be my disciples.

> John 15:8 (NIV)

10/03/09 (Saturday), 10:49AM-Jeff

Well it is Saturday morning here at the Krehbiels', and we are not getting around as early as usual. I did sleep fair last night, and the 4:00 mornings are coming around, but I am still tired, so I go back to bed and get a couple of extra hours' sleep. I think this is good for me because it allows my body to recouperate [recuperate] some.

Yesterday was an interesting day because of the scheduling with the doctors. I think they are getting it straight, and we don't want them to get it messed up now. I want to start this off right.

I went for a drive yesterday. It was the first time I had driven since the surgery, and everything went well other than my pickup is a manual transmission and the clutch was a bit of a challenge. I just went to look at some wheat and then over to Dad's and back home. Last night we went to the football game. Hinton got beat by Sayre. It was a good game. Hinton has a very young team this year, but with a little help, they will be better in the future.

My legs seem a little better today, but they always do in the morning. They started out pretty good yesterday and then went bad about 10:30. They seem to be doing the same today. By yesterday afternoon, they were the worst they had been in a long time. I believe this will get better over time, but I am ready for that to be right now, and that is not God's timing.

—Jeff K.

10/04/09 (Sunday), 9:01AM-Jeff

It is a misty damp Sunday morning, and this is good. I had a pretty good night last night but still have issues with my legs. I am preparing to move on with or without them as the case may be because I am tired of gripping about them and it doesn't seem to be doing any good. Again, I would like to thank everyone for their prayers, and continue to pray for Karen and Brittany. This journey has only just began, so let's move to the future.

It is a great Lord's day today. We are about ready to leave for church this morning. We are meeting some friends for lunch and then back to the house for a little football, if I was guessing.

I will keep it short today.

—Jeff K.

10/05/09 (Monday), 6:05AM-Jeff

We had a nice day yesterday. We went to Church in the morning and then went to Wong's for lunch with cousin Monte and Cindy Lee from Texas. After lunch they all came to our house for a little visitation time. I also watched a little NASCAR and Dallas football.

My legs seem to do pretty good until about 9:00 AM, and then they tighten up on me. I am very persisitant [persistent] that this will eventually go away, and some other things can take over my thought process.

Continue to pray for Brittany and Karen as they go through this journey with me. I will be told what to do, but they have to put up with me while I am going through these treatments. We still don't know what the treatments are, but as soon as we do, we will try to get that on the Internet. I think most of you know that the appointments that were scheduled for today have been cancelled until they get all the drugs worked out and ready to use.

Have a good day.

—Jeff K.

10/06/09 (Tuesday), 10:16AM-Jeff

We need a little prayer going here. I appologize [apologize] for posting late this morning, but I was waiting for information on how my treatments will be handled. I got a call late yesterday evening wanting to know about my size and weight because they

wanted to get my chemo medicine ordered. We were not able to do that then, so I told them I would call them back today with the numbers and we would set up an appointment to get stuff started. They want to start me on radiation and Avistar [Avastin] chemotherapy at the same time. This will be a first time for this oncologist and the radiation therapist to have a patient with this type of treatment. This has been approved to be done, but the insurance company has to approve it, and my insurance has not done that yet. This method was only approved about 3 months ago. Please include in your prayers that the insurance will approve this coverage and it will fall under my insurance coverage.

We meet with them on Thursday Oct. 8th at 2:30 at Mercy in OKC. They will do some blood work, and then we meet with the nurse practitioner.

I feel pretty good this morning. I have found that if do my morning chores, then my legs start to really tighten up. I rest for an hour or so, and they feel a little better. Yesterday morning, I went to Dad's about 9:00, and we went to look at pivot and some dirt work we are doing on one of my farms. We came back to Dad's and did a little work on the computer, and then I went to Weatherford to the bank and Sonic. I also stopped at Cummins and visited with Chad and the guys. I believe yesterday my legs were a little better for the first time since the surgery. Hopefully, this will continue. I was gone from the house most of the day, but it was good being out and about.

Continue to pray that the insurance will pay for this new drug approch [approach] and continue to pray for Karen and Brittany.

—JK

10/07/09 (Wednesday), 5:51AM-Jeff

Brittany went and got her flu shot Monday, and now she is sick. We don't know if it is the flu or if it is strept [strep] throat. She was a little sick yesterday with sore throat, and we figured it was a carryover from the flu shot, but she is sick at her stomach and not feeling well. She was really excited because it is homecoming week, and she had different constumes [costumes] for the next 3 days at school and was looking forward to having a good time. Hopefully, this won't last long and everything will pass quickly.

Yesterday was a good day, and Brittany got a finishing wire on her braces, so she is on the downhill side of having her braces completely off about Christmastime. We also never got her anything for her birthday, and she wanted a pair of boots, so we got her a pair of boots for her birthday.

My legs seem to be improving. I don't know if it is because I have decided to go about my business and see if they will get better or what, but they don't hurt as much now. I just go for a few hours in the morning, and then I have to let them set for an hour or so, and then I start moving again. I can't hardly walk. I just shuffle along, but I believe if I keep moving, they will get better.

I believe that the medicine for my chemo will be approved, but continue to keep that in your prayers. This will be our next step, and we will know more Thursday evening.

—JK

10/08/09 (Thursday), 5:18AM-Jeff

I will just make a short note because we are having lightning here, and the last thing we want right now is a lightning hit on our computers.

Brittany took a short nap yesterday morning and got to feeling much better. I took her to school for second hour, and she went all day and felt pretty good. It was peace day at homecoming week, and she dressed like a hippy yesterday. She was first in her class and finds out today how she did on the schoolwide basis. Today they are to go like a Disney character. She is going as Cruella DeVilla [de Vil] from 101 dalmations [*101 Dalmatians*]. I believe it was the flu shot that made her sick, but I don't know that.

Karen and I are going to the city today to meet with the oncologest [oncologist]. They are going to work on my chemo drugs and get a schedule set for me. I don't know more than that right now but will update later when it is all layed [laid] out. This should be an interesting day with a lot of questions answered.

Please keep Karen and Brittany in your prayers and pray for God's hand to control the work that we are to do today.

> "I know the plans I have for you," declares the Lord, "plans to prosper you and not to harm you, plans to give you hope and a future. Then you will call upon me and come and pray to me and I will listen to you."

Jeremiah 29:11–12 (NIV)

—JK

10/08/09 (Thursday), 10:29PM-Jeff

We had our meeting this morning with the nurse practitioner for Dr. Keefer, who is the oncologist. They drew some blood, weighed me, asked my height, and then determined the amount of drugs I would be taking every day. The current drug arrangement is for me to take Temodar by mouth for the next seven weeks. This is a pill type of chemotherapy. I will take a pill for nausea in the evening and then wait for 45 minutes. After 45 minutes, I will take the Temodar and go to bed. This will happen every night for the next 7 weeks. I will be monitored, and they may change dosage. We will also start the radiation at this time. I will go to OKC every day during this time period for 5 days a week, and they will run the radiation on the cancer cells. This procedure is the basic procedure that they have used recently. Dr. Keefer wanted to add Avastin to the drug mix but, after consulting with other doctors, decided not to do that. This will allow them to use Avastin at a later time if they need it. This current therapy should be approved by the insurance company without any trouble.

My legs seem to be better. They don't hurt now like they used to, and I can walk a little without much trouble. I still have trouble straightening them out, and they are still week [weak], but I think they are much better. As far as tasting and eating, I can't taste stuff, and all food is very bland. This is from the steroids I am taking to keep the swelling in my head down. I am talking about actual swelling, not just the big head. They told me that this would remain for a long time and would eventually get better, but it would be a while before they could reduce the amount of the steroid dosage. I really miss the taste of good food, but I will get through it.

—JK

10/09/09 (Friday), 5:58AM-Jeff

I just wanted to share a quick story about my appointment at the doctor's office in OKC yesterday. They called me in to get some blood, and the guy that drew the blood commented that I was from Hydro. He is about my age and made the following comments. He said that the only funeral of a patient that he has gone to was Travis Payne's. Everyone that knew Travis really appreciated his love for the Lord and the way he wanted to spread the good news. I didn't have to ask what the closeness was for this gentelman [gentleman] and Travis, but I could guarentee [guarantee] the Lord had a hand in it.

It seems like the doctor's office visits take a long time, but I believe once the treatments start, they will go much faster. Things are looking like they will start next week with chemo and radiation.

Later.

—JK

10/10/09 (Saturday), 6:15AM-Jeff

Yesterday was a good day at the Krehbiel house. When Karen and I bought the house, part of the deal was for us to put in a new water softner [softener] because the old one was broken and had been removed. When we were in OKC Thursday, we picked up a new softner and brought it home. Yesterday Alfredo came over and helped me install it. I took Brittany to school and picked up some plumbing supplies and came home to install the softner. It went pretty well. I even soldered in a new fitting to hook it up, and it didn't even leak. That's pretty good, considering I hadn't ran [run] a sodering torch on copper in years. Alfredo's connections leaked more than mine did, but he assured me that was a sign of a good plumber because a good plumber never overtightens a fitting. He only gets it tight enough that it doesn't leak so if you have to take it appart [apart] again, it will retighten and seal. It took 3 trips to Hinton, but we got the water softner installed. I think it works, but I didn't notice any effect this morning when I took my shower. I think it will get better over time, but I need to give it a day or two.

We also cleaned the garage a little, hauled off the trash, rearranged the freezer and old refrigerator, took the leftover shingles to the barn, and fixed it so Karen could get her car in the garage. Little chores that needed to be done and just needed a little time.

Another thing we did was put a television outlet in my office upstairs. I think every room had a television outlet except that one. Alfredo did an excellent job of bringing it in through the roof [attic] and right into the room where I needed it.

It was a big day, but we got a lot done, and I really enjoyed it.

This evening was homecoming in Hinton. They played the dreaded Mangum Tigers, and the Tigers nailed them pretty good. I left with about 4 minutes left, and the score was Mangum 41 Hinton 6. Mangum is coached by cousin Lorna Lee Lewis's husband Larry. So see, there is a silver lining sometimes. I think

Larry has done a great job there, and the team seems to be doing better every week. I also must say that Hinton is under a new coach and the team is very young with only 4 seniors. They will be better in the future. This morning I am looking forward to the OSU vs T a.m. game. It should be interesting.

Until tomorrow.

—JK

10/11/09 (Sunday), 7:12AM-Jeff

It is a beautiful Sunday morning. As I look back over the last several weeks and the events that have transpired, I realize that I have missed some important things that I would like to comment on. Because of this tumor, I didn't get to comment on Raymond Unruh retiring from our church and moving to Kansas.

Raymond and DeMaris [DaMaris] were very special people for our congregation when we needed a little healing and God's love to help our congregation. We got that and much more. Everyone that had an opportunity to meet Raymond really enjoyed his company, and he will be missed. I have gone to hospitals with Raymond to visit the ill. He took care of the people in his congregation but also people from the town or friends of mine. I asked him to go see a friend of mine from down at Valliant that was in the hospital in OKC. He was glad to do that. Raymond spent a number of trips meeting with Karen's relative in OKC that had a terrible gunshot wound. I know they spent hours together. These trips don't include the countless other trips that I don't know anything about or can't remember. He meet [met] with other people from the Hydro and Hinton area on many occasions. Raymond had a very special way of ministering to the sick, and that will be missed.

Raymond has a way of ministering to the congregation on Sunday morning also. It was very complicated. Take the book called the Bible, open it to the scripture you want, and then let the Lord give you the words for the congregation. I realize there was a lot more to it than this, but it seemed like that was the mission every Sunday morning. And every Sunday morning, we recieved [received] a heartfelt message. His true guidance on church-related matters were [was] a blessing to our congregation.

Of course, we can't forget the once-a-month Wednesday- night dinners at the parsonage. We had such a great time and the pies. Don't forget the pies. What great friendships enhanced and stories that were told. The food was outstanding, and we always helped out as much as Raymond would let us. Hopefully, this will continue.

Raymond is a dear friend. I love him for his committment [commitment] to the Lord, to his family, to the people he loves, and to the people he will commit to the Lord in the future. I miss his calm, soothing voice on occassion [occasion], but I know all I have to do is call and he will do what ever he can to help. I asked him how he wanted to be referred to in an introduction. He wanted to be called Pastor. I was a little shocked because that was not a term that we used often. After using the term a few times, I realized that there is no doubt Raymond Unruh is a pastor in every sense of the word.

—JK

10/11/09 (Sunday), 4:18PM-Karen

It was just a month ago, September 11, that we visited the doctor's office with what we thought was a flu bug. God has been with us through this fast-paced month, opening doors that in the secular world would not have opened so quickly, if they even opened at all: From diagnosis to surgery in ten days, out of the hospital in only three days and recovering so well from surgery. Thanks to answered prayers, Jeff has had a lot of good days this week, and his legs are much better. He's able to do almost anything he wants to do. We want to thank each of you for your prayers. We'll

keep posting updates as Jeff starts chemo and radiation. We'll let everyone know where the need seems to be so you can focus your prayer. I'm humbled that each of you take time to "checkonjeff." There are so many other things you could do with your time. We're blessed to have so many wonderful friends and family that care so much.

…I thank my God through Jesus Christ for all of you…

Romans 1:8 (NIV)

25

10/12/09 (Monday), 6:19AM-Jeff

We had a good day yesterday here at home. Watched a little football and NASCAR and ate 3 great meals. I am feeling better now. My legs don't hurt as much as they used to, and mostly, they hurt from walking on them all the time. They get very tired. I keep walking trying to build them up. The Lord has granted me the confidence today that the chemo and radiation schedule will get worked out to his satisfaction. The chemo doctor and the radiation doctor want to start this at the same time, but the chemo drugs are not here yet, so they can't set the radiation times yet. I believe this will get worked out this morning, and prayers for that would be good. I don't know how this will effect [affect] my everyday life, so that is on my mind. As I said before, just the last 3–4 days, I have been feeling better. My taste buds do not work well. I can't taste anything, and I want to eat because of the steroids. I have gained about 5 pounds of the weight I lost back, and I am trying my best to keep that down because I feel so much better. I lost about 30 pounds before and during the surgery.

I think I am going to go for now and may post later today when I find out when I am going to have the chemo and radiation.

—JK

10/13/09 (Tuesday), 6:03AM-Jeff

Well, yesterday was not as eventful as we had hoped. I thought we would get my chemo drugs and move forward from there. The drugs didn't show up, and after several phone calls, we are still not sure where they are at. The oncologist doesn't want me to start my radiation until I have started taking my chemo drugs. The radiation Dr. [doctor] wants me to start radiaton [radiation] and start the chemo when they come in. I talked to both doctors, and we will start the radiation after I get my chemo just like Dr. Keefer wants me to. Dr. Keefer's (oncologist) office will call me this morning when they find my drugs and determine when I will get them. Yesterday was a holiday, and I believe that is one of the reasons they were held up. I believe I am ready to move on with this process, but the Lord's timing is what is important.

I did have a big day, though. I fixed breakfast and then went to the office for a while. I am having trouble getting the printer to work like I would like for it to, and I am trying to decide what to do there. It wants to work on the network, and I am trying to decide if I want to change that. I did some work on the computer and also worked moving some things around in the house. I hung my OSU tie rack in my closet, and Karen and I went out to the barn to determine if we should take out some trees so we can get a trailer into the shed.

This evening Karen's brother Phillip and his wife, Donna, came by for a visit. They live at Fort Supply, and Donna has just went [gone] through a bought [bout] with cancer. She had cancer in her tonsels (sp) [tonsils]. They removed them, and she had to go through radiation with a mask similar to what I am going to have to do. They ate supper with us, and we had a great visit. She is completely done with her treatments but has to go to OKC once a month to make sure the cancer doesn't come back. Phillip had a new 55-inch TV in his pickup, and I offered to keep that for him because it looked a little like rain, but he didn't seem to want to leave that here with me to see how it would look in our living room.

Continue to pray for healing and God's perfect work in our lives. Continue to pray for Karen because there is tax deadline this week that she really needs to meet, and the pressure with the radiation, chemo, and tax is a load for her to bear. Brittany is doing well and looking to the future. Continue to pray for the ladies in my life.

—JK

10/13/09 (Tuesday), 9:21PM-Karen

Thanks for checking in on us again. I spoke with the pharmacy today (more than once) that is sending Jeff's chemo drug, Temodar, as well as the Rx for nausea. They ship UPS, and it should be here tomorrow. Jeff has gone to OKC tonight to be fresh for the October Oklahoma Wheat Commission meeting tomorrow morning at eight thirty. I looked at their agenda. It looks like it could be a long meeting. (Pray for strength.) It will be good for Jeff to see all the other commissioners. Jeff will go in for radiation therapy tomorrow at 3:00 p.m. for another MRI and a double check on the fitting of the mask for his treatments. Assuming the Temodar arrives tomorrow as expected, Jeff will start live radiation on Thursday. The oncologist will be out of office on Thursday and Friday of this week, so they want to doublecheck everything in case they need the oncologist for something before starting treatments on Thursday.

I often go with Jeff to his commission meetings, usually to shop with the other wives, but I stayed home to finish a few income tax returns. I should be working right now, in fact; but I wanted to relay everything I learned today.

Jeff has been doing great this week. He has been driving for a week or so and can do about anything he wants. But if he's on his legs very long, they get weak, so he takes a break and usually regains his "get up and go" pretty quickly.

Thanks so much for all the encouraging posts, and especially for the prayers. Wonderful "peace that passeth all understanding" continues, and we know it's a direct answer to prayer.

> And the peace of God, which transcends all understanding,
> will guard your hearts and your minds in Christ Jesus.
>
> Philippians 4:7 (KJV)

Thanks for the prayer!

10/14/09 (Wednesday), 6:35AM-Jeff

I woke up this morning at a hotel in OKC. We have a Wheat Commission meeting today, and I am here to get ready for that. I slept well last night and didn't get up until 5:30am. That is about 1 hour longer than normal. I figure it was the company I had for supper last night that wore me out. I am really looking forward to our meeting today and hope we can help the wheat producers in the state of OK.

After our meeting, I go to radialogy [radiology], and they will do another test and determine where the radiation needs to go. They will not start the radiation right now, but they will have it ready for tomorrow. I am supposed to get my Temador [Temodar] today on UPS. This has been a little bit of a hassle, but Karen worked hard on this yesterday and got it through. I have considered raising Karen's "well patient in care box" dollar amount to cover all the extra work she is doing for my insurance, but I am not well, so it wouldn't matter. I should take my first round of Temodar tonight. I am concerned about this, but I feel it will go well.

I ran off and forgot my boots. Now I have to wear my tennis shoes with my suit for my meeting. I feel like I am in Africa and they lost my luggage. It will be kind of fun actually.

I may post later.

—JK

RADIATION AND CHEMOTHERAPY

10/14/09 (Wednesday), 11:21PM-Karen

We received the UPS air packages about seven forty-five this evening from the specialty pharmacy. Jeff had a 3:00p.m.appointment with radiation therapy—no radiation, just a test fit on the radiation mask and lining everything up for a real radiation treatment tomorrow. Everything went fine, and Jeff even grabbed a short nap while he was on the treatment table. His first radiation treatment will be at nine forty-five tomorrow morning. Tomorrow evening he'll take the RX for nausea, and then forty-five minutes later, he'll take the first chemo treatment, in pill form. He'll take the pills in the same manner every night for about seven weeks. Radiation will be Monday through Friday.

I don't know how to adequately thank each of you for your prayers for Jeff and our family. I know the peace in our lives is an answer to each of your prayers.

I'm reminded this evening of the history of Esther from the Bible. Everything that happened to her was to prepare her personally and to arrange the circumstances so she could approach the king and request that he spare the lives of her kinsmen. The verse that comes to mind is when her uncle, Mordeciah, says, *"And who knows that you have come to royal position for such a time as this."* I had to open the concordance on my computer to get the chapter and verse. It was Esther 4:14 (NIV). I do believe God has prepared our family for this time. He has a purpose for these events. It may not be a purpose we'll ever understand, but I'm confident...

All things work together for good to them that
love God, to them who are the called according to
his purpose.

Romans 8:28 (KJV)

10/15/09 (Thursday), 7:32AM-Jeff

The day is finally here. I am sure most of you read Karen's update
on the medicine arriving last night, so today we will start the chemo
and radiation. I am looking forward to this and dreading it also. The
uncertainty of how my body is going to react has me a little nerveous
[nervous]. I am trusting God will provide what I need to get through
this in excellent shape.

Moving on to yesterday. Man, did I have a big day. It was great to
be at the Wheat Commission meeting and participate there. We had an
exceptional meeting and covered several topics that are very important
to the wheat producers in this state. Due to Mark Hodges being gone
and no representative from the Wheat Growers, the meeting went a
little shorter than normal, but we still covered some new ground. I am
strongly looking forward to making the commission more effecient
[efficient]. I greatly appreciate Sen. Justice and Rep. Arms adding their
imput [input] on the future of wheat in OK.

I also went to the radiation Dr. yesterday afternoon. They put me
on the table and lined up the mask and stuff on my head. It went very
smooth because I was asleep most of the time. It took about 30 minutes.
After that I went to Office Depot and got a new printer for my office. I
am going to take the old printer and put it in the secretary's office. I then
went to Lowe's and got a new kitchen sink faucet. The old one we had was
all froze up. After I got home, I got it put in, but the hoses were too short.
Brittany and I went to Weatherford to get a new hose, but they didn't
have one at Wal-Mart, so we are still without water in the kitchen until I
get a new hose. Finally, to bed at 10:30 this evening. I went right to sleep,
but I don't sleep very long, and I am awake. I usually sleep about 1 to 1.5

hours, and then I am up for a little while, then back to sleep for an hour or so. A good long sleep would be nice, but I will take it when I get it.

Karen is working on the last 2 tax returns that are due today. She thinks she will get them done in good shape, but she will not be able to go with me to OKC. I think I will take Dad with me just in case I have any trouble. Well, I think I will start some breakfast.

—JK

10/16/09 (Friday), 5:27AM-Jeff

Once again, I must thank the Lord for a good night. This was my first night of chemo, and everything went very, very well. We had tacos for supper last night, which is one of my favorites, and I was curious about how that would effect [affect] my stomach. I took my pills for nausea about 9:00 p.m. and then my chemo pills about 10:30 PM. I then went to bed. I watched the sports and went to sleep. I slept until about 1:30 AM, used the restroom, and went back to bed. I slept until about 4:00 a.m. and then had a cramp in my foot. I had to get up and walk on it a little to get it loosened up. It was no big deal other than I had to work it out a little. I couldn't go back to sleep, so I took my shower about 4:30, got dressed, and drank a new bottle of Gatorade and a banana and posted here. I am very pleased with the way the chemo medicine worked last night. I am sure it will change over time, but last night was good, and I am anticipating that it will continue that way for a long time.

Yesterday was a good day. My dad went with me to OKC for the first radiation treatment. We had a good visit, and it was nice to have someone along just in case I had trouble. Karen wanted to go, but she had a couple of taxes that were due and wanted to get them out because the tax deadline was yesterday also. The radiation went very well. I went in and laid [lay] on a table similiar [similar] to a CAT scan table. They have made a mask from a plastic liner that is placed over my face and then fastened down to the table I am laying [lying] on. I am on the table about 15 minutes while they run the radiation treatments. They encourage me, and I try to just go to sleep during these treatments. It seems to work well for me.

After the treatments, we went to Lowe's, and I finally got the hose I needed to get the sink hooked up in the kitchen. I took Britt to piano lessons and then back home again. I was really tired this afternoon, so I took a nap and basically didn't do much until after supper. That is when I hooked up the TV in my office. It is just hooked to the antenna, but it works pretty good, and I think I will enjoy it.

Today we go back for another radiation treatment. Karen and Brittany are going with me.

Once again I cannot tell you how much your prayers are appreciated, and I am fully convinced that prayer is the reason I am getting along so well with the treatments and peace of mind that I have right now with how the treatments are going. This journey is just starting, and I ask that you continue to pray for healing, comfort, and strength.

Until later.

—JK

10/17/09 (Saturday), 4:39AM-Jeff

I had another good night last night. I went to bed about 11:00 and slept until 1:30. A quick trip to the restroom, and then I slept until 3:30. I have had my shower, my Gatorade, my banana, and am typing on CarePages at 4:30. I am so thankful that I have had no sickness and feel pretty good. I am still a little weak, but that is getting better. I do wish I could get a little more sleep at night. According to my family, and I find this terribly hard to believe, I get a little cranky in the afternoon and want to take short naps when available [possible]. I can believe that I want to take short naps, but I am quite sure that me being cranky is out of the question. I am sure a little more nighttime sleep would be good for my body.

Karen has been looking for some living room furniture for the last few years for our house. Even when we lived in our old house, she was wanting to replace what we had because of its age. Yesterday she found what she wanted. We didn't bring it all home, so I will pick part of it up next week, but she bought some new living room furniture. I am happy she waited until she found exactly what she wanted, and I am glad that we have such a nice place for it.

I had a good day yesterday. My radiation went well, and I anticipate that for a while I will be going by myself for radiation. Continue your prayers that this process will go well and according to schedule.

Until later.

—JK

10/18/09 (Saturday), 6:59AM-Jeff

I had another good night with no side effects from the chemo or bad effects from previous radiation. I can't believe the Lord is providing me with this treatment and few side effects. I am a little tired, but I can do about what ever my body will endure. I hope to increase that over time. I continue to drink a lot of water and Gatorade as recommended and am having trouble wanting to eat all the time. I have gained back about 8 pounds of the weight I lost when I was sick, and I need to be careful there. I know I would be much happier at less than 250 lbs than over 250 lbs. At one time in the last 2 weeks, I was at 255. I still only sleep about 5 hours a night, and usually I wake up 2–4 times per night during that [those] 5 hours. I would like a little longer time frame, but I am very happy to wake up if that means I don't have any side effects from the chemo.

Yesterday we looked at trying to lay out a circle drive in front of our house. We are still looking at that and how we want it to be. We only have one problem. Karen wants it symetrical [symmetrical], and I want if functional. I think we will get it worked out today so we can start on it next week. I feel like getting more work done in the office, and I plan on working on that next week some more.

Have a great day.

—JK

10/19/09 (Monday), 5:57AM-Jeff

I continue to have good nights while taking the chemo drugs. I only sleep about 4–6 hours, and they are interupted [interrupted], but I am thankful for that, and with no side effects, I am happy. I will get a nap in when needed. I can't believe how much I am drinking. I have already drank [drunk] a 20oz Gatorade this morning, and I have a new pitcher of iced tea waiting in the kitchen as soon as I am done with my post this morning. My appointments at OKC for radiation are at 10:45 this week. They will try and move them earlier in the day as time goes by and people come off of radiation. I would like to have them a little closer to 9:00 PM.

We had an uneventful day here at home yesterday. We watched a little football and bought a few groceries after lunch. Of course we went to church in the morning, and I plan on being Worship Leader next Sunday. This will be my first time since the diagnosis. It will be a little bit of a challenge, but I need to get back in practice.

Until later.

—JK

10/20/09 (Tuesday), 5:49AM-Jeff

Visited by royalty. I have had the pleasure of knowing many people in the agriculture industry over the past several years through my involvement with the wheat industry. Yesterday Karen and I had the pleasure of welcoming Jimmy [Jimmie] and Judy Musick to our home. Jimmy is the current president of the Oklahoma Wheat Growers Association and is doing a wonderful job. I just wanted to say thanks to Jimmy and all the work that goes into this job that is never compensated for. Jimmy had to stop and get some paper work for the meeting in Utah starting tomorrow and they were on their way to OKC to catch an early flight in the morning.

I wish I was going to that meeting, but do [due] to my radiation treatments, I couldn't go. I am sure it will be a good meeting. I trust someone will send me an e-mail occasionally [occasionally] so I don't miss much.

I had a good day yesterday, and again I am not having any side effects from my treatments. I went to OKC yesterday by myself with no trouble. I need to be a little more careful about being tired while I am driving. I think a short nap before I leave would be good.

Until later.

—JK

10/20/09 (Tuesday), 10:38PM-Karen

Just a quick update to confirm the good reports. Jeff's doing exceptionally well. God has been very good to us in many ways. We heard many horror stories about sickness that could accompany chemo and radiation. Jeff hasn't had any side effects to this point. At his radiation appointment today, he spoke with a doctor from the radiation therapy team. He discussed with her his unhappiness with the steroids he's taking. Seems she was very empathetic to his concerns but left him with "That's fine, but you still have to take them." Everyone with medical letters after their names acknowledge the steroids are probably the culprit stealing his sleep hours. He sleeps about five hours a night, broken into hour-and-a-half naps. The doctor he met with today told him he could try Tylenol p.m.to help him with the sleep issue. Pray that change will be effective and allow for a better night's sleep.

I'm thankful for each of you who are faithful in praying for Jeff and our family. God has blessed us beyond measure. I don't drink coffee oreventea,but I'mreminded oftheanalogyfrom a catchy little song: "I'm drinking from the saucer 'cause my cup has overflowed!" We are truly blessed you take the time to check on us and to pray.

10/21/09 (Wednesday), 5:18AM-Jeff

I had a good day yesterday. We managed to get the combine set and cut a few soybeans yesterday afternoon. I am not sure how they are doing, but we cut about a semi load. Of course, the irrigated were good and the dryland are not good.

Karen went with me to theropy [therapy] yesterday. Everything went very well, and the short nap before I left home yesterday morning helped me stay awake. We decided on lunch at Sid's Diner in El Reno. It was good to have a fried onion hamburger.

I tried the Tylenol PM last night to help on my sleeping. It did not do any good. I couldn't tell any difference from taking it or not. I may try again, but I didn't think it helped.

To all my good friends in Utah at the wheat meeting, I regret not being able to be there this week. I had to stay home to get my radiation treatments for this week. I am doing well and feeling good so far. Please continue your prayers for my continued recovery.

Until later.

—JK

10/22/09 (Thursday), 5:22AM-Jeff

Once again, the treatments are going very well with little or no side effects except for lack of sleep. Hopefully, that will get better with time. It rained most of the day yesterday and shut down bean harvest. We did get one semi load cut on Tuesday and took it to Minco to Braum's dairy. After my radiation yesterday, I went to Weatherford to get the oil changed in my pickup. I also knew I had some front ball joint trouble that needed to be worked on, so I had them fix it. What I didn't know was the wheel bearing was out on the front wheel, and that was part of my trouble. Just short of $1,300 later, I had new ball joints, new wheel bearings, changed oil and full of diesel. Isn't it amazing what can be fixed for a little money and time.

Mike, thanks for the updates from Snowbird. I appreciate them very much, and it helps me keep up with what is going on there. Also, pay no attention to Ken Davis because he is from Texas and would lie about me just because I am not there to adequately defend myself. However, if there is anything I could add to this conversation from Oklahoma just to keep it honest, let me know. We sure wouldn't let Ken's "wheels" run off of the scales, if you know what I mean.

Later.

—JK

10/23/09 (Friday), 5:44AM-Jeff

Treatments continue to go well, and I am thankful for this. The wind chill this morning is in the low 30s. We had rain yesterday, so there was not much field work done. They are predicting some drying weather, so maybe we can get some of these crops out and finish sowing wheat.

This evening I think we are going to see Corn Bible Acadamy play football at Mt. View. They play 8 man, I think. We have a young man from our church that plays for CBA. He is only a freshman but is doing really good. He used to mow our yard a few years ago and could hardly run the gas-powered weed eater. Now he could run it just for football practice.

I have a question for my friend Don Schieber. Since he is missing his football game this evening, does someone fill in for him, or does the rest of the umpire team just not miss him? Just interested.

Later.

—JK

10/24/09 (Saturday), 7:20AM-Jeff

Well, I am a little late getting started this morning. Our hot water heater tripped a breaker this morning, and I don't know why. It took me a little while to figure out what the deal was, but it is heating now, and we should have hot water in a little while. This house has circulating hot water, and it takes it a while to get the water traveling through the floors to the other rooms. I hope we don't have another problem that needs to be fixed, but I am sure that it won't be much if we do. I also slept pretty good last night and got about 4 hours' sleep at one time.

There for [Therefore] I didn't wake up until about 5:30. This was very much appreciated and an answer to my prayer.

We went to Mt. View last night and watched Andrew play football. They did pretty good for the first 1/4 or so, but Mt. View was pretty good sized and had about twice as many players as Corn Bible. Corn held with them and then lost by about 3 touchdowns I think. I got a little cool in the middle of the 4th quarter and went to get the pickup started. It was a beautiful evening though. Cierra went with us to the football game.

I am looking forward to a good day at home because I don't have to go to OKC for treatment and I can spend some time here at the house doing some things that need to be done. It sounds like they had a good meeting in Utah for the wheat producers. I wish I could have been there, but I had to stay home for radiation treatments.

To anyone this may concern. I understand there were helecop- ter [helicopter] rides to the top of Sheep Flat Mountain for less than the fee of the taxi cap ride. Everyone with a little animal science knowledge knows that sheep don't flat, they roll, so no telling where Sheep Flat Mountain is.

Later.

—JK

10/24/09 (Saturday), 9:37AM-Karen

We are so blessed Jeff hasn't had any sickness with the chemo and radiation. Or as the little girl from *It's a Wonderful Life* would say, "not a smidgen" of sickness! We know Jeff's protection from the sickness that often accompanies chemo and radiation is a direct answer to prayer.

Talking about *It's a Wonderful Life*—that old movie is a favorite of my dad's, and over the years, it has become one of my favorites. For those of you who haven't been watching TV during Christmastime for, say, the last fifty years, I will summarize. The main character hits a patch of very tough times, thinks everyone would be better off without him, and wishes he has never been born. His wish is granted for the bulk of the movie, and when he decides he wants his life back, that wish is also granted. He finds out the whole town has rallied and that he's blessed in many ways.

Well, to my knowledge, Jeff hasn't been on any bridges lately, but we've certainly discovered how blessed we are. Blessed that so many of you from so many different connections are checking on us and so faithful to pray and petition God on our behalf, blessed that close friendship is a gift from God that isn't bound by miles and blessed God loves us and will use these things *"to work good for them that love the Lord"* (Romans 8:28 KJV).

Thank you for spending your time reading our daily posts, and especially for the prayers. Jeff's cancer is certainly not a path we would have chosen for ourselves, but we're convinced God will use it for good.

10/25/09 (Sunday), 5:59AM-Jeff

Our Sunday school lesson this morning tells us that it is easier for a camel to pass through the eye of a needle than for a rich man to enter the kingdom of Heaven. Thankfully, nothing is impossible for the work of our Lord. Healing sickness, believing in Jesus, or getting me up and down those stairs one more time without breaking my neck are all within his time schedule.

Now to a little more lighthearted banter. Do you all have one of those DVR machines hooked up to your TV? We happen to have one and really enjoy it. We don't watch commercials, and they are very handy after lunch or during lunch. Yesterday I ran to the TV to watch the OSU vs. Baylor football game, but I had some duties I needed to do before I could enjoy the ball game. I set the TV on pause to start recording, took care of the things I needed to do, and started watching the ball game about 30 minutes late. I sped through the commercials. By the time halftime was there I was caught up with the regualar [regular] game. Again with pause, and a plate of nachoes [nachos] was in the works for lunch. After the nachoes during the football game, a nap set in, and I had to back up the DVR about 4 times to catch what happened. I got the ball game watched, the nachoes ate, and didn't miss a single play of the ball game. How cool.

We had a hot water heater element go out on one of our water heaters. I changed that this afternoon. It went really well. The only thing I didn't do was take the shop vac and suck the stuff out of the bottom of the tank before I put the new one in.

Later.

—JK

10/26/09 (Monday), 4:44AM-Jeff

Yesterday was a big day for me. I was worship leader for church, and that went pretty well. I was still out of practice, but with a little help, it will get better over time. Clifford filled our pulpit for the Sunday and did an excellent job. Charles Rickel has been employed [employed] as our interim pastor for the upcoming months. I am excited about this and think he will do a good job for us.

After church we went to Clinton for lunch, and then to Atwoods. After Atwoods, we went to Wal-Mart in Weatherford. After that, to Ace Hardware for a showerhead and then to Braum's because we needed milk. It was 5:00 before we got home yesterday. What a big day for me. You would think after all that I would be ready for a good night's sleep. After all that running around, I still didn't sleep very well at all. However, I am getting around good, and I feel pretty good. The Lord has truely [truly] blessed us and will continue to do so. We have a busy week this week and would continue to ask for your prayers.

Later.

—JK

10/27/09 (Tuesday), 6:30AM-Jeff

Well, I had a good night last night and didn't get up until about 5:30. Then I found out that the shower didn't have hot water again. I am about to call a professional and get this fixed once and for all.

We had a good day here yesterday. I went to radiation, and that went well. I had to stop on the way home and take a little nap because I was tired, but I had been up since 3:00 AM, and it was about 3:00 p.m. when I decided to stop.

I am still doing good on the treatments, and I am not sick. I am having trouble gaining weight. I have gained back 15 lbs of the weight I lost when I was sick, and it tends to go up every day. I don't want to gain the weight back. I am eating like a harvest hand and working like a church mouse. Pray that I can control my urge to eat all the time.

Isedro brought a couple of men over today, and they started work on our circle drive. I am really excited about it, and I think it will look good when they are done. I had them take the grass that they are digging out and moving it over next to the house. Over the years, some of the grass that was there had melted down or eroded away, and now it is being replaced with this good burmuda [bermuda]. It really looks pretty good. I need to get some fabric to put down underneath the gravel that I want to get hauled in over the next few days.

My radiation theropy [therapy] will be at 10:45 for the rest of this week, and then it will move to 9:30 starting November 2 for the rest of the time I am on radiation. This is the time frame I wanted, but it took them a couple of weeks to get it set up this way.

Aunt Valeta, I tried the new G2 Gatorade, and I really like it better than the old Gatorade. Thanks for the tip.

Later.

10/28/09 (Wednesday), 6:28AM-Jeff

I had another good night last night and slept until 5:30 this morning. I seem to be getting in a little extra rest after my 3:30 wakeup time, and I really like it. After my theropy [therapy] yesterday, I met with Dr. Shaffer, the radiation doctor, and she was concerned about how much my face had swelled and how much weight I had gained. She had me cut the amount of steroids I am taking. I am only taking 1/2 pill at night. This is a 25% reduction in steroids. I am excited about this and hope it helps in reducing the amount of weight I gain, helps me sleep better, helps my sense of taste, and my all-around good nature. All this glory goes to God.

After my treatment, I had the opportunity to eat lunch with the 2009 Plant and Soil Science Outstanding Alumni, Mark Hodges. We talked about the meeting in Utah and how things were going with the wheat industry. We had a very good visit, and Mark is doing an excellent job with PGI and OGI.

I did have a hot shower this morning, but I am not sure that I have the hot water deal all figured out yet.

The boys are getting along very well on the drive. I need to find some stuff to put under the rock so we don't have grass coming out from under the rock.

Since I am running a little late and need to fix breakfast, I better let it go. I think bacon, eggs, and homemade bread, toasted if you like.

Later.

—JK

10/29/09 (Thursday), 6:18AM-Jeff

I woke up about 3:00 this morning and watched the rain and lightning move in. We received 1.1 inches of rain since 7:00 last night. I went to the basement and turned on the TV. I saw just enough to know that the Pillsbury Doughboy got his cinnomon rolls out of the oven on time before I fell asleep. I slept a little over an hour, and when I got up, the storm was over.

As most of you know, the hot water heater situation in this house has been a small pain for the last couple of days. I had good hot water this morning, but I am still not satisfied that the problem is repaired, and I am still running tests. As most of you know, I have had some experience with electrical appliances, electricity, computers, and that type of stuff for a while. Most of it is based on the same electrical functions, and you build off of that. My problem is that those basic functions that I have used for years are not coming back to me easily. Therefore, I have to rebuild those principles and then base the problems back on those basics. My favorite father-in-law was here, and he helped me work on the hot water heater some. With his help, I was able to see that it is the basic functions in my mind that were not coming back to me. It takes a little time to get them restored, but once I get them, it seems to come back easier. I think a little time will help me a bunch now that I understand the drawback. It takes me a while the first time, but I remember them for later and they come easier. There seems to be life lesson here that I had not thought about. Even though they removed part of my brain and I am having to rebuild some of those areas, that rebuilding is a life-changing experience. Because once they are rebuilt, they will function the same way for a long time.

Breakfast time. Didn't forget how to eat or cook!

—JK

10/30/09 (Friday), 6:29AM-Jeff

You better have your warm underware [underwear] on this morning. It is 39F this morning with a wind chill of 33F. I guess the winter time is coming, whether we want it or not. I really like the winter myself. Jerry Clower always told the story that the senate in Mississippi wanted to pass a bill that would move February between July and August because it was a short cool, rainy month and that would be a good time to have church socials. I don't think they ever got that done, but I believe with the leadership of Ron [Justice] on the senate side and Don [Armes] on the house side in OK, we might be able to do that.

I overslept a little this morning, and I am wondering if the reduction of steroids is letting me sleep a little better. I meet with the oncologist, Dr. Keefer, this morning at 8:00 a.m. in OKC. After that, I have my radiation, and then I am sure we will be headed back home. Karen is going with me to make sure I don't miss any of the information.

I had a good day yesterday, but I seem to be low on energy. I am still tring [trying] to figure out what is wrong with Brittany's clothes washer in her bathroom. It has turned into a challenge for me, and I only get to work on it for a short period of time, and then I get called away. I think I can figure it out, but it is new to me because it is a Maytag, and I was trained in Whirlpool. The wiring diagram is similiar [similar], but a little different. It is going to take some time, but I'll get it.

Brittany had her concert last night and did a great job. This was all the grades from 5th through seniors. They have a new teacher in Hinton, and before the concert, the teacher asked if anyone wanted to do a group prayer. No one stepped up, so Brittany said she would. She led the prayer for the entire group before concert. God is good!

I need to get ready because we need to leave in a little while to make our 8:00 AM.

Later.

—JK

10/31/09 (Saturday), 5:53AM-Jeff

Why are so many people born around Halloween? And the funny thing is they are so easy to pick out of the crowd. Most of them are wearing some type of costume. Just something to think about this morning.

Karen and I went to OKC yesterday morning for a meeting with Dr. Keefer, the oncologist. It went very well. They drew blood and said all of my tests were normal. My white blood cell count was very good, my bone marrow was good, and they didn't have any trouble with anything. They think the treatments are going good and didn't change anything so far. I don't ask an abundance of questions, and I just do what they tell me to. I have an abundance of faith in the people that are making the calls on what I need to take, and I leave that all up to them. I don't believe they would move the radiation beam a 1/2 inch to the left if I ask them, so I just let them decide where it needs to be aimed. I also believe that the Lord is healing me now, so it doesn't matter where the radiation or chemo is going. He is using it. Positive prayer is always the key!

Karen is taking Brittany and some classmates to All State Chier [Choir] auditions in Chickasa [Chickasha] this morning. I ask for safe travel and that they will sing to the best of their ability. We ask that nervousness be kept in control and they have a good time.

Later.

—JK

10/31/09 (Saturday), 3:54PM-Jeff

I couldn't put it on the Internet this morning, but Linda Beerwinkle had a birthday breakfast for Dale this morning. It was really pretty neat, and there were about 20 there. We had scrambled eggs, biscuits, homemade bread, pork chops, bacon, gravy, and other things that I can't remember. I really had a good time, and thanks for inviting me.

This afternoon, I am putting corn in the deep freeze. Dad planted some corn late and sprayed it a couple of times. It is very good. I have 54, no 53, ears to get in the freezer. I have them cooked and in the water cooling down. It has been a good day so far, but I am getting a little tired.

Later.

—JK

11/01/09 (Sunday), 7:41AM-Jeff

I had a good night last night sleeping. Still there are no troubles, and I hope it continues this way. I keep thinking that it will get worse, but the doctors don't think it will be any worse in the future as well as I am getting along now. I guess I really enjoyed my extra hour because Karen changed the clock after I went to sleep. Somehow I made it to the bathroom twice within about 6 minutes and got an hour of nap in between.

I just ate my Gatorade and banana this morning and realized how my Cowboys felt last night playing Texas. Texas is a better football team and deserve to be in the in the title game later, but I don't think they are that many points better. My quarterback had a bad game, but that will happen sometimes. The reason I tied this back to the banana and Gatorade is that I have been eating a banana every morning for a while, and when I went to eat my banana this morning, it was in very good shape. The skin was bright and beautiful, the color was perfect. This was a good banana. When I grabbed on to the stem to peal it, the banana broke in half in the middle and center of my banana was not good under a perfect skin. That's the way my cowboys were last night. The skin was right. They looked ready to play, but under the skin, they just didn't quite make it. I don't know where the saying comes from, but between Karen and her sister Janice, they say life is to short for "brown bananas." Last night the Cowboys had a brown banana.

Still no word on how Brittany did in her choral review yesterday. She is hoping to find something out on the Internet this afternoon, I think. Randy, Jake, Lenzy, and some other friends are coming to Mom and Dad's for lunch today. I haven't seen them for a while, and it will be good to visit. I think it may be steak and shrimp for lunch. With my limited amount of taste buds that actually work, all the food tastes exactly the way it is supposed to. If it doesn't have any flavor, you might as well have it taste just like you want it.

Later.

—JK

11/02/09 (Monday), 6:42AM-Jeff

It has been 42 days since I had my surgery. I don't remember much about that Monday morning on September 21, 2009. I know we got up early and went to OKC. I got ready for the surgery, and before I knew it, I was out, and I woke up later in the ICU room in Mercy Health Center. I also remember that the staff there was very, very, good. One thing I also don't remember is what they were going to do. I think I knew they were going to operate on me, but to say they were going to take part of my brain out didn't really hit home until about 3 days later. The good part of that is I never had any fear of what was going to happen in the surgery. There has been a steady peace about this process that is very hard to explain without laying it at Christ's feet, and I am very happy with that. Not once have I worried about what would happen if the surgery went wrong, the treatments didn't work, or any of that because

I couldn't fix those things. I have had some pain with my legs, but nothing like some people have, and I seem to be getting better. I don't know what God's plan is, but someday I will.

Brittany found out yesterday on the Internet that she didn't make the Junior High All State Choir. She was a little disappointed, but maybe next year she can make it.

My brother Randy and his daughter Lenzy and her husband Jake came out from Tulsa yesterday. We had lunch at Mom and Dad's and then came over to the house for a while. We had a good time, and Lenzy is going to have a little girl in March, I believe. They are very excited.

My radiaton [radiation] therapy has been moved to 9:30 in the mornings. This works pretty well for me because I can take Brittany to school on the way to OKC so she doesn't have to ride the bus as early in the morning. I also have a Wheat Growers meeting this afternoon. It is going to be a very busy day today.

Later.

—JK

11/03/09 (Tuesday), 6:16AM-Jeff

Karen is going with me this morning to the radiologist. On Tuesdays we meet with the doctor. Also, we need to do some grocery shopping for men's supper tomorrow night. If you are coming and didn't sign the list, put a post up here, and I will cook for you.

I had a good day yesterday. After my radiation, I went to the Oklahoma Wheat Growers meeting yesterday afternoon and stopped by Ross's True Value on my home and picked up a thermostate [thermostat] for the water heater. I had a very good visit with Tom. I bought a $20 thermostate, and he gave me $50 worth of popcorn, caps, and soda. Man, what a deal.

I put the thermostat on last night, and it was working this morning. I will give it a couple of days to see if it works before we call if fixed.

I had a good night last night, but Karen noticed last night at supper that my hair was falling out on the left side of my head.

This is the side of my head that the tumor was on. Before the radiation started, they told me that it would fall out, so this is not unexpected. I don't think I will lose all of my hair, just part of it on that side of my head. We will just have to wait and see what happens. I think Brittany is already getting the camera ready for pictures in a couple of days to see if there is a fashion statement here that needs to be recognized.

Later.

—JK

11/04/09 (Wednesday), 6:01AM-Jeff

I had another big day yesterday. Karen went with me to OKC. We got to meet with the radiation doctor. Last week she cut my steroids by 25%, and I was very happy about that. It seemed like last week I would ask her a question and she would say the steroids were causing the trouble. So she had me cut the dosage of the evening steroids by cutting the pill in half. Again this week, I would ask her about certain troubles I was having, and again she would say it was the steroids, so again she cut my morning pill in half. So now I am taking half as many steroids as I was a week ago. I hope this works out well and allows me to get my taste buds back in line and my legs will work with more dependability. After meeting with the doctor and having my radiation, we did a little shopping, ate lunch, and then went by Baptist Hospital to see Kim Spady. She is battling colon cancer. She seemed to be doing well but is trying to get through that after-surgery shock that I have decided everyone goes through after a major surgery. We headed to Hinton to get Brittany because she had an orthodontic appointment in Yukon. After her appointment, we went to the grocery store in Yukon and were pretty impressed with the Homeland on Czech Hall road. We ate a hamburger at Wendy's and then came home. Aunt Valeta and Uncle Lester came by last night and visited for a while. They have been over at Mom and Dad's putting up corn for the winter. I think Valeta said they put up over 250 ears in the last couple of days.

Later.

—JK

11/05/09 (Thursday), 6:35AM-Jeff

I had another good day yesterday, but man, was I tired yesterday evening. I went to my radiation therapy and then hurried home to get ready for the Church Men's meal we had here at our house last night. We had about 12 or so. We had ham and beans, fried potatoes, salad, corn bread, cake, and ice cream. I enjoyed it and hope everyone else did also.

I had a good night last night, and yesterday I got pretty tired because I was on my feet most of the time cooking. I could not have done it without the help of Karen and Brittany. I helped cook my first cake yesterday, and I thought it went pretty well. I am not ready for a competition, but in a bind, I could cook a cake with the proper instructions.

Today looks like a day that I don't have a lot going on. I have radiation this morning and then home. Maybe I can get Brittany's washer fixed today and check on a couple of other projects around the house.

I believe God is working in our lives, and I believe he is healing me now. Please continue your prayers for healing and strength for me and my family.

Later.

—JK

11/06/09 (Friday), 6:17AM-Jeff

I was pretty tired yesterday. After my treatment, I came home, and after lunch, I rested for a while. Then I worked a little on Brittany's washer, but I couldn't get it running. This afternoon, Karen's parents, Glen and Sue Burkhalter, came for the evening. They spent the night with us and are headed to Enid to the Mennonite Sale. They will stay with Janice and Larry. While Glen was here, I had him help me with Brittany's washer. He finally found that there was a corroded terminal on the washing machine lid, and after he cleaned it up, it worked! Brittany was excited about it. We also fixed the shower control in the spare restroom. Everything seems to finally be coming together. The water heater worked again for another day. All these little jobs are finally getting done.

Today the Farm Bureau State Convention gets started. After my treatment this morning, I have a meeting with the Commodity Council for Farm Bureau. Some of you will remember that I was national chairman of the wheat committee last March, so this is a continuation of that duty and passing this position on to someone else. I always look forward to State Convention. Also, the Wheat Commission will have their booth set up to give away cinnamon rolls and bread.

Later.

—JK

11/07/09 (Saturday), 6:14AM-Jeff

Karen and I are at the State Farm Bureau Convention at the Cox Center in OKC. I came here right after my radiation yesterday, and I have really enjoyed the meetings so far. I had a good night in the hotel. Today at the convention, we have some general sessions and then start on the resolution part of the program. I really enjoy the resolutions because it sets the course for the future of the organization. Karen and I are both delegates for Caddo County.

The Oklahoma Wheat Commission has a booth set up here, and we are making cinnamon rolls and bread for the people attending the conference. It is always a big hit, and you can smell the bread baking all over the Cox Center.

I am a little short on words this morning, so all I can say is later.

—JK

11/08/09 (Sunday), 6:23AM-Jeff

Karen and I spent the night in OKC at the Farm Bureau Convention. I had another good night. I really enjoy the Sunday meetings here at convention. They manage to have some very good music and speakers for their Sunday morning services. I am always uplifted by there [their] messages. The service starts at 9:30 this morning.

Karen is going to give a devotional at a women's breakfast this morning. I am sure she will do a great job, but prayers are always helpful.

After our morning meeting, we will be done for the convention. I have enjoyed the convention and am already looking forward to next year.

Later.

—JK

GONE HUNTING

11/09/09 (Monday), 6:56AM-Jeff

I was up 5 times last night, but I slept late this morning. I woke up at the 6:00 a.m. alarm. That is the first time I have heard that while I was still in bed for a long time. It was a good night though. It cuts my mornings a little because I need to get breakfast for my girls.

Karen's devotional went very well, and I believe she did it on Mary and Martha. Very appropriate for a group of outstanding ladies who are presidents of their county Farm Bureau Women's groups. Don't get caught up in the details and miss the function of the meeting.

We had a good speaker at the church service Sunday morning at FB. She is a former Miss America and is deaf. She told of growing up and how things in her life had shaped her Christian life.

It is very foggy here this morning and will probably cause the drive to be a little longer. I have radiology this morning and then back home.

That's about all today.

Later.

—JK

11/10/09 (Tuesday), 6:25AM-Jeff

I had an okay night, but nothing special.

Mark Hodges and his son Clay came by last night and helped me a little with our computers. Clay did a lot of work, and Mark and I watched. He made a little progress, and I think we found the problems. With a little time, we can fix the problems. Thanks to Clay for all of his work.

Things seem to be going okay here. Karen is extreamly [extremely] busy with her CPA business because it's the first of the month. Please keep her in your prayers that the numbers will come together and she can get the reports done for her clients that are due the 10th.

Brittany had her first basketball game yesterday in Minco. She done very well and scored 7 points of the 24 I think they had. Karen went, but I stayed at home with Clay and Mark. Karen said she played very well. I hope I can go watch them play Thursday. Brittany has been practicing with the high school because they needed more people on the high school team to scrimage [scrimmage]. It has really helped her get accustomed to the speed of the game on a higher level.

Later.

—JK

11/11/09 (Wednesday), 6:57AM-Jeff

I met with the radiologist yesterday at my treatment. They tell me that my energy may start to get less as I get further into my treatments. Yesterday was my 19th treatment of the session. I will take 35 radiation treatments, but the chemo will continue, and I am not sure for how long. Energy has been the limiting factor on what I can do, so a decrease is not exactly what I wanted to hear. I trust that this can be prayed to a minimum. I am still feeling very good.

Karen had a good day yesterday, and the book work that she was responsible for went without a hitch. Thank you for your help on that. She was done by about 4:30 yesterday afternoon. Now on to another project.

This seems to be just another day for me today. I need to cook breakfast. I think we are going to have biscuits and gravy.

Later.

—JK

11/12/09 (Thursday), 7:01AM-Jeff

We have a foggy morning here. The weather man says it will take a while for it to burn off. Britt has not been feeling up to her full self the last couple of days. She has not missed any school and seems to be getting better but didn't practice basketball yesterday afternoon.

Karen's sister Janice had surgery this week in Enid. I believe she will be going home today or tomorrow. She seems to be doing good. Pray for Larry. He needs it.

Also remember the Spady family this week. They have now reattached Kim's colin [colon] and ran into some infection problems. She will be in the hospital for the rest of the week. Keep her and the family in your prayers.

I have a friend coming Saturday to do a little quail hunting. Since I have limited ability to walk, I will be able to ride a 4-wheeler to hunt quail. Now, I am quite the optimistic person, and I am really looking forward to this possibililty [possibility]. Brad has some very good dogs, and the weather is going to be good. I figure a 46-year-old man with brain cancer, that is taking steroids, who's [whose] vision is a little impaired, with a loaded shotgun, on a moving vehicle, chasing a bird dog, and with a severe lack of sleep—this could be fun.

Later.

—JK

11/13/09 (Friday), 6:07AM-Jeff

It is Friday the 13th. Sounds like fun to me. Yesterday was a good day for me, and we had a Caddo County Farm Bureau meeting last night. I was reelected to the office of vice president. For those of you at the State Convention last weekend, I look forward to filling the job description that Matt Muller outlined in that meeting. Matt pointed out that vice president may be the easiest job on the board. Also, there was considerable discussion about the money lost in the insurance industry over the last couple of years. Farm Bureau is taking action to secure the financial structure of the insurance company.

We got our first load of rock on the drive way yesterday. They are going to bring another load today. Today they are going to bring another load. We are thinking about 4 to 6 loads. We are glad to get this project moving forward.

Brad called and was looking forward to bird hunting this weekend but was a little concerned that the Kevlar may not arrive before the weekend.

Later.

—JK

11/14/09 (Saturday), 9:46AM-Karen

Jeff just left to go hunting with an old friend from the southeast corner of the state. He brought two men with him, so the four of them are off to hunt birds. I believe Jeff's excited to go. I know they will come home with stories and memories and, with a little effort, some quail.

Yesterday I went with Jeff to Oklahoma City to his radiation appointment. I believe it was number 22 of the thirty-five scheduled. While he had his treatment, I went to see an RN in the oncologist's office. I had called earlier in the week to get a refill shipped on Jeff's chemo prescription. The package was shipped, but when it arrived, it was not correct. Jeff takes two capsules every night: a 140mg and two 20mg capsules for a total dosage of 180mg. When the package arrived, there were only 140mg capsules without any 20mg capsules. I called the national pharmacy on Thursday evening when the prescriptions arrived. There seemed to be confusion between the oncologist's office and the pharmacy having to do with the refill. I think it's resolved. We're awaiting a next-day air, Saturday delivery of the 20mg capsules.

After Jeff's radiation appointment, they pulled a blood test to check the blood counts and a few other numbers. All tests on the blood came back good. As we understand the situation, a low white cell count could cause alarm, and possibly change the flow of treatments. Jeff's on track to finish his radiation the first week of December. I haven't put a pencil to the calendar yet, but I think that will be the third or fourth. After the lab stop, Jeff caught a short nap in the waiting room. The radiation seemed to have drained him a little, but the short nap seemed to renew his energy. After his nap, we met with our assigned RN in the oncologist's office. Brenda is her name. She laughs with Jeff and is very helpful in answering our questions.

Jeff didn't forget about you this morning, but I offered to post so he could be on his way with the guys. Please know each of you is treasured. We're so humbled God has blessed us in so many ways. One of those big blessings is our friends and family. Some of you are friends of friends or family of friends. You are treasured as well. My overall prayer is that through our lives, God will reach others with the message of Jesus Christ. After all, once we have accepted Christ's death as payment for our sins and are reconciled to God...we work for Him.

> Not that I have already obtained all this, or have already been made perfect, but I press on to take hold of that for which Christ Jesus took hold of me. Brothers, I do not consider myself yet to have taken hold of it. But one thing I do: Forgetting what is behind and straining toward what is ahead, I press on toward the goal to win the prize for which God has called me heavenward in Christ Jesus.
>
> Philippians 3:12–14

Thanks for taking time to "checkonjeff."

11/15/09 (Sunday), 8:37AM-Jeff

Quail season is under way in Oklahoma. We really had a good time yesterday morning. I was suprised [surprised] that we found as many quail as we did. Most people said that they had not seen many quail this year, but we found about 6 coveys yesterday morning. Most of them were small (8–10 birds), and the birds seemed to be young, but they looked very healthy. We harvested 8 birds, and the guys I hunted with were good enough to give me the birds. This is just enough for us for supper tonight. My good friend Brad brought the dogs, and I must say it was a joy to watch Brad as his dogs busted every covey of birds we saw, and we didn't get a good covey rise the whole time. I asked Brad if his dogs had to see the quail before they went on point or if their noses actually worked. I have hunted with Brad on many occasions, and he always has good dogs. Brad's dogs are good, but the damp weather on land that still has grass and weeds that have not had a freeze on them is still causing the dogs trouble smelling quail. Anyway, I sure had a good time teasing Brad about his dogs. I do appreciate Brad and his friends taking me with them yesterday morning, and I had a great time. It was a little difficult getting good shots on quail, and I didn't get too far from the 4-wheeler because my legs were not very strong. I only got one shot and made it count.

Curt McMurtry came by this afternoon. He came to Willow to see his son and came by to see me on his way home. It was good to see Curt again.

I have some pictures that should be up later. Brittany is taking care of that.

I have to get ready for church.

Later.

—JK

11/16/09 (Monday), 7:10AM-Jeff

This morning after I take Brittany to school and then go to radiation, I have a Wheat Commission meeting. These meetings are very important to me, and I hope that my decisions will have a positive impact on the wheat industry. I feel it is important that I do everything in my power to make sure that the producer money that is given to the wheat industry is used to improve the industry and not to increase the coffers of the state. This happened in Arizona about 2 years ago and is happening in Nebraska now. We can keep this from happening in Oklahoma, but we must start now.

I had a very busy weekend and survived it in good shape. Thanks so much to Karen for driving most of Sunday so I could catch up on my sleep. I was worship leader Sunday, and that went well. Our new interm paster [interim pastor] is doing a great job and has added some stability to our church service.

Many of you have asked about my radiation treatments. I have some pictures that were taken Friday, and I have put them in the pictures here for you to look at. This should give you some idea of how they tie me to the table and apply the radiation.

Have a good day.

Later.

—JK

11/17/09 (Tuesday), 7:07AM-Jeff

I am looking out the window at a beautiful sunrise this morning. It is supposed to be cloudy and cool today.

This morning I put captions on the pictures that I put up yesterday. It should help you through the process a little. That is why I am late posting.

I had a big day yesterday. I went to radiation and then went straight to the Wheat Commission meeting (all ready [already] in progress). The Wheat Commission meeting was good, and we accomplished somethings I have felt needed to be down for a few years but the timing was not appropriate until now. It is not my time line that counts.

I got home just in time to get Brittany from school but she had basketball practice for about 30 minutes and then stayed with a friend of hers until the bus left for Calumet. I practiced with my La-Z-Boy for about 45 minutes before we left for the ball game. The La-Z-Boy worked fine, and it left me in just enought [enough] of a stupper [stupor] that Karen drove to Calumet and I slept some more. Brittany's team won, but Karen and I don't remember the score.

Later.

—JK

11/18/09 (Wednesday), 7:07AM-Jeff

Last week the oncologist told me that my energy would start to decrease a little as the radiation and chemo continues. I don't know if it is because she told me this or if it really has, but I seem to be more tired lately. However, with this, I seem to be sleeping a little more at night, which is good. I feel good, and I don't have any side effects, so that is still good.

Back when I was in high school, the 4-H agent was J. D. Nelson. J. D. retired while I was in high school and, a few years later, died of cancer. Before he died, he sent word that he wanted to see Brad Wheeler and me. We were at college at OSU, so we went to Anadarko and met with J. D. He gave us each a nice wooden box of OSU pencils with a Pistol Pete on it, and then he gave us a "round toit." I didn't know what it was, but J. D. explained it. It is a wooden coin a little larger then a quarter that had printed on one side "round toit." He explained that often we have so much to do that we don't get everything done, and when people ask if we got the job done, we say "I didn't get around to it." J. D. assured us that if we carried this coin, it would help us complete the tasks at hand. I don't carry this coin, but I have thought about J. D. many times when I run out of energy and don't complete a job that because "I couldn't get around to it." I think I will go look for my "round toit."

Later.

—JK

11/18/09 (Wednesday), 11:20PM-Karen

I went with Jeff to his radiation appointment this morning. Then we met with a radiation oncologist. We really didn't have any questions, and the visit was very short. Jeff has only nine radiation sessions left and will finish on December 3. He won't have radiation on Thanksgiving Day or the Friday after Thanksgiving. The radiation oncologist we saw today suggested Benadryl to help with Jeff's sleep. We intend to try that tonight to see if Jeff can get more sleep at one time. He's only been sleeping about an hour or an hour and a half at a time. Then he's awake for ten or fifteen minutes before he can go back to sleep. It chops his rest up quite a bit. Everything indicates this is a side effect of the steroids.

I had a nice reminder of God's provision for us today. When I was sorting through some of the cancer insurance papers, I came across a copy of the application for insurance. It was signed on September 11, 2003, exactly six years to the day prior to Jeff's first diagnosis of his cancer. I was reminded of the fact that none of this is a surprise to God—not the cancer, Jeff's treatment, or the side effects. Not even our future is hidden from Him. He knew before the foundation of the earth what we would need and continues to send reminders that He's in control.

When Jeff's chemo prescription arrived last Thursday, the dosage was not correct. After multiple phone calls over two days, the corrected dosage took a plane ride from Florida or Illinois and arrived at about nine fifteen Saturday evening via private courier from the airport. Jeff takes them at ten thirty. Once again, God provided, and surprisingly, I kept my cool, which was definitely God at work!

Someone asked me the other day, what one scripture have we held on to that seems to help us get through this time? My answer to him was that there really isn't just one. I have found comfort, strength, and peace in so many different verses that I've memorized over the years. There's no way to explain how important it is to memorize scripture. Of course, I rarely remember the reference and end up researching the verses to find them, but God planted the verses in my memory so that when I needed them, I would have them. Again, God provides.

> My God shall supply all your need according to his riches in glory by Christ Jesus.
>
> Philippians 4:19 (KJV)

11/19/09 (Thursday), 7:02AM-Jeff

Yesterday was a pretty good day. Karen went along, and she drove to OKC and back, so I got to do a little sleeping and telephone time.

We picked up some irrigation parts in OKC and ate lunch and then came home.

We got our second load of rock on the circle drive yesterday. I think it needs another load or two on the drive, and then it should be in good shape. Now the decision is where do you stop? I would like to do more of the drive, but I don't know where to stop.

Karen is going with me to radiation this morning. We have a couple of things she wants to do. When she goes, I get to rest, and that way, I can do more in the afternoon. Yesterday I tried to hook a scanner up to a printer in the office. It went well, but I have a problem with some software that won't allow me to scan directly into a computer. I think it is a small thing, but I ran out of time and energy yesterday. Maybe I can fix it this afternoon.

Not much to say today.

Later.

—JK

11/20/09 (Friday), 6:32AM-Jeff

Including yesterday's treatment, I had 9 treatments left. Yesterday they changed my treatment. If I understand what they have done, they have changed the radiation to a more exact type of treatment. The radiation is concentrated on a more exact area per dose. This allows them to pinpoint more where they want the radiation to go. It took them a little while to get the pictures taken and the machine set the way they wanted it, but I could not tell the difference in the treatment while or after they were doing it.

We finally got the new front door window installed in our house. They took it out about a week ago, and it was returned and installed and fixed yesterday afternoon. It looks very nice. While the man was here, he also fixed the door to Brittany's bathroom, and we really appreciated that.

Speaking of Brittany, her basketball team won their ball game in the Calumet tournament and will play for the tournament championship on Saturday. They play Okarche. It should be a good game.

Again, we want to thank you for all of your prayers. Please continue to pray for stamina for me. It seems like I run out of stamina before I run out of things to do. This also plays a roll [role] in how I deal with other people, and I am getting more short tempered. Pray for me in this area. Pray for Karen and Brittany because they are the ones that have to put up with me!

Later.

—JK

11/21/09 (Saturday), 6:39AM-Jeff

Well, Saturday is finally here. Brittany is excited because her junior high basketball team is in the finals of the Calumet basketball tournament. I think they will play Okarche at 2:00 this afternoon.

In the morning, I always make a mental list of what I would like to get done that day. I never get any of the list done, it seems like. I run out of time or stamina, or something gets in the road. I mentioned something to Karen last night that the week was gone, and I didn't know what I got done this week. As usual, her wisdom pointed to all of the things that did get done that were not on my list but needed to be done. Most of them were small jobs but needed to be done, and it worked out fine. It is not what my desires are that count.

I have one job that I would like to do today and without radiation or other distractions, maybe I can get it done. I refuse to tell anyone what it is until I finish it. Maybe today is the day.

Later.

—JK

11/22/09 (Sunday), 8:24AM-Jeff

Yesterday was quite an exciting day. Brittany needed to be at school around 10:30 to go to the basketball game, so Karen took her while I stayed at home. Karen came back after me, and we decided to go on over to Calumet to the tournament because Hydro was playing. We could watch Cierra play for the Hydro girls and Tyler Entz play for the Hydro boys. They were both playing for 3rd place in the tournament. Both teams won. Brittany's team wasn't that fortunate. They lost to Okarche. However, they play okay, and Okarche is always tough to beat. We left for the ball games about 11:00 and didn't get home until about 5:00. I was pretty tired when I got home, so I took a nap.

As for my project that I wanted to do yesterday, I didn't get to even look at it. Karen had another problem that she needed some help with. It seems that her dishwasher was not attached to the countertop, so every time you open the door and start loading or unloading it, the thing wanted to dive out of the hole in the counter and onto the floor. We had to pull the dishwasher out of the counter and mount some wooden blocks under the counter so we had something to screw into. The water valve for the dishwasher didn't work, and we had to turn the water off for the house. I finally figured out how to do that the other day, and it worked fine. Then I didn't have the right screws, and Karen had to pick some of them up for me. I finally finished it after we got back from the ball games, and it seems to be working good now. I may try to work on my "special project" today. When I get it done, I will let you know.

Later.

—JK

11/23/09 (Monday), 7:45AM-Jeff

We got home yesterday from church and lunch, and I wanted to take care of my special project. I got some of the tools together and began this little job. I had started on this project several weeks ago. I wanted to put in an electrical outlet near my sleep- infected (La-Z-Boy) chair in the basement. I have been running an extension cord across the floor to the chair so I could run the laptop and the telephone near my chair. I had put an outlet in the wall, but when I went to the existing plug that was down the wall a short distance, it did not have power. I got discouraged and gave up on the project for a while. Yesterday, I installed a new wire and hooked it up to the electrical outlet. It took me about twice as long as it should have, and Karen helped me a little, but the job is accomplished, and Karen is glad that the wire across the floor of the basement is now put away. I am now looking for another project.

Yesterday was a good day. It is always good to be at church even though sometimes I think while I am getting ready that it would be nice to rest once in a while. We had a good church service yesterday.

Radiaton [Radiation] until Wednesday, and then we will be off until Monday, Nov 30.

Later.

—JK

11/24/09 (Tuesday), 6:59AM-Jeff

On my way home from radiation yesterday I stopped at Braum's and got some $.39/lb bananas. I know now why they were only $.39/lb was because they needed another $.25 to finish getting ripe. That one I just had was a little green. We all know that they will be good by the time I get to the end of them.

Brittany played basketball at Lookeba last night and won one game and lost the second. The first game didn't include the 9th grade, and her team won. The next game did include the 9th grade, and that team lost. I think all of the boys teams one [won]. Today she goes to Weatherford and participates in the choral contest and is singing in a concert this evening. This is one of the contests that she was selected to participate in a month or so ago.

Yesterday we had another man come and look at fixing the internal roof damage in our house. I hope to get something started on that before too long.

Later.

—JK

11/25/09 (Wednesday), 8:10AM-Jeff

Well, my $.39 Braum's bananas only need another $.10 worth of time this morning, so they are coming along nicely. I worked on the computers a little yesterday afternoon and accomplished a few things on putting a pivot quote out for a customer. That felt pretty good since sales have been down for a while. My dad brought the GPS over, and that is what I worked from. He also brought the information we needed for the dam we built on another farm. That turned into a bigger project than we thought it would. It felt good just to get a few things done like that.

Brittany had an honor choir concert in Weatherford yesterday. She went over yesterday morning and practiced all day, then had a concert yesterday evening. Unfortunately, I got a chair in that concert hall that had the sleep active gene in it. Therefore, when I sat in it, I kept falling alseep [asleep]. I knew I should have taken a nap yesterday afternoon, but the nap didn't happen. I knew the concert was good because after every song, the clapping woke me up.

Karen's mom and dad showed up yesterday afternoon and went to the concert with us. Fortunately, I was able to get Glen to help me with a small project here at the house. The ovens are built into the wall, but no one had ever mounted them, so they would fall out onto the floor if you set something on the door. We pulled them a little ways out of the wall and used some small wood screws to secure them to the wall. It works very nicely now.

I am going to my last radiation for this week. I don't go back until Monday. I am looking forward to the 4-day brake [break].

I can tell over the weekends how much the brake helps so 4 days will be interesting. Glen is going to drive me today.

Later.

—JK

11/26/09 (Thursday), 1:33AM-Karen

"Be joyful in hope, patient in affliction, faithful in prayer" (Romans 12:12, NIV). This verse seems to fit our situation so well. We have a

hope that goes beyond the physical, and being faithful in prayer keeps us somewhat patient.

Only four radiation sessions remain—Monday through Thursday of next week. Then we meet with Dr. Keefer on Friday. He'll tell us what he has planned for Jeff's next phase of treatment.

Jeff's energy level has dropped pretty drastically this week. I'm not sure whether it's the more focused radiation or a cumulative effect of the radiation and chemo. Jeff drove himself on Monday and stopped for a short nap in El Reno before coming on home. Both Tuesday and today, he had a chauffeur, which allowed him to sleep a little more. A special "thanks" to both of you.

I want to wish each of you a blessed Thanksgiving. I'm considering leaving the food on the stove until after the prayer. This year's list of things to be thankful for could lead to cold turkey and dressing.

Thanks for the prayers for our family. God is good and continues to provide.

11/26/09 (Thursday), 6:46AM-Jeff

It is a little after 5:00 a.m. on Thanksgiving morning. Karen is up putting the turkey in the oven. I got up to help her a little. She had a hard time getting the neck out and we had that thing thawing since yesterday morning. She finally got it out and the turkey is on the spicket. My Brother Randy and his son Jay are coming for lunch as well as my Mom and Dad. Tomorrow we are going to Karen's sister's for her side of the family's Thanksgiving dinner.

Yesterday the radiation treatment seemed about the most extream that I have had. The mask was terribly tight, and I have developed a partially stopped-up nose that makes breathing through the mask a more difficult challenge. I made it through the treatment, and hopefully, it will get better before I am finished with the treatments. Relaxation and short prayer was the answer to this problem.

It seems like if you go on a trip and you think it is going to take two hours and it winds up taking 4 hours, I get stressed that it took extra time. Same thing if you go on vacation. If it is supposed to take three days and you start on the third day, you are ready to get home. I think that is the way with this radiation. If they would have told me that it was going to take forty days and then cut me off at thirty-five, it would have been a pleasant suprise [pleasant surprise], and I would have been happy. Now all I can seem to get to is thirty-five treatments. I am sure that this will work out fine. I am sure that the good Lord will provide me with the patience I need.

We have many things to be thankful for in this home. As time goes by, we learn how fortunate we are. Please remember where these good things come from and celebrate them in ways of the Lord.

Later.

—JK

11/27/09 (Friday), 7:29AM-Jeff

It is now the day after Thanksgiving, and we only have one left at Karen's sister's at Kremlin. We plan on leaving about 8:00 a.m. If I eat and sleep as much as I did yesterday, I am sure I will be a lot of fun.

We had a good time yesterday and had a good visit with Randy and Jay.

Not a lot to report today, so I think will finish for the day. Later.

—JK

11/28/09 (Saturday), 8:44AM-Jeff

It is Bedlem [Bedlam] game day here at the Krehbiel house. I went to bed last night with a bad feeling about today. I finally realized what it was at 4:00 this morning. The game wasn't listed on my television guide that Dish network provides. I started doing research and found that when we changed house, I had Karen reduce the number of channels that we had in the house. One of them was Fox Sports, and they were broadcasting the game today. I looked for the bill for Dish network and found a customer number. I called them, and they were not open until 5:30 a.m. mountain time. I had to wait about 20 minutes before I could get the television channels changed like it needed to be, but as soon as I told them I would pay them their fee, they agreed to allow me to watch the football game on my own TV. And it was turned on immediately. I was about in search of someone to help me enjoy this festive day, but the mission has been accomplished, and we are now ready for the festivities here at our house. Bring on the chips and salsa.

Yesterday was a very interesting day for me. I got up showered about 5:30 AM, wrote in my journal, got ready to go to Janice and Larry's, and watched a little TV. We headed to Kremlin, and I slept three-quarters of the way. When we got there, I slept until about 1:00 p.m. when lunch was ready. I therefore slept from 9:00 Thursday evening (in one hour stretches) until 5:30 a.m. on Friday, then from 9:30 a.m. (in one hour stretches) until about 1:00 p.m. on Friday. I stayed awake until 11:30 p.m. last night. I watched a TV show, that is pretty uncommon for me to stay awake for an hour after 10:00 PM, and we even went to Atwoods for an hour. Maybe I am trying to push to hard and need to sleep more. Which reminds me, I better take a nap before the ball game starts at 11:30 AM.

This Thanksgiving has been a wonderful time, and I have learned to appreciate more and more being with family and enjoying a good nap. I hope everyone has had a wonderful time this year. We are so blessed with the things that God has provided.

Later.

—JK

11/29/09 (Sunday), 8:47AM-Jeff

OU played poorly a week ago against Texas Tech and came back this week to play a very good defensive football game. OU play well and beat OSU on both sides of the ball. I was downhearted for about 15 minutes. Once that piece of cherry pie and ice cream got onto my plate and it started kicking in, I was in good shape. Isn't it amazing how much the satisfaction of your stomach can make everything better? We did eat good with nachos, hotdogs, Frito chili pie, and, of course, leftover pie and ice cream.

Our scripture for our Sunday school comes from 2 Peter 3:1, and it talks about the second coming of the Lord. It expresses how we do not know the time because a day is like a thousand years and a thousand years is like a day to the Lord. As I go through this journey, I must remember God's time and not my own timing of events.

Brittany had a friend of here [hers] come and spend the night. I think they had a good time because I went to bed at 11:00, and they were still doing something to make a racket.

Next week is going to be busy for me. They moved my radiation meeting to 3:00 tomorrow afternoon and then back to 9:30 for Tuesday, Wednesday, and Thursday. I need to get a water sample for the meet canner tomorrow and take it to the DEQ lab. I have a Wheat Growers meeting tomorrow that I may skip. Friday we meet with the oncologist to find out what our next step is going to be. Please keep us in your prayers and allow God to guide us and the doctors in these decisions.

Later.

—JK

11/30/09 (Monday), 7:58AM-Jeff

Another busy Monday. I am going to Hydro to get the water sample for the meat canner that is coming next week. I have to take it to DEQ today so we can get the report back in time for the inspector. I also have a Wheat Growers meeting this afternoon. They also moved my radiation treatment to 3:30. On top of that, I overslept a little, so I am running behind.

I have a lot of travel today, so pray for safe travel and alertness. Also, we are finishing up my treatments this week, so keep that in prayer.

Later.

—JK

12/01/09 (Tuesday), 7:25AM-Jeff

I had a big day yesterday, but everything went well. I made all of my appointments and didn't have any tired moments while driving. However, I did take about a 10-minute nap during the Wheat Growers meeting. My brother Randy tells about Henry Bellmon being able to sleep during meetings, and no one was able to catch him doing it. I think I could go ahead and protect [perfect] this lost art and do some further research to increase its popularity.

My radiation treatment went well, and the mask didn't fit as tight as it did last Wednesday. That allowed me to relax a little during the treatment.

Karen is going with me today to radiation. I also meet with the radiation oncologist and Karen wants to be there for that meeting. This may be the last meeting with Dr. Morrison, but we don't know that for sure.

The water sample for the meat canner was delivered to DEQ at 11:30 a.m. yesterday. We should recieve [receive] the results today sometime.

Later.

—JK

12/01/09 (Tuesday), 7:10PM-Karen

I went with Jeff to his radiation appointment, and then we met with Dr. Morrison. She cut the steroids in half again. Starting tomorrow, Jeff will take half of one tablet each morning and will cut out the evening half pill he'd been taking. Since the steroids are producing the most visible side effects, we're glad to have this reduction in medication. Thursday will be the last day for Jeff's radiation and for chemo before bedtime. He'll have a month off from appointments with Dr. Morrison and then have a follow-up visit in early January. She's planning an MRI for the same day prior to Jeff's appointment.

I know for Jeff it has seemed like a long time to get through the radiation and chemo, but we certainly recognize the blessings: no bad weather driving to OKC, safe travel, strength during the duration of the treatment, friends that let Britt stay for an hour or two after school and before games so we didn't need to make an extra trip to town, so many faithful to pray for our family during these days, and, especially, the blessing of God's provision for every need along the way. Thank you for your part in asking for *His* guidance and peace during this process. We are truly blessed.

Two days to go!

We better get gone. Britt's team plays basketball in Hinton tonight, and I don't want to miss the tip-off.

> In all thy ways acknowledge Him and he shall direct thy paths.
>
> Proverbs 3:6 (KJV)

We continue to trust God will direct our paths—one step at a time.

12/02/09 (Wednesday), 6:27AM-Jeff

According to Mesonet, it is 39 degrees this morning and 34 degrees wind chill. It is the coldest morning that I have had since I have been going to radiation. I have only worn a coat into radiaton [radiation] once or twice since I started. Today I probably will. Everything is going good, and I am very excited about getting my radiation finished. I couldn't sleep very well last night and was up before 4:00. I am also having trouble controlling my body weight. I have exceeded my weight before I was sick by about 5 pounds. I realize this is a problem for everyone, but it is making it hard on my legs to hold me up. Just pray that I can control how much I eat and, as I come off of some of the drugs that I am taking, that things will get better.

Brittany's ball game went well, and her team won. She played most of the game.

Later.

—JK

End of Radiation

12/03/09 (Thursday), 6:41AM-Jeff

Today is the last day of radiation. I will take my chemo this evening, and they tell me that will be the last day for chemo for about a month. Tomorrow I meet with Dr. Keefer, and he will tell me the rest of the plan. I look for them to take a MRI or something in about a month or so. Of course, I wonder if all of the chemo and radiation has worked to this point, but I have faith that God has taken care of that and everything will be good when we get all of the tests back.

Karen and Brittany went to church last night to help with hanging of Christmas decorations. LeElla even sent me a cinnamon roll for breakfast.

Karen is going with me to OKC today, and I am glad for that. I seem pretty tired this morning, so the extra [backup] driver will be good.

Later.

—JK

12/04/09 (Friday), 4:42PM-Karen

Jeff and I just got home from OKC. His blood work looked good. He's been turned loose until January 5, when he'll have lab drawn and then meet with Dr. Keefer's PA, Brenda, to review the results and touch base. Dr. Keefer has given us the outline of the next stage. Starting the Monday after *Christ*mas, Jeff will have five days of chemo (a higher dosage) and then take 23 days off. He'll do this six times, or roughly six months. As I mentioned in a post yesterday, the radiation therapy department will schedule an MRI for mid-January to check the status of the site. Dr. Keefer told us today that he believes that's a good time frame to have the first MRI. Any earlier and scar tissue could/would distort the MRI images, and the results would not be as accurate.

Dr. Keefer wrote a prescription for a stronger antibiotic to kick Jeff's cold/allergy/sniffles and cough. Although we all know, it won't be the antibiotic responsible for healing; all credit for Jeff's progress goes to God! If your prayer list has a few lines left, help us put this matter in God's hands as well.

Since I took Jeff today, he was able to sleep both directions and some additional time while I ran an errand in Hydro, one in Weatherford, one south of Hydro, and one in Hinton. Poof— most of our day is gone. Jeff's planning to work on a couple of our computers this evening. I plan to put up the *Christ*mas tree. Not sure if Britt will help me or go to the Hinton vs. Hydro basketball game tonight.

Saying "Thanks" in these updates doesn't seem like enough for each of you who take the time to checkonjeff, and especially for those who are so faithful in prayer for our family. Please know it's sincere. Your words of encouragement are effective, and even if you read the updates and never post, we have access to the login records and can tell you've been here. Thanks to all of you for investing your time in our situation. It's our prayer God will touch your lives as you touch ours.

12/05/09 (Saturday), 10:17AM-Jeff

It seems like a huge relief not to have any more radiation treatments. I seem to have slept a little more over the last couple of nights than I did the previous 3–4 nights. I even slept until about 7:30 this morning. I was up about every 1 1/2 hours, but I could go back to sleep. I have also slept quite a bit while I was riding with Karen. I hope I get caught up on my sleep and things start to level out over time.

We have a big weekend. Raymond and DaMaris Unruh are going to stay with us this weekend, and Raymond is going to bring [deliver] the message at church tomorrow morning. We are having our dedication for our new church fellowship hall, and we asked Raymond to come and help with that because he was so encourageing [encouraging] with getting the building built. I am really looking forward to seeing them again.

Later.

—JK

12/06/09 (Sunday), 10:45PM-Jeff

I am sorry for not replying until late today. It was a very busy morning. Raymond and DaMaris spent the night with us, and we had a great visit. With all of the activity this morning and getting ready for church, I didn't have a chance to write on CarePages.

We had a good church service this morning. Raymond brought [delivered] the message, and I was the worship leader. I really had a good time as worship leader this morning. I was not able to be worship leader the last couple of times I was supposed to be because of my brain cancer, so this was a great opportunity that I felt I had missed a few weeks ago.

I also taught Sunday school this morning, so by the time the church service and lunch was over, I was worn out. I took my

own pickup, so I came home after lunch and didn't stay for the dedication this afternoon. Karen said the dedication went well.

Later.

—JK

12/07/09 (Monday), 7:50AM-Jeff

I believe that this is the first week since September that I don't have a doctor's appointment or something going on all week. I am supposed to recover this week and get ready for more chemo in a few weeks. I am hoping my energy will come back and I will be able to do some things around the house. Yesterday was a big day, but I made it through okay. I was a little tired, but I am looking forward to this week.

Dad and a couple of hired men went to Hastings NE to the T-L service school early this morning. We have some guys coming to work on Dad's dam below his house because we are running out of time on getting the government money appropriated for fixing the dam.

It is still a busy time of year, with ball games and Christmas parties. Karen and Brittany started decorating the house over the past few days, and I think they are going to find a place for every Christmas tree.

Again, we ask for energy for me, and stamina. Grant us saftey of [safety for] the holidays and remember our church as we look for a new pastor.

Later.

—JK

12/08/09 (Tuesday), 7:16AM-Jeff

Mesonet says the temperature is 28 degrees with a wind chill of 19 degrees. That makes it tough to work outside. It looks like this is a good time to be in Nebraska at pivot school. We have a lot of work to do, but the weather is going to slow us some.

I think we are going to have a busy Christmas season here. Karen's family is coming for a day or two, and I imagine my family will be here. Also, the collage [college] roommates and there [their] families are going to be here for New Year's, so it should be a busy time around the homestead. The Lord has truly blessed us with this home, and it is totally our intention to share it with others. When we were buying this house from Dean, I asked him if he was sad to sell it. He said, "It wasn't mine to start with. It all belongs to God. So how do you get upset with something you were allowed to use for a period of time?" I hope that I can keep that frame of mind for a long time while we have the use of this home.

Later.

—JK

12/09/09 (Wednesday), 7:59AM-Jeff

Accordingd to Mesonet, it is 13 degrees and -3 with a wind chill. The wind is blowing 17 mph. It is by far our coldest morning of this winter. Brittany has 4-H Share the Fun today at Carnegie. She is looking forward to that.

I have been working on getting a new computer installed, and I think I am getting pretty close. I think I will get done with that today.

Dad and a couple of our hired hands are in Nebraska at an irrigation meeting. They are wanting [want] to come home this morning, but that could be a problem because of the snowstorm they are having there. I think they will be fine if they don't leave until a little before noon. I need to do a little more Internet searching [research] before they are ready to leave.

I am feeling pretty good, and I think I am getting some of my strength back. I only got up two times last night, which is

pretty good for me. I am hoping that I can get on a good sleeping schedule.

Later.

—JK

12/10/09 (Thursday), 7:20AM-Jeff

On the medical front, it looks like they are going to increase my chemo to 400 mg of Timodar [Temodar] per day for 5 days and then off for 23 days. This is a large increase from the 140 mg I was taking every night before. I will not start taking this for a while, and maybe after the first of the year. Therefore, this dosage may change between now and then. The oncologist says that if I didn't have trouble with the previous dosage, this should not cause me much trouble either. I hope he is right.

Britt's team won! Brittany's Share the Fun team won the county contest. I don't understand what all happened, and I also don't even know what their skit was about, but their team won, and she was happy about that. I know they worked pretty hard on it the last few evenings to get it ready.

Dad and the hired men made it home from Nebraska yesterday evening. They got home about 7:00. He said the roads were slick until they got to Salina. Today they are setting up at the farm show in Tulsa. They have already cancelled the one in Wichita Falls, Texas, this year. I am wondering if the farm show is going to fall by the wayside.

I got the computer moved downstairs, and now if the printers and scanners will work, I think we will be on track for Kim to have more of a permenant [permanent] place to do her work.

Later.

—JK

12/11/09 (Friday), 8:57AM-Jeff

I slept in a little this morning. Not because I slept well but because I was up several times, and when I finally went to sleep, I slept longer than expected.

We have our Caddo County Farm Bureau Christmas party this evening in Anadarko.

I am going to try to work on overdue irrigation books today. This is going to be a challenge for me. I hope everything works out they way it should.

Later.

—JK

12/12/09 (Saturday), 8:25AM-Jeff

We had a good time at the Caddo County Farm Bureau Christmas party last night. I had the pleasure of meeting Lisa King, who has been following me on Facebook. I didn't realize she was Garrett King's mother, and she is a delightful lady.

They are having the annual Oklahoma Wheat Growers State Convention today at the Express Convention Center on Northwest Expressway. Congressman Lucas is going to talk, and I am sure he will hit health care and global warming. Cinnomon [Cinnamon] rolls at 9:30 and program at 10:00.

Janice and Betsy are coming today to help Karen decorate the house for Christmas. I really think they are coming for free diet Dr Pepper and Gatorade.

Well, I am headed to OKC.

Later.

—JK

12/13/09 (Sunday), 7:16AM-Jeff

The Oklahoma Wheat Growers had a very good meeting at the Express Convention Center yesterday. I was a little late but had the opportunity to visit with lots of good friends, and they had some great information available to the wheat producers.

When I got home, I just had to take a nap before supper. Sometimes I think I have more energy, and sometimes I think I have less. After my nap, we ate supper, and then I worked on the agenda for the business meeting at church this evening.

I need to study some more for the Sunday school lesson today since I am the teacher this month.

Later.

—JK

Neutrophil Counts

12/14/09 (Monday), 2:12PM-Jeff

I had a fever last night when I went to bed. I took some Tylonal p.m. [Tylenol PM], and that seemed to take care of my fever. When I woke up this morning, the fever was back. I took some more Tylonal. At one time, my fever was up to 102.2. I am feeling pretty good now, and hopefully, I will get better soon.

Please remember my mom, Fern. She had some tests run today. They claim there is no sign of cancer, but a good report would be appreciated.

We had our annual business meeting at church last night. I was church chairman and conducted the meeting. It turns into a bigger job than I remember from the past, but we got the business taken care of.

I appologize [apologize] for posting so late this afternoon. Mostly do [due] to sickness, I think. Please pray for strength for me because we have a big week ahead with lots of company.

Later.

—JK

12/15/09 (Tuesday), 12:35AM-Karen

It's been a while since I left an update. I've been busy with my taxi service. Britt had a junior high basketball game at Geary this evening. Hinton did very well, and Britt got to play quite a bit. Jeff wasn't quite up to the trip, so he stayed home and rested. He said this evening that maybe watching TV in the basement makes him want to sleep more. I expect him to make an adjustment to see if he can get more *awake* hours in his days. I have started some *Christ*mas baking. I really enjoy spending time in the kitchen.

I continue to be humbled by the activity on Jeff's CarePages. I can't believe how many friends are checking on us—and praying! That peace that we wrote about early in Jeff's diagnosis still has a comforting effect on our lives. Many of you understand exactly what I'm talking about—the comfort of knowing God's in control of our lives, He knows the plans He has for us, plans to prosper us and not to harm us. All we have to do is ask Him. He'll guide our decisions.

Thanks for your time, and especially, your prayer time.

12/15/09 (Tuesday), 11:13AM-Karen

Jeff's running a fever again this morning. I gave him some Tylenol, and that brought it down some. Tried yesterday to get a doctor's appointment, but they were booked solid all week. We're on standby. I'll call again this morning to see if they've had a cancellation. Please pray Jeff's fever will go down and whatever is causing the fever will go away.

12/15/09 (Tuesday), 9:48PM-Brittany

Tonight I would like to bring an important prayer concern before you all. You know Dad hasn't been feeling well the last few days and has been running a high fever. This afternoon Mom took Dad to Convenient Care in Weatherford. They took blood samples, and his white blood cell count was almost nonexistent. Dr. Keefer recommended that Dad go to OKC, to the hospital. Dad will go to the Mercy emergency room, where he'll be admitted and get an IV antibiotic. I want to thank you for your continued support and prayers through this difficult time. God is fully in control. That statement alone gives me courage. Mom will try to update again when we know more.

—Britt

Karen Remembers:
God's Protection

On Tuesday evening, December 15, 2009, after Jeff and I left the Weatherford ER, we went by our house to get a few things. We weren't sure how long he would be in the hospital.

The school Christmas vocal concert was that night. I tried so hard for Brittany to have normal days. I took a guess at what time her class would sing, did a little math in my head, and figured with a little strategic timing, I could probably still hear Britt's class sing.

Jeff stayed in the car. I popped into the back of the multipurpose building, staying as far from the crowd as possible, listened to students one year younger than Brittany and then Brittany's vocal class. Brittany never saw me at the back of the room, but it was important to me to be there. I didn't talk to anyone and quickly left as soon as her class finished singing.

As I look back, I know God must have compensated for my stupidity as I entered a crowded building in the middle of December. Then I went back to the car where Jeff was suffering from a zero white blood cell count with absolutely no way to fight infection. My ten-minute detour could have proved deadly had Jeff contracted anything during his days without a white cell count. Truly, God watched over us that night.

12/16/09 (Wednesday), 5:27PM-Karen

As we suspected, when Brittany posted last night, Dr. Reeves (oncologist on call) with the Cancer Care Associates admitted Jeff to Mercy and ordered a round of IV antibiotics that was completely administered in the ER before Jeff got a room. They took a chest x-ray, which came back clean—no sign of pneumonia or other chest issues.

They also pulled about 6 vials of blood to run tests. His white blood count was extremely low. In Weatherford, it was .8; then on the second sample, it tested 1. The count at the Mercy ER was .9, so Jeff was admitted. This morning his fever was still in the 99 range. As I understand the issue, when white counts bottom out like Jeff's has, that can cause the fever. Jeff doesn't appear to have any infections or viruses, and he has tested negative for the flu.

Dr. Keefer made rounds about noon and ordered an injection to boost white blood cell count. He thought it would be Thursday before Jeff could be released. Jeff's resting well this afternoon. I'll probably run home this evening and catch up on a few things.

Keep up the prayers. We'll trust God to do the rest.

12/17/09 (Thursday), 11:31AM-Jeff

I am at Mercy Hospital in OKC. My white blood cell count is very low, so I can't have any visitors or flowers. They are trying to keep me from getting an infection. When I was admitted Tuesday evening, my white blood count was at .9. This morning it was at 1.0. This is not much of a change so I may be here another day.

—Jeff

12/17/09 (Thursday), 11:31AM-Karen

They gave Jeff an IV of a combination of two antibiotics overnight. We expect to see Dr. Keefer about noon for an update and possible plan. I know this is frustrating for Jeff. He would like to be at home.

We thank each of you for your time checking on Jeff, and especially for the prayer. We continue to believe God is in control. He knows the future and will provide for each need. In fact, each issue that arises is an opportunity to watch God provide.

12/17/09 (Thursday), 7:43 p.m.Jeff

Dr. Keefer came by this afternoon, and he is very concerned about my low white blood cell count. Especially the Nutrifils [Neutrophils] in the white blood cells. My current white blood cell count is about 1.0, but very little in Nutrifils. Dr. Keefer said when I get my Nutrifils up to .5%, then he will let me go home. He doesn't know if that will be tomorrow or next week. He is giving me medicine to bring that count up.

Brittany's team won their basketball game this evening, and Britt said she played pretty good.

Continue to pray for an increase in white blood cell count, and especially for Nutrifils.

Later.

—JK

12/18/09 (Friday), 1:20AM-Karen

I believe it may be time to summarize where we are.

Jeff finished radiation on December 3. He also stopped the chemo pills he took seven days a week while he was undergoing radiation five days a week. The plan was to restart chemo after Christmas or the first week in January with a five-day-a-month 400 mg/day dose of Temodar. This regimen was to last six 28-day cycles.

Jeff felt congestion coming on in mid-November, so his primary physician prescribed Amoxicillin to fight any infection.

Jeff finished that antibiotic shortly before seeing Dr. Keefer, the oncologist, on December 4. Because Jeff felt the symptoms had not changed, Dr. Keefer ordered Augmentin, another antibiotic. Jeff finished that prescription on Tuesday. However, Jeff started running a fever on Sunday evening. Although the fever was low grade and seemed to respond to Tylenol, it still caused concern and only seemed to be a problem in the evening and overnight— in other words, his fever stayed down during the day Monday and Tuesday. As I understand it, the low white blood cell count is what is causing the fever, not any infection. All tests for infection, flu, or viruses are negative.

Jeff's low on all white blood cells, but it's the Neutrophils type Dr. Keefer seems to be most concerned with. Jeff's getting an antibiotic Vancomycin IV each morning and an injection of Neupogen each afternoon. The Neupogen stimulates production of white blood cells. In addition to these, Jeff's back on blood pressure meds. He's still taking the steroid Decadron to suppress swelling inside his skull and Keppra to prevent seizures (hasn't had any seizures; this is preventative).

Dr. Keefer said today that Jeff won't start the six-month Temodar treatment until his white blood cell counts have stabilized for at least 1 week. He also indicated that once Jeff's white blood cell counts have decreased to this extremely low level, each future round of chemo will have a higher chance of a severe white cell reaction. Once affected, it can take a while for the count to increase. He also said it's always the patient's choice whether to proceed with the chemo treatment. This severe reaction causes some patients to pull back from the treatment. He strongly recommended against stopping the chemo, especially when dealing with glioblastoma, the type of cancer Jeff had.

Once again, we are reminded all is in God's hands and his timing will be perfect. Our earthly minds cannot fathom the whole of His wisdom in these matters. We are promised *"all things work together for good to them that love God"* (Romans 8:28 KJV). When we consider that God has planned for these days since before the foundation of the world, we have to trust He is providing the care Jeff needs on a daily basis. We hold to the truth that medical science will always be inferior to the knowledge and wisdom of God. Maybe it's the *"peace of God which passeth all understanding"* (Philippians 4:7 KJV).

Thanks for your prayers for our family.

12/17/09 (Friday), 5:19PM-Jeff

Dr. Keefer was just here and decided that I would not go home today. He said we had to wait on the blood count to come up some more. Evidently, I am confused on how much it needs to be in order to be adequate, but when he tells me I can go home, I will. I will be looking for the nurse at 4:30 a.m. tomorrow to pull that blood.

Thanks for your prayers.

—JK

12/20/09 (Sunday), 5:48PM-Karen

Jeff's still in the hospital with low white blood cell counts. This afternoon he's running a temp of 102.3. They are working on cooling him down. He's not very happy with their tactics. Please pray the white blood cell count will increase and the fever will go down and stay down. If I understand the results of his blood counts, his Neutrophils are at 5 percent, and they need to be within a range of 36 to 70. His discharge from the hospital hinges on these counts. We ask for specific prayer in the areas of temperature and white blood cell counts.

12/21/09 (Monday) 6:16PM-Karen

Jeff's fever came down yesterday evening but was back this morning. It was only low grade, and Tylenol wiped it out. It hasn't been back up this afternoon. Jeff lost the proper bacteria balance in his digestive tract, a condition the staff calls CDif. He should start receiving a new med for that later this afternoon. CDif won't keep him from going home once the white blood cell count gets up to its target. The Neutrophils count was 365 this morning, and we're still waiting for it to reach 500. Sometimes we get the results as a count, and sometimes it's a percentage, which is a little confusing.

Because the count doesn't seem to increase very quickly, Jeff has been doing the math and doubts whether Christmas morning will be in the new house. I'm still holding out for "home for Christmas." I know Jeff's frustrated with the amenities, cuisine, and absence of a sleep-infected La-Z-Boy recliner.

Please continue to pray for patience. We trust God has a plan. Our prayer is He can use this to His benefit, in whatever way He finds best.

Thanks for the prayers. God is answering.

12/22/09 (Tuesday), 2:46PM-Karen

Jeff's Neutrophils are down to 0 on the blood count printout today. We had been told it was a long process to get them up. We were frustrated with slow, but back to 0 is definitely a discouraging setback. We haven't seen the doctor yet, so we don't have much information. I will post again after the doctor's rounds. Sometimes they come in by midafternoon.

Keep up the prayers. We trust God will take it from there.

12/22/09 (Tuesday), 8:21PM-Karen

Brittany came to the mall in Oklahoma City with a friend and her family today. What a sweet thing to do for Britt so she could have some fun. Late this afternoon, I met them and picked up Brittany so she could come back to the hospital with me to see her dad. Of course, while I was gone, the doctor came by. After he left, I spoke with Jeff on the phone, and he had a glimmer of hope that today's results were in error. The doctor didn't seem to think it was an error, but tomorrow morning's lab will prove whether the count is up or down. The doctor thinks it will be midweek next week before Jeff's counts will be up again. This news has left Jeff in low spirits, and because "the two shall be as one," I'm sad too.

The Neupogen Jeff takes to boost white cells has started showing some side effects in the way of achy bones. Because white cells are stimulated in the bone marrow, the ache is a result. I choose to believe if the side effects are there, that's a sign that the drug is working. Jeff isn't on any pain medicine at this point.

I can't imagine how nonbelievers would cope in these situations, without the peace we have—all because God sent his only son so we could be pardoned and have all the blessings salvation and a relationship with Christ bring. Of course, our biggest blessings aren't of this world, but are spiritual in nature. Life with Christ, even with cancer treatment or post-cancer treatment, still trumps life without Christ.

Thanks for checking on our family. We treasure your prayers, and we know all will be completed in God's time.

> For this cause shall a man leave his father and mother, and shall be joined unto his wife, and they two shall be one flesh.
>
> Ephesians 5:31 (KJV)

12/24/09 (Thursday), 12:41AM-Karen

Thanks for taking the time to checkonjeff, Brittany, and me. We are so blessed to have so many friends checking on us. We're glad you take the time to read our posts. When I type them, they become my therapy sessions. Truly, putting into words the events and emotions of the day is therapeutic. Besides, I would forget what happened each day. This has become a thorough journal of our journey.

The Neutrophils count this morning was a disappointing zero. Brittany went with me to the hospital again today. Jeff can only have immediate family visits because his immune system is very low. Any bacteria, or germs no matter how mild, could cause a severe infection. We are required to wear gloves, mask, and gown every time we enter his room. Even the hospital personnel are under these precautions. As I understand it, that's for our protection as much as for his health.

Jeff had a tough day emotionally. Today pushed him over the one-week mark on his hospital stay. I think he may have set today as a cutoff for whether he could be home on Christmas Day. Since that notion is past, maybe we can again take each day as it comes and humbly accept the blessing it brings.

Brittany had practice tonight for our church's annual Christmas Eve service, so we left the hospital about five thirty. The weathermen are still changing the forecast but are expecting snow in the state tonight and tomorrow. I asked Jeff if he ever remembered a Christmas Eve service being cancelled because of snow. He didn't think so. I guess we will have to quiz a few "old- timers" and test their memories.

As important as tradition is, whether it's a Christmas Eve service, the lighting of Advent candles, or the singing of Christmas carols, those traditions are not the most important aspect of Christmas. And it isn't about tinsel, lights, Santa, reindeer, or even our treasured gift exchanges. If we really "get it"—I mean really understand the concept of Christmas—that *"God so loved the world that He gave His only begotten son that whosoever believeth in Him should not perish, but have everlasting life"* (John 3:16 KJV), then each day should be an opportunity to serve the King. That means whether we spend our day basking in the sun on vacation (doing something we want to do) or in a hospital (doing something we don't want to do), we will praise Him. *"Worthy is the Lamb"* (Christ) to take away the sin of the world!

Merry *Christ*mas from the Krehbiels

Saying with a loud voice, "Worthy is the Lamb that was slain to receive power, and riches, and wisdom, and strength, and honour, and glory, and blessing."

Revelation 5:12 (KJV)

12/25/09 (Friday), 12:56AM-Karen

One for the record books. Fourteen inches of snow in OKC. The most ever recorded in a twenty-four-hour period. Bet our family won't forget this one either. Brittany and I were able to get out for the Christmas Eve service in Hydro. Jeff's parents, a mile north of us, couldn't get out. Their road was drifted closed.

We spoke with Jeff on the phone several times today, and even once on Facebook. Every time we spoke, he sounded weak. Because of the blizzard, we weren't able to go today, and going tomorrow is unlikely.

Please pray with us that Jeff will gain strength, his white blood cell counts will increase and stabilize, and we'll have peace and patience.

Merry Christmas!

—The Krehbiels

12/25/09 (Friday), 5:06PM-Karen

Brittany and I came to the hospital today. It really wasn't too bad. We drove on mostly dry pavement, some wet pavement, and an occasional patch of packed snow. The packed snow was mostly at overpasses. From Country Club Road in El Reno to Mustang Road in Yukon it's only about thirteen miles. In that stretch of I-40, Brittany counted fifty cars and six semis still in the ditch from yesterday's record-setting snowstorm. I suppose it was good we didn't try to come yesterday, but it was hard not being with Jeff. We hadn't seen any stranded vehicles until we got to El Reno. It seemed like there was a line at that exit where the heavy snow started. I really think if there was fourteen inches in the areas we drove through, it had already blown south.

Jeff's white count was .02 today on the Neutrophils. That doubled yesterday's count of .01. If my math skills are good and if my memory of cell division is anywhere near accurate, the more white cells you have, the quicker they double. I'm optimistic the counts will turn a corner and really show improvement.

Since we got here, Jeff has showered and is getting IV fluids. He's resting a little. Everything he does makes him tired, and he needs naps often.

Thank you for checking on us, and Merry Christmas.

12/26/09 (Saturday), 12:40PM-Karen

Jeff's total white count is up to 2.3 from 2.0 which is good news. However, the Neutrophils are back to 0 again this morning. Certainly, you can imagine how disappointing that is to Jeff. He really wants relief from this room.

Foods don't taste good to him; consequently, he doesn't eat. He's on IV liquids to provide the nourishment he isn't getting from the food that doesn't taste good to him.

Please pray he'll be patient in this extended hospital stay, that I can be a caretaker with a servant's heart, that God will provide wisdom for the doctors as they treat the low white blood cell count issue and develop the overall cancer treatment plan from this point forward, and for Brittany's continued strength.

As always, thank you for your prayers on our behalf.

12/27/09 (Sunday), 8:31PM-Karen

Still at Mercy. Jeff's total white blood cell count is 1.8, down from 2.3 yesterday. Based on the chart we get with the blood cell counts, the normal range is 4.5 to 11.0. The Neutrophils are up to 2.0 from yesterday's 0 with a target range of 36 to 78. The doctor has ordered a change from the Vancomycin antibiotic to Amoxicillin in an effort to get the white blood cell counts out of this slump. On a strange level, this is almost reassuring. If his white cells were affected by the chemo, any cancer cells remaining after surgery have also been destroyed. If that's the case, this will all be worth it.

Jeff's spirits seemed better today. I came to the hospital first thing this morning, and Jeff's parents brought Brittany over this afternoon after church. Jeff's visitors are still limited to immediate family to reduce the risk of infection, because of the low white blood cell counts. He played on the computer for a little while this afternoon and is watching football this evening.

I'm optimistic the new week will bring the results we're waiting for. Please continue to pray with me that Jeff's blood counts will increase. I don't know what God has planned, but I know "all things will work together for good."

12/28/09 (Monday), 2:14PM-Karen

Neutrophils are down to 0.0 again. Total white count is the same as yesterday at 1.8 with a target range of 4.5 to 11. I spoke this morning with Jeff's PA about these white blood cell count numbers. She confirmed that bringing the white blood cell counts up will be a slow process, with ups and downs, but encouraged us not to give up.

God has blessed us tremendously in having the relationship with this woman and her staff long before the cancer was diagnosed. We had always used a doctor in Weatherford. Several years ago, Jeff needed to see someone for strep throat or something seasonal, but our family doctor was booked solid. We called, and I think he had an appointment with the PA the same day. Since then, Jeff has continued to see her for all his medical care. She and the staff at the clinic have been very caring and always willing to spend a little extra time with him each visit. I know she cares about all of her patients, but I believe she has been sent by God to care for Jeff. She had a history that made her the perfect choice for God to use. And she's willing to give God the credit.

Thanks for spending a few minutes of your day to check on jeff, and thanks for the prayers. God is sustaining us through these days.

12/29/09 (Tuesday), 10:43PM-Karen

Jeff's total white blood cell count was 1.3, down from yesterday's 1.8. His Neutrophils were up to 1 today from the 0 yesterday. Dr. Keefer explained the target of 500 during his visit today. The 1.3 is read as a total white blood cell count of 1300. The Neutrophil percentage of 1 is multiplied the total white count of 1300 and yield a Neutrophil count of 130. So, 130 with a target of 500. Dr. Keefer remains confident the count will increase, although slowly. So we wait, one day at a time.

Today is day 14 of this hospital stay, and I must admit, my patience is running low. I feel pressure to work on year-end financial tasks in the office but know that right now it's important to be with Jeff at the hospital. I try to come over every day and quickly address the urgent items at home either in the evening after I get home from the hospital or in the morning before I leave.

I believe Jeff's gaining strength as the days progress and know the white blood cell counts will follow shortly. Please pray for Jeff's continued healing from the cancer as well as the side effects of the chemo and radiation.

Brittany was able to go with Jeff's parents to OSU cowgirls and cowboys basketball games today. She was even able to take a friend. I know she'll come home with lots of stories that will probably be a needed boost to my morale.

Thanks for checking on us.

12/31/09 (Thursday), 12:49AM-Karen

Jeff's total white blood cell count was 1.7, or 1700, but Neutrophils are back to 0 today. Dr. Keefer assures us the counts will go up. He said he's never had a patient whose white blood cell counts didn't eventually come back up.

Jeff's weak but restless. He really wants a change of scenery from the hospital room.

I spoke with my sister, Janice, this evening. We discussed the concept that perhaps we were in the hospital to be able to witness to someone. She suggested I get busy witnessing so we can go home. Sounds a little oversimplified; nonetheless, that is our mission: to be used wherever God places us, in whatever way He sees fit.

Since God has a plan (Jeremiah 29:11), and since all things work together for good to them that love the Lord (Romans 8:28), and since we love the Lord, then there is a reason why it's taking so long for the counts to come up. So we'll accept each day as God gives it and be thankful.

> This is the day that the Lord hath made, We will rejoice and be glad in it.
>
> Psalm 118:24 (KJV)

Keep up the prayers.

01/01/10 (Friday), 12:42AM-Karen

Day 16 of Jeff's hospital stay: The total whites were down to 1.3, or 1300, but the Neutrophils we've been waiting for were up to 3 percent. That's a Neutrophil count of 39 with a target of 500. Dr. Keefer was again positive we would see some progress soon. He said once the Neutrophil count stops fluctuating and starts climbing, it will climb consistently.

We close this year thankful for many things, with Jeff's life high on our list. Our family and friends are even more a treasure than they were just a few months ago. May your 2010 be blessed with health, happiness, and hope.

Thanks for praying for my family.

01/02/10 (Saturday), 1:19AM-Karen

Jeff's white blood cell counts are still not high enough to allow his discharge from the hospital. Dr. Keefer has the weekend off, and Jeff saw Dr. Reynolds, not the Reynolds who was his surgeon, but another Dr. Reynolds in oncology. The total white blood cell count was 1.1, the same as yesterday, and the Neutrophils were a 2. This may be down on the counts, but somehow works out to be a higher Neutrophil count. I thought I understood the math, but apparently, I was mistaken.

Please continue to pray for patience for our family through this long and tiring hospital stay. Jeff requires a lot of sleep, and his appetite is hindered by the blend of prescriptions he's taking. We aren't sure which one is causing everything to taste funny to Jeff. I guess even if we knew, it wouldn't change the fact that he needs each of the meds he's been prescribed.

We hold to the wonderful peace that God is in control and nothing has slipped by Him. The creator of the universe is awake and on the job. I yield to His plan.

01/03/10 (Sunday), 12:45AM-Karen

We're not home yet. We are watching the white blood cell counts and still waiting. That reminds me of a gospel song my aunt used to sing—"Watch and Wait."

Today's total white blood cell count was up to 1.4 from yesterday's 1.1, and the Neutrophil percentage was the same as yesterday at 2 percent. Still 2 percent, but 2 percent of a higher number! We seem to be moving in the right direction.

A big thanks to Jeff's brother, Randy. He came to OKC to sit with Jeff today and tomorrow. This let me get some work done in the office today and allows me to spend some time with Brittany. We went to OKC to see Jeff late this afternoon and stayed a couple of hours before heading back home.

Thanks for all the encouraging messages and prayers. It's in God's hands as it's been all along. Even Jeff's oncologist said Thursday he had prayed Jeff's counts would be up because he hated to come in again and tell us they weren't.

If you find yourself with lots of free time, consider the spiritual analogy of waiting to get out of the hospital to understand the wait for Christ's return. Are we actively watching and waiting?

01/03/10 (Sunday), 11:51PM-Karen

Another day at Mercy. Both of the white blood cell counts are up today, however still not quite enough to come home. The total white blood cell count was 2.2, up considerably from yesterday's 1.4. The Neutrophils were also up a full point to 3 today. Dr. Reynolds acknowledged the counts were up but wants Dr. Keefer to handle the decision of whether to let Jeff come home on Monday. The ray of hope was welcomed. Jeff seemed to be stronger today, which I attribute to the higher blood counts and, of course, God's provision.

Hope all of you had a pleasant Sunday inside, where it's warm. Brittany has one more day of Christmas vacation, and then it is back to school. She has a basketball game tomorrow, but no school.

Randy stayed with Jeff today. That allowed me to go with Britt to church. It was good to be surrounded by our church family, but I sure missed having Jeff there with us.

Please continue your prayers for Jeff's strength and patience for all of us.

HEADED HOME

01/04/10 (Monday), 9:34AM-Karen

I got up and called Jeff this morning, as I do most mornings. He hadn't seen a nurse or doctor yet. They had drawn blood, but he didn't have the results. He called back and said the counts are in the normal range. It looks like he's coming home! He asked the nurse to call Dr. Keefer. Hopefully, he'll be released as soon as I can get there. I'm on my way to OKC!

As earnestly as you have prayed for Jeff, please offer a prayer of thanks to God for this good news.

01/04/10 (Monday), 1:06PM-Karen

Jeff's nurse just left the room. She's working on the discharge paperwork and getting prescriptions lined up.

Yesterday's total white blood cell count was 2.2; today it's 4.7. His Neutrophil percentage was 3 yesterday. It jumped to 22 on today's blood work. Again, if my math's correct, that's a total Neutrophil count of 1034. Dr. Keefer promised to release Jeff when the total Neutrophils hit 500. The last few days, he was even willing to negotiate that number to something lower in an effort to get Jeff out sooner. No negotiation is necessary today— the numbers are where they need to be!

We are definitely giving all credit to God for this blessing. No matter how much research was done on a drug, it's still in God's hands to make it effective. We are so glad Jeff will be going home!

01/04/10 (Monday), 11:28PM-Karen

We made it home about seven or seven thirty this evening, and Jeff took a nap in his own bed for an hour or so. And then he asked if Britt had gifts she could open. So we opened Christmas gifts. Of course, the best gift today was coming home. Britt goes back to school tomorrow, so we beat the deadline of sharing our family Christmas before school starts back.

Jeff's still terribly weak and will need frequent breaks and naps. We'll be protective of his immune system for a while, I'm sure. I'll be able to work a little and still be available if Jeff needs something.

Funny how God has a way of making things work out really well. If either of us had a nine-to-five job and answered to an unrelated boss, taking time off for medical reasons might be a big issue. With both of us self-employed, our hours are flexible. December is not typically a heavy month for me. I have some end-of-the-year work, but my busy time is about to start. Busy season for the farming is usually through the summer and fall, so often, there is a lag during the winter. We have several loyal men that have been with us for many years, so they know the routines. Jeff's dad, Wayne, is retired in theory but has kept things moving on the farm-and-irrigation side of things.

I really can't thank each of you enough. Your comments are a source of encouragement, and even when you don't leave a message, we know you have been logged in to "checkonjeff," and that too is encouraging.

Please keep up the prayers. I know God is answering and providing for our needs.

01/05/10 (Tuesday), 10:13PM-Karen

Jeff's resting well in his own bed. He seems to be eating better. The diet he was on in the hospital was very bland, and I think he's glad to have some flavor. I made hamburger stew and cornbread for lunch, and we reheated a bowl for supper. With the chill outside, it was nice to have a hot meal.

I believe Jeff stayed awake most of the afternoon. I know he played on the computer a little and watched some TV. He ventured up to my office for a while and was in the basement some. I think he's enjoying the freedom from the IVs.

He's supposed to have blood tests tomorrow to confirm all is well with the white blood cell counts. We will have that done locally and fax the results to Dr. Keefer.

It's such a humbling experience to know so many people have Jeff on their prayer list.

01/06/10 (Wednesday), 11/26AM-Jeff

Jeff here. I don't know how to explain the changes that have taken place over the last 3 weeks. I am still extreamly [extremely] tired. It is great to be home. Being couped [cooped] up in the hospital room and not being able to have company was very tough. I know it was difficult for some of you that wanted to drop by, but it worked out for the best. If you are not familiar with all of the troubles I went through, Karen documented them in earlier posts.

I cannot tell you how your prayers brought me through some very tough times while in the hospital bed in the middle of the night. I often wonder why I am worthy of His grace, love, and healing when there are so many others that are more deserving. Without your special prayers, my wife's special love, and my daughter's special faith, I would have had a much tougher time getting through this ordeal.

Later.

—JK

Karen Remembers: Goodbyes

Jeff later told me watching us leave each night during this lengthy hospital stay was one of the hardest things he ever had to do. It was equally hard for us.

01/08/10 (Friday), 10:20AM-Karen

Jeff's still weak, but Brittany and I both believe he's getting stronger with every day. Our appointment at Dr. Keefer's office is the first week of February, so Jeff has a little break. He had blood drawn Wednesday at Weatherford, and we had the results faxed to us. I still haven't received my medical degree yet—and don't plan to—but my analysis of the lab printout says both the whites and the Neutrophils have more than doubled since Monday's release from the hospital. A definite praise!

Jeff got up at six forty-five this morning and started breakfast. He had the bacon cooked and then needed a rest. Brittany came downstairs about that time and scrambled the eggs. I was taking the dogs outside, one at a time. They've been in dog crates in the garage since Wednesday afternoon. We were concerned it would be too cold for them in their pens. When I took Britt to school this morning, the thermometer read four degrees.

We have two border collies and one little mutt. The mutt was a dropoff at our old house, and his current name is Little Dog. He has turned into a lot of entertainment. So you can enjoy the laugh with us, one night last week, we came home from seeing Jeff at the hospital and came into the driveway but didn't see Little Dog. I rolled down the window to get the mail, and we both heard a clop. Brittany immediately thought something was wrong with the car. Then we saw him. Little dog had a glue trap stuck to one paw and was bouncing out to see us. Clippity clop, clippity clop. We have speculated how he got the glue trap but don't have any definite answer to that question. In case you are wondering and are ever in a similar situation, Goo Gone will take a glue trap off a dog's foot! We laughed so hard. Guess we needed a laugh!

Things are leveling out a little, and we're working on new routines. We're still so thankful Jeff's home with us and no longer in the hospital. God is so good to us, and we have blessings far beyond what we deserve.

I had a dream last night that I was sharing John 3:16 with some college students at Braum's. In the dream, I shared how it's all about God wanting us to choose a relationship with Him. He could have created us without a choice, but that would have decreased the value of the relationship. Consider a lady that enjoys flowers. If she has to ask for flowers, then when she receives them, she doesn't know if the giver gave them because she *asked* for them, or if it was because they *wanted* to give her flowers. But when she gets flowers she didn't ask for, then she's thrilled because she knows the giver acted on his own.

I'm still learning, but that's kind of how it is with God. He's told us what will please Him—a personal relationship with Him. Everything God has done—from Creation to giving us a free will to preparing Heaven for us—is all about us choosing to have a relationship with *Him* and His eternal fellowship with those who want to be with Him.

John 3:16 (KJV) says, *"For God so loved the world that he gave his only begotten son that whosoever believeth in Him should not perish, but have ever lasting life."*

God knew from the beginning how sweet eternity will be with those who chose to have a relationship with Him. We had to have a choice. That choice led to sin, sin led to a need for a savior, the need for a savior led to Christmas, Christ's birth, and the cross and then to the resurrection. How do we approach our relationship with God? Do we consider it a joy to spend time with God in prayer and in the Word because we want to give him a bouquet of our love?

I continue to tell you how much we appreciate each one of you taking time out of what I know are busy days to check on our progress and how much we appreciate your prayers for our family. "Thanks" doesn't seem like enough of an acknowledgment, but it's the best word choice I can find. So "Thanks!"

01/09/10 (Saturday), 10:23PM-Jeff

I haven't written for a little while, so I thought I would let you know how I am doing. I am still very tired, and with very little effort, I am often worn out. I find my hardest decision is whether to sit in the La-Z-Boy or just go to bed and take a nap. Simple tasks like walking to the kitchen or going to the restroom take most of my strength. I don't feel bad, but I don't feel good either because of the stress. The blood counts seem to be good.

Continue to pray for stength [strength] and stamina for me, and for Karen and Brittany also.

Later.

—JK

01/11/10 (Monday), 10:46PM-Karen

Jeff continues to gain a little more strength every day. Today he even asked for Mexican food from our favorite local Mexican cafe—make that our *only* local cafe. Anyway, a favorite. He ate about half the to-go order and said his taste buds still aren't back completely.

Britt and I went to church on Sunday but left Jeff at home to rest. We were concerned he was still too weak to be out and about.

I know what seems to be "waiting time" is really part of our journey. We're reminded daily of our blessings, and we're enjoying the treasure of having Jeff at home.

Thanks for your continued prayers for our family.

01/12/10 (Tuesday), 9:27PM-Jeff

I've had a pretty good day today. I cooked breakfast this morning for the first time since I got out of the hospital. I don't know if I will be able to do it tomorrow, but maybe in a little while, I will get part of my strength back. Karen took me to Hydro, to the barbershop. We went to Weatherford and got milk and vanilla ice cream. We got home about 5:30 this afternoon and I slept for a while and that helped a little. I am still pretty weak, but maybe a little improvement today.

Later.

—JK

01/13/10 (Wednesday), 9:35PM-Jeff

Lately it seems easier to make entries in the evening. I have been sleeping more at night and only waking up in the middle of the night. In the mornings, it takes a lot of my energy to get ready and shower, and I am out of energy before I get everything done. I am still having minor indigestion problems. It is very tiring, though. I went to Hinton with Karen this afternoon to get Brittany. I am just trying to get out of the house for a little while everyday to help build my stamina. I am still very tired most of the time.

Please continue your prayers for strength and healing and remember Karen and Brittany. Their strength is unbelievable.

Later.

—JK

01/14/10 (Thursday), 4:47PM-Jeff

Brittany is in a basketball game in Fort Cobb, and I don't know if I should go, but I am thinking about it. I am getting a little stronger, and I think it may be a good outing for me. I don't have a lot of stamina, but if I don't push it, I don't think it will ever get better. Not much going on today, so I didn't use a lot of my energy so far.

Later.

—JK

01/15/10 (Friday), 1:53PM-Jeff

Karen has been helping with the billing on the irrigation business the last couple of days and wanted a copy of the T-L program on her computer. I have installed this many times, and I have not had any problems. After the ball game last night, I decided I would install this program on her computer. I started the installation, and everything seemed to have went [gone] well until I tried to reboot her computer. Now I have the blue screen that says there is an error and the system is shutting down. I have exhausted all of the avenues I know, so I guess we are going to take it to Weatherford and see if we can get the info off of the hard drive and then reformat the hard drive. That is what I have been doing most of the morning. I didn't sleep well because I worried about this, but maybe we can get it running.

I seem to feel a little better, and my strength is slow in coming back. I think I will take a nap as soon as I finish this blog. Karen took Britt to school and then went to run some errands. She isn't back, yet she has promised to bring food.

Later.

—JK

01/17/10 (Sunday), 5:12PM-Karen

Jeff continues to gain a little strength with each day. Jeff wanted to go to church this morning but wasn't sure if he could hold up for Sunday school, the worship service, church meal, and the pastoral search committee meeting, so we took separate vehicles. Jeff came for church, stayed for the meal, and then came back home.

Our church had a prospective minister preach today. He and his wife stayed Friday and Saturday nights with us. It was nice to have guests, and Jeff had good strength. Last night, the pastoral search committee and their wives came to meet the couple. The menu was potluck Mexican food. It was delicious.

Thanks for your prayers for Jeff, Brittany, and me. We know it's all in God's hands, and we're thankful for His guidance.

01/17/10 (Sunday), 10:15PM-Jeff

I am in my office for the first time in a long time. This has been a busy week, and I would like to share with you the blessings that have been given my family, my church, and myself. We have had the great experience the past 3 days entertaining a prespective [prospective] new pastor for our church. Bob Sprunger and his, wife, Linda spent a couple of nights with us, and they were great guests. Don Troyer picked them up at the airport in OKC and brought them to our house. Dad came over for supper on Friday evening, and we had a good visit. On Saturday, Bob and Linda were given a tour of Hinton, Hydro, the Church, and seeing the countryside. They even made a trip to Clinton to Wong's for lunch. Saturday evening we had a large Mexican supper here at our house and with about 20 present. We had a great time talking about the future. Sunday morning was again busy helping getting everything ready for the morning service that Bob was going to preach at. They had some minor difficulties getting things ready, and I went to church a little later because I didn't think I had enough stamina to go to Sunday school and church and then the dinner. When I got there before church, Brittany and I was able to get it all fixed, and the sound system worked fine. We had a great time with the Sprungers and was glad to have them. We asked for prayers that God will let his desires be known to us.

Before the Sprungers came to visit, I was going to install a T-L program on Karen's computer, but after I tried to install, it the computer locked up. I worked on it a little but didn't have the attention span that I needed at the time. Karen worked on it and again couldn't get it to boot up either. I finally went back to it this afternoon, and again, after a short talk with the Lord, the computer booted, and Karen was able to move all the data that needed to be moved to another drive. My next intention is to format the hard drive on her computer. She is not happy about doing it as tax season starts, but I am so happy we recovered the data that I was scared we lost.

I am gaining strength everyday, but it is slow. I actually drove to church this morning. This is the first driving since I went to the hospital over 5 weeks ago. It felt good to be out and about.

Later.

—JK

01/18/10 (Monday), 4:38PM-Karen

Jeff has served on several farm organization boards on both state and national levels. One of the big blessings that emerged with the responsibilities is meeting a variety of individuals. Some of those acquaintances soon became friends, and some of the friends became close friends. We've had the opportunity to meet many quality people over the years. To back that statement up, I offer the following:

Five professors from the Department of Plant and Soil Sciences will be competing in the upcoming OKC Memorial Marathon as a relay team to honor Jeff. The members of the team are Drs. Brian Arnall, Kefyalew Desta, Chad Penn, Jason Warren, and Dave Porter. They will run a total of 26.2 miles during the race. As a relay team, these men will trade off and keep one team member running the entire marathon. Their team, Krehbiel's Krew, is raising funds for the American Cancer Society. It's such

an honor these men chose Jeff as the namesake for their team. It will be fun to have runners to watch during the marathon.

Dr. Porter says they are the best agronomists in the whole marathon!

Thanks to each of you, and a special "Thanks" to each of these kind and generous men.

01/20/10 (Wednesday), 6:31PM-Jeff

What a big day. We took Brittany to school a little early and then went to OKC for the Oklahoma Wheat Commission meeting. Everything went well. We had a good commission meeting and the commission is concerned that we protect the wheat varieties that were developed by Oklahoma State so they are not used without just compensation from independant [independent] operators that would like to use them in biotech wheat in the future. Also the national meeting for US Wheat is the rest of this week in Washington D.C. I will not be going this week. This will be the first time in several years that I have not gone to Washington D.C. That is one trip I will definately [definitely] miss.

After the meeting this morning and lunch, we went to Ultimate Electric and got an HDTV for the living room upstairs. Karen's brother Phillip is coming on Saturday to help install the TV. Actually, he is going to do it, and I am going to watch and tell him what he is doing wrong. I can't fix it, but I can give my opinion.

Karen and Brittany went to church this evening. They are having a singing group come sing this evening. I didn't think I could make the trip.

Keep praying for us.

Later.

—JK

01/21/10 (Thursday), 9:14PM-Jeff

I have been pretty tired today. I loaded some anti-virus software on the two computers. I have been pretty tired today, so I took a nap this morning, and then this afternoon, I went Hinton to get Brittany. Brittany helped me this afternoon. We hooked up one of the TV's, and they are going to hook them up on HD tomorrow. We are excited.

I feel pretty good, and about half the time, I am sleeping most of the night. I am sleeping later in the morning, and that makes it harder to write in the morning. I will try to get back in the habit as soon as possible.

Later.

—JK

01/23/10 (Saturday), 11:53PM-Jeff

Well, we skipped a day. Karen's family came out today, and we finally celebrated Christmas. They decided to put it off during the Christmas season because I was in the hospital at that time. A gambler will say he drew to an inside straight or hit a lucky horse. I simply got a lot more than I paid for with my in-laws. They were all here today, and I got a TV hung on the wall, the sound system put on it, and I got to watch it this afternoon. They did a wonderful job, and I appreciate all of their hard work.

Fortunately, I got to see OSU beat Kansas State. This was especially interesting when Karen's niece's husband is a K State fan. After that ball game, a short nap was in order. Then after some supper, a short nap was in order. Then I worked with getting the remote on the TV to work like I wanted, and that didn't take long before it was time to go to bed.

Glen and Karen are going to sing in church tomorrow morning. This morning we had a deacons' meeting at the Mark Restaurant in Weatherford. We had a very good meeting, and we intend to suggest that the congregation give Bob Sprunger a call at the next church meeting in a couple of weeks.

Later.

—JK

01/26/10 (Tuesday), 12:05AM-Jeff

I seem to be sleeping more at night, and I think that is good. This morning we worked on getting more irrigation bills sent. Karen and Dad have really worked hard on this, and I am glad they are making progress. My next project is the wheat seed reports that were due at the first of the year. I am very appreciative of all the help several at OSU have shown toward me during this difficult time. I planned on doing the reports before Christmas, but my hospital stay put an end to that.

After lunch I worked on the television for a while trying to get the programs for the dish network. We then went to Fort Cobb to Brittany's basketball game. The 7th and 8th grade won their game. But the junior high lost by 5 points. The boys lost both of their games.

Later.

—JK

01/26/10 (Tuesday), 11:02PM-Jeff

I seem to be sleeping better then I have since I have been sick. I usually sleep 7–8 hours a night and just a short nap during the day. It if feels really good to get long periods of sleep at one time.

Tax time is here, and Karen is working on 1099s. I went with Karen today to Clinton. She had to drop some stuff off at the Social Security office. This was after we ate lunch at Wong's cafe. We stopped at the pharmacy in Weatherford and the dry cleaners to get some pants I was having pressed. We went to Hinton and picked up Brittany at school and then came home. After that trip, I needed a nap. I then took Brittany back to school because she had to work at the concession stand for the high school basketball game. Girls won, and boys lost.

My family decided not to have Christmas at Christmastime because I was in the hospital and the weather was not good at the time. We were going to have it this weekend, but again the weather does not look good, and Lenzy has other obligations. We may have to do this later in the year.

Later.

—JK

01/29/10 (Thursday), 3:42PM-Karen

Jeff has had good days and hasn't needed very many naps. It's good to have him up and around more. Brittany didn't have school today. In fact, they called it prior to the end of the school day yesterday. I guess they trusted the weathermen. Turns out they were right this time. We have a clear layer of about a 1/2 inch of ice, and it's been sleeting for an hour.

Wayne was able to help me get caught up on the billing for the irrigation business last week. We got the invoicing in the mail on Monday, except a few accounts needing special attention. I'm almost done with 1099s and W-2s and then it's on to taxes.

Thank you for all your prayers. We still have a wonderful peace that seems to engulf us and keep us from worry. There are still many unknowns. I'd like to think all the bad parts are behind us, but the truth is...we really don't know, and yet, there is peace.

I've always been a music fan and always been able to easily remember words to songs. I often catch myself with a "song in my heart," so to speak. I've noticed that lately I'm especially susceptible to the emotion in hymns. I find myself pitying the songwriters for having to experience such pain in order to write such touching songs. The line from the song that seems to fit right now is "Many things about tomorrow, I don't seem to understand, but I know who holds tomorrow, and I know He holds my hand."[3]

Thank you for checking on us, and especially for the prayers.

"For I know the plans I have for you," declares the Lord, "plans to prosper you and not to harm you, plans to give you hope and a future." Jeremiah 29:11 (NIV).

01/30/10 (Saturday), 11:00AM-Jeff

It is a beautiful morning here. The snow or sleet has covered the ground, and the view out of the living room window is really pretty. We have been very lucky because we have only short outages of electricity. Usually less then [than] a minute of outage a few times yesterday. I feel good, and the family is well.

Brittany had piano practice yesterday and then met with the church youth group this afternoon for some sleding [sledding]. They went to Grandpa Wayne's and slide [slid] down the hill on Chris and LeElla's sleds. I think they really had a good time when they hooked the sled behind Grandpa's Polaris Ranger and went for a spin. They did get pretty cold, but they had a good time. I can't figure out how Chris knew how to hook a sled behind a tractor and go sleding. I don't remember anything like that ever happening around there about 30 years ago.

Later.

—JK

02/01/10 (Monday), 11:48AM-Jeff

The frozen fog that has engulfed our home is making me wonder when this is going to pass on to someone else. I haven't been out of the house in 5 days, and I want to get out, but I don't think it is worth the risk. Dad wants me to go to Stillwater to the basketball

game. I don't think I am going to go because of the parking lots, and I don't know if I have the stamina for the trip.

Yesterday we called off church for the first time in several years. I can't remember when we called off church last.

They called off school in Hinton for today. I hope that by tomorrow the roads will be okay.

Later.

—JK

02/02/10 (Tuesday), 10:35AM-Jeff

I finally talked myself into going to the ball game last night. Dad, Brittany, Cierra, and I went to the Texas-OSU basketball game. We had a good time, and I think the girls enjoyed themselves even though OSU lost. The roads were good except right here in country. There were more electric wires down than I thought there would be. When we were out, we saw several high line wires that were on the ground. We have only had some minor outages, but with the number of wires down, we could have had more power outages.

We lost Internet [connection] yesterday, and they said it was a power problem on the telephone grid. We have a DSL Internet here at our house, and in the past, we had a wireless system. This system seems to work better, but there is a problem when the electricity goes out. For some unknown reason, the FCC seems to think that the telephone service is more important than the Internet. We didn't even know what the Internet was for the first 40 years of my life, and now we think we half [have] to have it.

Britt went to school today, so she was ready to get back to school today. Maybe things are getting back to normal.

Later.

—JK

02/03/10 (Wednesday), 2:12PM-Jeff

My trip to Stillwater seems to have taken a lot of my stamina. I have been sleeping some during the day and trying to catch up. I have been doing pretty good, though.

We have this little dog that showed up right before we left the old house, and with the cold weather, we have been letting him in the house lately, and he has been doing pretty good, and no messes yet. Karen has given him a bath or two, and he seems to like it. We put him in a carrier at night, and then we let him out first thing in the morning. He may be alright [all right] in the house after a while.

Brittany invited all of the youth group out for ham and beans for supper. One of our hired hands is going to come and clear my sidewalk for the youth group.

Brittany got a new phone today because her old one broke. It was under warranty. She also has a dental appointment this afternoon. She is getting close to having her braces taken off soon.

Later.

—JK

02/05/10 (Friday), 10:03PM-Jeff

I took Britt to school this morning. The snow cover is still on some of the fields. By this evening, most of the snow cover was gone.

I went to Weatherford about noon and went to Western Equipment. They have my combine their [they're] being worked on. I need new cylinder bars and straw chopper knives. There were several things that needed to be changed, and I think I am going to have Western fix some of the stuff, and we will do part of it also. From Western, I went to Cummins and picked up Karen. We ate lunch and then went to the eye doctor.

Dr. Franz said that my main trouble with my vision was I had not been to the doctor in 3 years. She said the primary trouble with my eyesight is that old age is causing my eyesight to be stressed. I think changing the lenses in my glasses will help. My eyes are in good shape for my age, and the theropy [therapy] has not caused me any trouble with my eyes. I go to my oncologist Monday, and he will have some input, but I think I will get my lenses changed next week.

After the eye doctor, we headed to Thomas to Brittany's basketball game. It was a junior high game, so Britt didn't get to play much. Thomas has a new gym, and it is very nice. We ate supper in Weatherford on the way home.

Later.

—JK

02/06/10 (Saturday), 10:46PM-Jeff

Karen and Brittany worked on the garage today. They are trying to get it cleaned up because we never got it cleaned up after we moved in. We could use two stalls, but the third one had a bunch of stuff in it. They did a good job, and I went out this evening and helped decide on what needed to go to the shed and what could stay in the garage. They also hauled a load of stuff to the ETC shop in Weatherford.

My Cowboys didn't fair [fare] well today on the basketball court. Hopefully better next week.

I am sure most of you have heard about the people in Haiti that have been imprisoned for trying to take children out of the country. I was a little worried about this and didn't know if this was a good or bad thing. We received an e-mail from a deacon in our church yesterday. His son, Ryan, is in seminary in Missouri, and he knows the people in Haiti that are in jail and has asked that we pray for them and their immediate care and safety. They are hoping to have them returned to the U.S. soon, but some of the reports have not been good.

Later.

—JK

02/08/10 (Monday), 11:56PM-Jeff

We got up this morning to another 3–4 inches of snow. We finally got all of the old snow to melt yesterday and Saturday, and we got more today. The roads were a little slick when we took Brittany to school. From there we headed to OKC to see Dr. Keefer. The highway was wet, but we didn't have any trouble. Our appointment was at 9:30, and we were on time. The only problem was the people that were supposed to be there before us also showed up at 9:30. They pulled blood, and the tests were all good. I was supposed to have an MRI back in January, but it was cancelled because I was having trouble with my blood counts. They were able to do the MRI today because of cancellations, but I won't have any results from that for a couple of days. There is some concern that my white blood cell counts could be bad if he puts me back on Temodar for chemo. The original plan was to put me back on Temodar at a higher rate. Keep this [it] a matter of prayer that Dr. Keefer will make the decision that is beneficial to curing my cancer.

Sunday was a big day also. I didn't go to Sunday school because I didn't think I would have enough energy. I was worship leader, and everything seemed to go well. No one came up and told me I did a bad job afterward. I enjoy being worship leader, but it does take more energy than you would think. Also, Sunday evening we had a business meeting, and I was chairman of that also. This was to extend a call to Bob and Linda Sprunger to be our pastor. I felt the meeting was very productive, and we had a unanimous vote to extend the call. I will follow up with that in the near future as soon as we have an idea if they accept the call.

Tomorrow I have to go back to OKC because I have a Wheat Commission meeting on Wednesday. I hope to get a good report from the meeting in Washington DC.

Thanks again for your prayers, and keep in mind the doctor's decisions that are going to be made in the near future. Also, pray for my stamina to be increased and for my mind to be sharp for the meetings.

Later.

—JK

02/10/10 (Wednesday), 12:46AM-Karen

We received a good report today. The thin rim of cancerous cells that wasn't removed during surgery in September is shrinking. Dr. Keefer will review the MRI and get back with us on the chemo schedule and dosage. The standard chemo treatment is given for 5 consecutive days a month for six months. Because Jeff had such a severe drop in white blood cells when he stopped taking the Temodar in December, Dr. Keefer wants him to take half that standard dose, based on calculated body mass, the first month, and then carefully monitor Jeff's white blood cell counts.

The objective is to have the dosage strong enough to have a negative effect on the cancer cells and yet not so strong to kill *all* the good white blood cells that fight off infections. Dr. Keefer was confident that with careful blood count monitoring and injections of Neupogen as needed, we can keep Jeff out of the hospital. Neupogen is a cell stimulator that targets the bone marrow where blood cells are produced.

I can't thank each of you enough for making time to check in on Jeff's progress, and especially for the prayers. Today's results prove God is answering our prayers! The peace we have written about before continues to be such a wonderful blessing. Life is so fragile, and we are so helpless, yet to know none of this is a surprise to God brings comfort

(Jeremiah 29:11, NIV). I think maybe the peace comes when we realize our future isn't earthly.

I have to give a big "Thanks" to all the Sunday school teachers that encouraged me to memorize verses. I often have to research the chapter and verse, but that hidden treasure has proved to be a great comfort to me.

02/11/10 (Thursday), 3:52PM-Jeff

I need to start with Tuesday. I took Brittany to school and came back home. I worked a little in the office because I need to get some book work done that has been hanging over my head for several months. I finally finished this job about 1:00 this afternoon, and it was a feather in my cap. Now on to the next project, and hopefully, it will work out well also. I headed back to Hinton this afternoon and got Brittany after school. I took a short nap after I got home, and that really helped me a lot. Britt helped me finish packing my bags, and I headed to OKC to for the Wheat Commission meeting tomorrow. We went to eat supper this evening at the Cattlemen's Steakhouse, and of course, an order of lamb fries for an appetizer was needed to start things off. After supper, we went back to the hotel. I was pretty tired, so I went straight to my room. I sat on the bed and was trying to find something to watch on TV. The next thing I know, it is 11:00 PM, and I am sound asleep with my boots, heavy coat, and cap still in place. I got up and got ready for bed. I really slept pretty good that night.

I was a little late getting up Wednesday morning, but I just skipped breakfast and made it to the meeting in good shape. I was still a little tired from the day before, I made it through the meeting, but I was tired. I stopped and got a little lunch and then headed home. I got home in the middle of the afternoon and took a good nap. I went to Hinton and got Britt after school, and she had her allotment of 4-H candy bars. By the time she got them home, there were 2 missing from the box. I told her where she was going to get the money for my candy bar, but I didn't know where she was going to get the money for hers.

I felt pretty good this morning. Karen took Brittany to school. I am going to Brittany's ball game this evening, and then down to Anadarko for the Farm Bureau meeting. I have been working on my GPS for my pickup because it didn't have the county roads on it. I tried to make it work, but it says it is short on memory. I think I have lost a memory chip out of it. I will work on it some later.

Thank you for keeping us in your prayers. Sorry the other blog didn't post, and I am sure I missed some things.

Later.

—JK

02/13/10 (Saturday), 8:03PM-Jeff

Yesterday we went to the basketball game in Carnegie. The junior high girls won. Brittany didn't get to play much because it was a junior high game. After the boys' game, we went to Weatherford and ate supper. It was a fairly good day for me, and I caught up on my sleep a little.

This morning we got up and headed to OKC. It was Grandma Fern, Karen, Brittany, and me. We were going to meet Grandpa there. He and I were going to the basketball game in Stillwater, and the ladies were going to a baby shower for my niece Lenzy. When we got to Hinton Travel Plaza, we stopped for gas for Grandpa's Suburban. I checked the tires, and one tire had a knot on it. We took it back to Grandpa's and got Karen's Yukon. We finally got on the road. We met Grandpa at the Flying J on I-35. I went with him to Stillwater, and the ladies headed to Tulsa. The ball game was very good, and we had a good time. Karen and Brittany are not home yet, so I don't know how the baby shower went.

I have been tapering down my steroids, and what I am finding out is my appitite [appetite] is going down. I think it is good because I need to lose some weight, and maybe this will help. I feel pretty good, and I am sleeping well most nights.

Later.

—JK

02/16/10 (Tuesday), 9:53AM-Jeff

Well, I haven't written in a few days. I don't know what the deal is, but I can't seem to get in the habit of writing in my blog every day like I used to. Sunday was a good day for us. We went to church and had our monthly noon meal. After lunch, we had a presentation by Roy Dick about a trip he took to Russia, and they also celebrated his 80 birthday. They were supposed to do that the other day but the snow called off church so they moved it back a couple of weeks. Sunday afternoon, I watched a little of the NASCAR race and the Olympics. Brittany had a couple of girls spend the night with her Saturday night, and Karen took them home Sunday afternoon. I think they had a pretty good time because they talked about (still) being up at 3:30 AM. After Karen and Brittany got home, they slept part of the afternoon.

Monday was President's Day. Brittany didn't have to go to school, so we were home most of the day. I worked on the computer most of the morning, trying to get my e-mail straightened out. It turns into a job when you turn on your Outlook, and it tells you that there are 350 e-mails to download. I went through all of them and took care of what I could. After that I watched the OSU vs. OU basketball game. Brittany hadn't seen it yet, and since it was such a good game, I could pass watching it on the DVR. Brittany had piano, so Karen and I took her to piano practice. She has really made a lot of progress on her piano playing, and I hope she keeps her interest. After piano, we came home and worked on the Dish network in the basement. We have had it for almost a month, and we were still having trouble. After two calls to Dish, we finally got it working. I think it is working, but I still have some reserves [reservations].

LeElla brought over supper this evening. It was a Mexican beef casserole. It was pretty good.

I took Brittany to school this morning, and then I tried to put one of those steering wheel covers on my pickup and that didn't go well. Karen had been looking a long time for one and found one that I would like, but I was having trouble getting it on the wheel, and I tore it. I am in bad trouble. Pray for her to grant [have] mercy on me.

Later.

—JK

02/17/10 (Wednesday), 9:44AM-Jeff

Houston, we have a problem. It is not a major problem, but it is a problem. Yesterday evening, I got up out of my sleep-infested La-Z-Boy recliner to take care of some personal business, and when I returned to the living room, I happened to notice that Brittany was not on the couch but had moved to the love seat on the other side of the room. I decided that this would be the perfect opportunity for me to try out this new couch as a laying-down [lying down] device instead of the old sit-up style type of furniture. As I reclined, I found the cushions to be very comfortable and firm. My wife brought over a small blanket and covered me up. About an hour later, I woke up, and it hit me: this couch is sleep infected too! Just like my La-Z-Boy chair. If you set [sit] in them very long, you wind up sound asleep. My usual length of sleep infestation is about an hour. Karen or Brittany usually wakes me up because they want to make sure I am alive and well. I think I am going to open a craigslist account. I am firmly convinced that if I could prove to potential customers that their furniture already has sleep infestation, it would be worth twice as much as brand new.

Later.

—JK

02/18/10 (Thursday), 9:33AM-Jeff

Yesterday morning, I worked in the office a little while, but I just kept falling asleep. I finally gave up. I was really tired, and I don't know why. Brittany was sick yesterday morning and didn't go to school until lunchtime. She was doing well that afternoon. Yesterday afternoon, we went to Mercy Health Center to see the new addition to the family. Karen's niece, Betsy and husband, Kelly Groves, are the new proud parents of a baby girl named Jasey Clare Groves. She was breach and had to be taken C-section, but mother and daughter seem to be doing very well. I wonder how she got such a nice room. It is three times bigger than the room I dwelled [stayed] in for three weeks while I was waiting for my blood count to come up, and they never told me that a room like that was available. I believe if I had to, I could have delivered a baby, or goat, or dog, or something for a room like Jasey's while I was at the hospital.

One little piece of advice while visiting someone at the hospital. When I was in the hospital, and especially towards the end of my incarceration, I was very tired and low on energy. When visiting, please keep in mind that the person you are visiting may be tired and need some rest. I know I feel like I must entertain people when they come to visit. That is just my human nature. Ten minutes holding a grand niece is not very long, but it can be forever if you just gave birth this morning.

Congrats to Betsy and Kelly, and may the Lord bless you. Later.

—JK

02/20/10 (Saturday), 9:54PM-Karen

Almost a week steroid free! I believe that makes Jeff more active, and the result of being more active? The need for more rest. Good thing is… he still sleeps well at night. We had both hoped his taste buds would recover after he was pulled off the steroids, but we haven't seen that improvement yet. He *has* noticed a decrease in appetite, which is a good thing. While he was on Decadron to keep the inflammation down, he often rummaged for snacks and almost always cleaned his plate. Now he seems to be okay with quitting a little earlier. I'm not sure if it's because he's getting the sense of being full or if he's bored with flavors that don't taste right.

Jeff's still a little weak. Five and a half months of limited activity has decreased his dexterity, and he wears down easily. He's spent more time in his office this week than he has in a while. I believe that's a good thing.

Some of you may have lived through events I have only seen in the old movies, where the family would hitch the team to the wagon and go to town once a month to get supplies. This morning we made a similar trek to Weatherford. It had been a while since all three of us went on this adventure. Counting lunch, we had eight stops. I drove but handed the keys to Jeff every time we got out. Some of the stops, he went in for a while and then headed to the car for rest. Some of the stops, he waited in the car. But he did make it in at Braum's with us midafternoon for a sundae. About six hours later, we headed home. It was almost a full day of activity for Britt and me, not to mention Jeff.

During Jeff's radiation days, when he started getting weak, we requested a handicapped parking permit. It has been a big help getting Jeff closer to the door. It doesn't seem to be quite as important on the way in as it is on the way out of stores.

A side benefit of our trip to town—a homemade lasagna for supper. Some meals require special ingredients that require planning or a special trip to town. Lasagna is one of those meals for us. We don't keep ricotta cheese around the house. I remember hearing a story once that if a redneck buys clothes, you can bet they're gonna wear them within twenty-four hours. Similarly, when ricotta cheese is on our shopping list, you can bet it's gonna be in the oven within twenty-four hours.

I know our day-to-day activities are probably a really boring read for each of you. But maybe they give you an idea of the status of Jeff's physical condition and an insight on how to direct your prayers.

I really wish we had a phrase that would convey our deepest appreciation for your continued prayers and your investment of your most valuable resource—your time—to check on Jeff's status. "Thank you" is the best response I can come up with. It puts me in the mind of some of the writings of Paul in the New Testament. He was always thankful of the people in other towns that kept up with him. Philippians 1:3 (NIV) says, *"I thank my God every time I remember you..."* The verse goes on to mention praying with joy because of those who were spiritually in partnership with him. Maybe that says it best.

02/21/10 (Sunday), 7:30PM-Jeff

Wake the kids and phone the neighbors I finally made it to Sunday school this morning. This is the first time I have made it to Sunday school in quite a while. I really enjoyed participating in the conversation.

After SS I went over to the church to get the projector ready for church. Everything worked pretty good, but I stay in the back in case something goes wrong and needs to be fixed during church. There are several cushioned chairs, and after trying out several of them, I have decided that the chair I sat in today was not sleep infected. I sat there for the whole service and fell asleep once. The last 3 Sundays, it has been a challenge to find a chair that is not sleep infected. I think a sleep-infected chair auctioned off at a fund-raiser could be interesting. Then you sell a non-sleep- infected chair to the other spouse. It would be very interesting who gets which chair.

Karen took Britt to Hinton practice basketball with some friends, and the Yukon quit working. I thank [think] it has a transmission problem. I went to town and pulled her home. Then we went to Grandpas and got their suburban so Karen would have something to drive tomorrow.

Later.

—JK

02/22/10 (Monday), 11:40PM-Karen

First thing this morning, Jeff drove the pickup, and I rode in my Yukon. Tow rope in between. The verdict: the transmission is out in my Yukon. It will be a few days before it's fixed. I'm thankful we didn't have any trouble getting the vehicle to Weatherford. When we got home, Jeff was ready for a nap. The Olympic curling events provide good background noise for his nap, but not quite as restful as the ice skating.

I was able to work in the office most of the day. Tax season is officially here. The first returns are headed out the door. Just fifty- two days left until April 15. God has blessed my practice, and I have some of the best clients in the world. They have all been so patient with me—another blessing God has sent my way!

Britt is in FFA this year and is working on her speech. They will enter several contests this spring. I know her topic is on agritourism, but she has done all the research and writing during class time. I'm anxious to hear the final version. She has accepted a commitment to play the piano offertory the first Sunday of each month. She was taking one Sunday a quarter and is bumping that responsibility up a little. I really enjoy her practices. She's a great kid. Jeff and I are so blessed. Do you see the pattern? Blessings are everywhere you look for them.

Having our daily activities summarized by bedtime each day has proven to be quite humbling. I start out each day with a list of tasks I hope to accomplish but go to bed without marking all the items as completed. Sometime back, I had a picture framed with an adapted version of the serenity prayer—you know, the one that says "God grant me the serenity to accept the things I cannot change, the courage to change the things I can and the wisdom to know the difference." I adapted it with three verses: Psalm 46:10 (NIV) that says *"Be still and know that I am God,"* Philippians 4:13 (KJV) *"I can do all things through Christ which strengtheneth me,"* and James 1:5 (NIV) that says *"If any of you lacks wisdom, he should ask God, who gives generously to all without finding fault, and it will be given to him."* I have a framed piece of paper on my wall that says I finished my formal education many years ago, but it seems that I'm still a student after all. God's still teaching, and I'm still learning. The concept of letting God direct my path sounds easy, but it's challenging. To let go of my selfish plans, my checklists as it were, and trust that He alone is able to choreograph my life, and that of my family's, to reach our potential is a daily challenge. I guess that's where John 10:10 (KJV) fits: *"I am come that they might have life and that they might have it more abundantly."*

My prayer is that God will use us in whatever way He sees beneficial to His plan, and that "me, myself and I" don't get in His way.

Thanks for spending time with us today.

02/24/10 (Wednesday), 10:47PM-Jeff

I have been feeling a little rough the last couple of days, and it seems like I am pretty low on energy. I have spent a little extra time in front of the TV. We are in the second week of the Summer [Winter] Olympics. They have been a lot of fun to watch, and some sports seem quite mind-boggling. Bobsledding and skiing are pretty easy. The fastest one down the hill wins. Then there is the ice skating that is based on whether you fall down or not. These sports are relatively easy to keep track of who is winning or losing.

Someone added hockey to the group of sports at the Olympics. Now some of you Northerners may know how to play hockey, and I do understand how the points are scored, but I don't know all the rules and penalties. It's easy to watch, and there are several teams that are fun to watch. I don't know what they are going to do when the men's and women's teams have to face off for the gold medal.

Another thing that blows my mind is curling. I don't know anything about this game, and in order to find out what the score is, I have to have the announcer tell me. However, I can turn this on in the middle of the afternoon, and I am so fascinated with speed this game progresses I am liable to sit and watch an hour of it, and I can't tell if either team scored a point. I think it even has a hoax on my sleep-infested chair. More info on that later.

Brittany pointed out that there was a possum at the dog dish. I promptly went and got my shotgun and a flashlight and went possum hunting. The possum headed around the house and got in the grass. I took my first shot and missed. This almost broke down my entire hunting prowess, but I managed to follow him around the corner of the house. I took a little extra time to aim more carefully. I pulled on the trigger, and the Lord called the poor thing home.

I seem to be gaining a little today over the last couple of days, and hopefully, that will continue. Thank you for your prayers.

Later.

—JK

CHEMO: ROUND 1

02/26/10 (Friday), 4:20PM-Karen

We received a call today from Dr. Keefer's office. The next phase of Jeff's treatment, a chemo regimen, will start on Monday. Jeff will take the same daily dosage of the Temodar he took last fall when he took it every day for fifty consecutive days. Starting Monday, he'll take Temodar on a schedule of five days on, twenty-three days off for six months. The nurse practitioner indicated they will keep close tabs on Jeff's blood counts. They'll start a white cell booster at the first indication the Temodar will affect Jeff's white blood cell counts. Please pray the white blood cell counts stay up, out of the critically low range, since that was the culprit for Jeff's extended stay at Mercy over Christmas and New Year's. Jeff's next appointment with Dr. Keefer is March 9.

Thanks for your prayers.

03/01/10 (Monday), 7:42PM-Jeff

Well, it is Monday, the start of a whole new time. I am going to be taking my chemo this evening, and it is the same dose and chemo that I took in November. It has not been as nice of time the last 3 months as I had hoped. As most of you know, the white blood count the end of December and the beginning of January really took a lot of energy from me, and I haven't recovered yet.

I am still very low on energy, and it is slow to build back. Food absolutely tastes bad most of the time, and very few foods taste like they should. I have been eating very little, but my weight hasn't gone down that month. A big meal for me is ¼ of a pork chop and small spoon of potatoes and a teaspoon of corn. If I get all that ate, I've done pretty good. That meal would last me all day. I am a little uneasy with not having good health and starting chemo again.

Yesterday I was worship leader for church. I debated long and hard about whether to pass it off to someone else or do it myself. I went ahead and was worship leader, and by the time we got home after church, I told the girls not to bother me because I was so tired. I slept from the time we got home until 5 minutes until 3:00 PM. I started watching the OSU vs. KU on the DVR recorder. I caught up with the real time about halftime. What a great game, and it is the first time OSU has beaten a #1-ranked team in a long time.

Please continue your prayers this week. Strength and peace of mind are the two most important so far.

Later.

—JK

03/04/10 (Thursday), 10:59AM-Karen

It's a beautiful country morning for our enjoyment. The beauty of God's creation is apparent on the first warm days after winter. It may be a short break from winter, but it's welcomed nonetheless.

Jeff's eating a little better, and I believe he's getting stronger. He still takes frequent naps, and even small tasks leave him exhausted. His eyesight has changed, and we're updating his prescription. With answered prayer, he'll be able to read and concentrate more easily. He takes chemo again tonight and tomorrow night and then has a break for three weeks. Brittany has semester tests today and tomorrow. I'm working on income tax returns for Uncle Sam.

Brittany and I went to a women's meal at church last night. The men were meeting for pizza in Weatherford, but Jeff didn't feel up to going. He was in his sweats, comfy in the sleep-infested chair, when we left. To be honest, I believe the thought of having to get up and change was a little daunting.

As a child, when we would drive to Amarillo to see my grandparents, if we arrived after dark, the porch light was always on. Granny would be waiting, expecting us and was preparing a well-lit path. Since our move last fall, we now have a porch. Jeff enjoys turning on the porch lights for Brittany and me when we get home after dark. If the outside of the house is dark, we don't see the house until we are almost in the yard. But last night, Brittany and I were still almost a half mile from the house when we looked at each other and grinned—the lights were on! Jeff remembered it was almost time for us to be home and turned the porch lights on for us! It isn't a difficult gesture for most people, but knowing how weak Jeff has been, it was even more special. It was a conscious effort to show us he missed us and he was waiting—possibly napping, but still waiting.

We appreciate each of you taking time from your day to catch up on our lives, what we are doing, what we are feeling…We know many of you are very diligent about praying for Jeff. Thank you.

I grew up with a preacher for a dad. That may not be much different than some of you who grew up in Christian homes, but with that history, I'm now going to preach a little. I want to ask one question, and it doesn't demand a written answer to me or to anyone else, but it's food for thought. Here it is: Are you ready? That was it. Are you ready?

If you haven't accepted Jesus' death as spiritual payment for your sins, you aren't ready for eternity. What will it take to get your attention, to get you to seek God? If you *have* allowed Jesus's death to pay for your sin, do you have a close relationship with

God? If not, what would it take to get your attention, to get you ready to seek God and become closer to Him?

The Bible says God is not willing that even one of us should perish (2 Peter 3:9). With that in mind, ask yourself this question: If God wanted to get my attention and wanted me to seek Him, what measures would he go to, or what would he allow to happen in my life? So what would it take? Cancer? Car wreck? Sickness? Earthquake? Or maybe the cancer, car wreck, or sickness of someone I love? Would it take hardship in your own life, or would God's provision, God's peace apparent in someone else's life—when from the outside, they should be experiencing turmoil—would that bring you to seek God? I believe God will do whatever it takes and allow whatever is necessary to give each of us *every* opportunity to seek Him. No one will be left with an excuse. His only holdback is you have to choose Him; he can't force your choice.

Spiritually speaking, the porch light is on! God is waiting up for you! But rest assured, He isn't napping, He's doing everything He can to get your attention. So what will it take?

We believe *"all things work together for good to them that love the Lord"* (Romans 8:28, KJV). We are content our situation has worked, is working, and will work to bring about good things for the body of Christ—whether that "good" is directly tied to us or will benefit someone we'll never meet. We know it will be good for God's family, which in turn is what we want all along—God's will and for Him to be glorified. I don't know if our situation is playing out to bring some of you closer to God or if it will be used for training and personal experience for a future event in our lives. It certainly has enhanced my personal relationship with God. His wonderful peace sustains us, one day at a time, whatever lies ahead...

03/06/10 (Saturday), 1:56PM-Jeff

I finished my last chemo treatment last night. I didn't have a lot of problems with the chemo, but I was low on energy most of the time, and I don't think that had a lot to do with the chemo. I have a large concern that my white blood cell count will stay up, and I don't have any trouble with it causing me trouble. The next 2–3 weeks will tell me what the count is going to do.

I finally got my wheat seed report sent in, to the delight of all involved. I went to Hinton yesterday because I had a bad battery on my pickup, and I needed to pick up Brittany at piano lessons. Britt has really improved at playing the piano.

Have a good day.

Later.

—JK

03/09/10 (Tuesday), 10:04AM-Karen

We are headed to OKC for Jeff's doctor's visit and lab. His appointment isn't until 1:00 PM, but we have several tax season- related stops. Jeff assures me he can sleep in the car as easily as he could if he was home. We need to go to Office Depot, Oklahoma Tax Commission, IRS, and then get a bite of lunch before Jeff's appointment. I think I will let Jeff choose the restaurant this trip. Maybe something will sound good to him. Sometimes things sound good, and sometimes they don't, and sometimes he doesn't want to choose. We will see how it goes.

Each week at our church, a different family provides the "special number." However, sometimes it's a selected congregational hymn, sometimes it's a piano number, and sometimes it's a reading. Last Sunday a special family in our church was in charge. They had an extended hospital stay a couple years ago after the birth of their daughter, which made their choice of the poem "Footprints"

especially meaningful. It got me thinking. That concept could apply to families as well. I believe this is one of those times when God is carrying us. For our family journey, there should be four sets of footprints, one set each for Jeff, Brittany, and me, as well as a set of footprints to reflect that God's walking this journey with us. I think it would be more appropriate to think there's only one set now because I definitely feel He's carrying each of us through this time—and that brings wonderful peace.

Thanks for checking on us, and keep up the prayers.

03/09/10 (Tuesday), 8:24PM-Karen

Red Lobster for the seafood lover in Jeff. Maybe it's not quite the ring the original commercial had. Jeff has always been a fan of Red Lobster, and since he hasn't been eating much, he wanted me to choose. We ate at Red Lobster. I have always given him credit for eating there. Turns out it may be one of my favorites too.

Jeff's lab appointment was scheduled for 1:00 PM, and then he met with the nurse to review the results. Her exact words were "Your blood counts are excellent!" After we left, she called Jeff on his cell phone. The potassium tests results show he's extremely low on potassium. She phoned in an Rx to our pharmacy, and Jeff has taken three of the horse-sized pills tonight. He goes back tomorrow for them to check his potassium level again.

I will be focusing my prayers on the effectiveness of the potassium pills. Again, pray God will use our situation and His provision for us to reach someone with His good news.

Thanks for keeping up with us. And as always, thanks for the prayers on our behalf.

03/10/10 (Wednesday), 8:22PM-Karen

Jeff woke up almost peppy this morning and offered words I have been waiting to hear. He said, "I feel pretty good this morning." What an answer to our prayer! I believe the potassium is adding back the nutrients Jeff needs.

Jeff drove to OKC for his lab work. He was told to wait for the results. When the numbers came back, the potassium was still very low. They let him go eat some lunch and then put him on an IV to add potassium into his system. The IV took about two hours to drip. He left the doctor's office with instructions to continue the potassium pills— one in the morning and one in the evening for the next week, and to discontinue his blood pressure medicine. The chemo drug lowered Jeff's blood pressure in the fall when he took Temodar, and Dr. Morrison took him off it for a while. They put him back on it when he stopped the chemo. However, now it's not low blood pressure but possibly the HCTZ (Hydrochlorothiazide) in the blood pressure drug that may be contributing to his low potassium level. So for now he's only taking Keppra (as a precautionary measure to prevent seizures) and potassium.

Brittany's eighth-grade class won second place in the Caddo County Curriculum Contest today, and the combined junior team won first place overall. Yesterday, Brittany participated in the 4-H speeches and demonstration contest. She won second place with a presentation of "The Earth as an Apple." Her point was that food production will need to triple in the next forty to fifty years to keep up with population growth and limited farmland. The available farmland on earth was illustrated by using the peeling from 1/32 of an apple. We are blessed to have such a wonderful daughter. As you might expect, I'm a little biased!

I want to continue to tell you how much we appreciate each of you. Every time I close an update, I'm reminded how valuable your time is and humbled you've spent a few minutes of such a precious commodity to check on us.

03/12/10 (Friday), 10:35AM-Karen

Last night was the Caddo County Farm Bureau Legislative and Clergy Appreciation Dinner. Our interim pastor, Charles Rickel and his wife Barbara rode with us—and Jeff drove—both ways! He's definitely tired today, and I expect he'll take a few naps to catch up. The potassium seems to have boosted his energy tremendously. In fact, I cooked the fried potatoes for the meal, and Jeff did almost all of the peeling.

Britt's softball team didn't win yesterday, but she felt like she played well especially for so early in the season. I think we'll look into a ball cap and dark sunglasses for Jeff. I think he could pull off a sleep infected lawn chair on the baseline!—In the shade of course, with a little sunscreen. It's exciting to think about spring softball. Hinton plays slow pitch in the spring and fast-pitch in the fall. Often it takes me a few games to remember the different rules.

It's tax season. I better get back to work. Thanks for checking in on us.

03/14/10 (Sunday), 12:43AM-Karen

Jeff's college roommate, Tom Gardner, and his son Zach came to see us today. He and Jeff got in a good visit.

I believe Jeff may be getting a little bit of his appetite back. For supper, he suggested Mexican cuisine from the local Mexican café in Hinton and ate more than he has eaten in one sitting in quite some time. He ate about a fourth of his meal. That's up from his recent norm of small portions. Flavors aren't what he remembers they should be. We really don't know what is causing the frustrating change in flavors.

I worked on taxes most of the day. Britt lounged and played Lego blocks with Zach. Our monthly church dinner is tomorrow, so I expect a tiring day for Jeff.

Thanks so much to each of you for your prayers, and please pass on our thanks to the prayer warriors in your churches who have Jeff on their list.

I know God is *able* to completely heal Jeff in one instantaneous miracle or overtime by providing doctors with skill, knowledge, and medications— either way, still a miracle. But ultimately, my job is to trust God's authority to use this situation to get the results He knows will be best.

> And we know that all things work together for good
> to them that love God, to them who are the called
> according to his purpose.
>
> Romans 8:28 (KJV)

Thanks again. Keep praying for the continuation of our miracle.

03/15/10 (Monday), 10:29PM-Jeff

Sunday morning I was very tired. I went to church, and we accept 2 new members. They have been attending for quite some time, and we are proud to have them as new church members. I came home after church even though they had lunch at church. I came home and went to sleep. I felt better and had a pretty nice evening.

This morning, with the time change, I didn't get up as early as I should have. I worked in the office for a while, and then about 11:00 AM, Brittany and I went to Brittany's dentist. We were there over an hour. After the dentist, we went to eat lunch at A&W/Long John Silvers. It was pretty good. After lunch, we went to OKC and got some pivot oil. We stopped back at the dentist so Brittany could get the rest of her stuff for her braces.

Later.

—JK

03/16/10 (Tuesday), 5:27PM-Jeff

Well, the lucky day finally came. Lenzy Krehbiel Burton, my lovely niece, and her husband, Jake, are the proud parents of a new little girl. Addie Krehbiel Burton is 6.6 lbs and 20 inches long. Everyone seems to be in good shape. I wish the whole family lots of happiness and a great future. I do know one thing: I believe I have found my lost money-making project. A sleep-infested baby bed. You just knew it was coming. I know new mom's and pop's out there that would give a mid-sized motorized vehicle for a bed like this. Just a quick pass by the bed, and the baby is asleep. For added convience [convenience] an on-off switch would be a great thing for when the grandmas show up. Just turn that bed off and let them feel bad about how long it takes the thriving child to go to sleep. I think I just made millions.

I have been feeling pretty good today. I almost concord one of those jobs that has been waiting around since we moved in here. I hooked all of our computers up to the printers. Know you can sit in the living room and print a document on the printer in my office or the secretary's office. This has taken me all day, and I have been getting along pretty good, but when you are loading software and cleaning up messes, it takes a while. I am not done, but I will be sometime soon.

Tomorrow I have doctor's appointments, and Karen takes the bread to the capital. I hope I can help here, but I have to stay at the doctor's office until I get my blood results back.

Later.

—JK

03/17/10 (Wednesday), 9:06PM-Karen

Jeff, Brittany, and I made the trip to OKC this morning. Jeff dropped Britt and me and a whole lot of bread at the capital, and then went to his lab appointment. They asked him to wait for the results. The test shows that his white blood cell counts and the potassium are at good levels. They left him on potassium twice a day, and he'll go back next

Wednesday to have another blood test done. We're so glad the blood counts are staying up.

In total, the Caddo County Farm Bureau group delivered 49 loaves of regular bread and about twenty loaves of sweet breads. Jeff got the results of his blood work and then came back to the capital and drove his taxi again. This annual event is a lot of work, but is a fun way to say thank you to a variety of people who represent our county and agriculture in general.

Jeff has stayed awake all day, and I suspect he'll sleep well today. He did not get in on all the walking, but still, a day out of the house is a big deal these days.

Thanks for your prayers.

03/20/10 (Saturday), 11:14PM-Jeff

I grilled steaks for lunch yesterday, and they were the best. I have some of my taste buds back, and that meat really tasted good. It is much better then [than] it was when Tom was hear [here] last week.

This morning we woke up to a snowstorm. If it would have snowed like this back in, December we would have had a foot of snow on the ground. It snowed until about midafternoon It snowed hard for a while. We stayed home all day and didn't do much but watch basketball. The OSU men didn't do very good and got beat yesterday. However, the women played this afternoon and started the second half 18 points behind and won by 7 points.

I made the decision to have church tomorrow, so that will be interesting. I don't know if I can get out of here tomorrow. They may be having church without me.

Later.

—JK

03/22/10 (Monday), 10:07PM-Jeff

We had church yesterday, but my family couldn't go. The eastwest roads were drifted shut on 3 different roads. I came home, and we waited on the roads to open tomorrow. Chris Lee and his girls came by this evening and said the county had sent out some road graders, and the warm weather this afternoon really helped clear the road. They had about 45 for church. I thought that was pretty good attendance considering the weather.

This morning I worked on the computer for a while and priced out a grain bagger. This afternoon, I went to Weatherford and took Karen's Yukon to have some oil leaks fixed. We had one on the rear end, and the water pump was leaking. They are going to try to get it ready tomorrow. Karen, Brittany, and I went to Yukon this evening because they had Brittany's new retainer. Then we ate supper at Primo's. While we were headed to Yukon.

Dad got Alfredo to help him load Mom in the pickup so Dad could take her to the hospital. She has an infection, and that caused her temperature to go above 102. By 8:00, the temperature was close to right, and Mom was feeling much better. They are going to keep Mom overnight and see if she will be better in the morning. She is terribly weak and needs help getting out of bed. Hopefully, some of her strength will come back.

Later.

—JK

03/24/10 (Wednesday), 3:43PM-Karen

I had my dates wrong. I wrote earlier we would see Dr. Keefer today. That will be Monday. Today's appointment was lab only, so Jeff went by himself. The white blood cell counts, including the all-important Neutrophils are where they need to be. As you continue to keep our family in your prayers, please offer thanks for the good test results.

Jeff has a Wheat Commission meeting this afternoon. Since I have tax returns accumulating in my office, I opted not to go with him.

We have good friends in the wheat industry, and I look forward to the meetings, when I can go with Jeff and catch up with these special friends.

Almost all of the snow is gone. I can still see a small flash of white in one of the canyons out back. I assume it was a very large drift, but if it stays much longer, I may have to go investigate. It may be junk that blew in with the snow. Oklahoma has had a very white winter. We had more snow this year than I ever remember in any one winter.

Palm Sunday is *this* week, believe it or not. The palm branches are ordered, and the kids will be able to march in Sunday morning singing "Hosanna! Hosanna!" Since we only have a handful of young children, one batch of palm branches goes a long way. What a wonderful time to reflect on the sacrifice made to reconcile us to God! As an accountant, I always like that terminology—*reconciled!* No matter what is on our side of the ledger, adding Christ's blood makes the records balance. Our role in the whole process is fairly minor, but without our acceptance, reconciliation never takes place.

> But now he has reconciled you by Christ's physical body through death to present you holy in his sight, without blemish and free from accusation.
>
> Colossians 1:22 (NIV)

Chemo: Round 2

03/27/10 (Saturday), 3:33PM-Karen

It's a rainy day in Oklahoma. Throw in a little wind, say 50 mph, and it's a really good day to be inside. Jeff got up and met the church board in Weatherford for breakfast this morning. His taste buds seem to be improving. He still asks if it tastes good to us, which tells me his taste buds aren't at a hundred percent. After a busy morning, he's parked in the La-Z-Boy, and I expect him to nap this afternoon.

Brittany's softball team participated in a festival yesterday. They had only played one game this season, so they were a little rusty. Our junior high team has no freshmen, three eighth graders, and the rest are seventh graders. I'm sure the teams we played were a little older. Experience usually comes with age. The wind blew hard, and Jeff and I opted not to get him out in the wind. We were able to sit in the vehicle behind center field and had a pretty good view.

Monday Jeff will have labs pulled at eight thirty and then meet with Dr. Keefer. He's on track to start the second set of five days of chemo on Monday evening. This is month two of six in a plan that normally has an increased dosage of Temodar. Because of the drop in white cells coming off the Temodar regimen, Jeff isn't taking a higher dosage but the same dosage he took last fall.

We don't know if Dr. Keefer will try to bump the dosage up or leave it the same.

We are thankful for the healing God has provided, and we continue to attribute it to answered prayers. Thanks for checking on us.

03/29/10 (Monday), 3:20PM-Karen

We took an early-morning trip to OKC for lab and a visit with Dr. Keefer. The blood tests show the white blood cell counts to be holding, which is a definite blessing.

Dr. Keefer's original plan last fall was to give Jeff Temodar and radiation at the same time, followed by a three-to–four- week break and then take a double daily dose of the chemo drug Temodar for five consecutive days each month for a total of six months.

However, when Jeff's white blood cell counts dropped to zero over Christmas, Dr. Keefer changed that plan. He now wants to ease into the double dose, testing carefully to make sure the white blood cell counts don't drop too far. So for the first month, he left the daily dosage at 180 mg instead of doubling it. That was the same daily dose Jeff had while he took radiation; only then he took it for fifty-one consecutive days. The double dose would be about 370 mg. Because the blood results over the last two weeks were good, Dr. Keefer increased the dosage to 280 mg, which is 75 percent of the dosage he really wants to give. He'll test the white blood cell counts weekly. We expect an increase to the full dosage next month if all the blood tests hold.

Increasing the dosage is a mixed blessing. The white counts are holding, which is definitely a good thing; the dosage of Temodar has increased, which under, the circumstances, is also a good thing. It will kill off more of the bad cells, if there are any; but the increase in chemo also means an increase in damage to good cell reproduction, which is not so good.

Last fall we moved into this house. Our first night here was a full moon. I vividly remember how bright it seemed. Of course, having some windows helped the view. According to the moon, that was seven months ago. What an incredible journey we've been on in that short amount of time. Jeff and I always liked the most extreme roller coasters! Up and down and turns at neckbreaking speed. Our lives are a little like that—hills, valleys, and unexpected changes. Well, there's a topic for another devotional, on another day.

Please continue to pray for good white blood cell counts, strength, and continued peace.

03/31/10 (Wednesday), 2:55PM-Jeff

I took my second batch of chemo yesterday evening, and so far, there doesn't seem to be any problem. I am not sleeping as well at night as I was before I took the chemo, but I am getting by pretty good. I am usually up 3–4 times and turning over in bed a lot. Three more days of chemo, and then we are off for 23 days. Continue your prayers.

I went to watch Brittany play softball Monday evening. They didn't win, but they didn't do terrible either. Brittany had a good hit, but the outfielder made a good play and put her out. The outfielder goes to our church, and her and Britt are good friends. Yesterday they played at Binger. I didn't go because I didn't want to fight the wind. They didn't win there either. Hopefully, they will get it straightened out before long and win a few.

Karen's dad has a dr.'s visit in OKC tomorrow, and we hope that it goes well. He is going to have an angiogram Friday at 9:00 AM. Pray for him and their travel.

Later.

—JK

04/04/10 (Easter Sunday), 5:54PM-Karen

I want to catch you up on what's happened at our house this weekend. Jeff finished cycle 2 of six monthly chemo treatments on Friday evening. He hasn't had many side effects from this round of chemo other than today he's been extremely tired.

The deacons had their annual Easter breakfast this morning. Jeff was down to bring the sausage, bacon, and scrambled eggs. This is the sort of thing Jeff and I really enjoy. We cooked his sausage yesterday afternoon and got up at four this morning to cook the bacon. Jeff cooked a couple of pans of bacon and needed a bed. He was so weak and tired he wasn't able to make it to the breakfast this morning. He slept until Brittany and I got home from church, and he seems to be caught up on his sleep for a little while. He gets to feeling pretty good and overdoes it. Then it takes a while to catch up on his strength.

For lunch we went to Jeff's parents' and celebrated the postponed Christmas with the Krehbiel family. We also met Jeff's brother, Randy's granddaughter, Addie, for the first time. We've added two great-nieces this year. They're both beautiful babies.

Good news! My dad had his angiogram on Friday. The doctor seemed pleased with the report, and he should be able to treat it with medication.

Have a blessed Easter, and thanks for checking on Jeff.

04/06/10 (Tuesday), 10:19PM-Jeff

Good evening, I have not been writting [writing] much lately, so I was encouraged to write on the blog more often. People like me to tell stories about what happened and try to add a little humor to their life. I worked in the office for a while this morning and then worked on a letter for the governor. We have a bill that has passed the House and the Senate and is headed to the governor's desk for his signature. This bill would allow the Oklahoma Wheat Commission to purchase needed items from other sources than Central Services. This is quite a money savings for the Wheat Commission on items they needed on a regular basis.

I am feeling pretty good today. The last two days have been good. I don't get a lot done, but I have been "movin' and shakin'" pretty good.

I took my pickup to Weatherford to get the air conditioner fixed. They gave me a Chrysler mini van to drive while they were working on my pickup.

Later.

—JK

04/07/10 (Wednesday), 10:45PM-Jeff

Well, today has been very educational. Brittany told me today that the difference between a minivan and an SUV is the minivan has sliding doors, and the SUV has regular doors. After looking at the vehicle I was driving, I decided she probably had a valid car talking point, and after looking on the Internet, I determined that the Chrysler Aspen that I was driving was an SUV. Now for western Oklahoma, I am officially a soccer dad, and I can be bought to pick up your kids for a price. Price will be determined when the kids are delivered.

We have been having a little plumbing trouble the last few days with one of our toilets. It is for the master's bedroom, and I was not going to walk all the way across the house in the middle of the night. I started working a little on it yesterday, but I had other jobs to attend to, and it was still working anyway. This morning, right after breakfast, I let her have it. I took the hold-down bolts out and pulled the baby out of there and found a bad gasket under the tank. I went to Hinton and met Karen for dinner and got me a new gasket. It is quite a ticklish deal to replace the bowl on the new gasket, and I had to get some help to lift the tank and bowl and put it on the new gasket. This evening, everything seems to be working fine, and it flushes and seals and everything.

This brings up another interesting point. That is the relationship between the sleep-infested La-Z-Boy and the importants [importance] of the properly working toilet. The PWT is so vital for the comfort and convenience of the person running the sleep-infested La-Z-Boy (SIL) that an evening without either one could be very detrimental. Therefore, I claim that any home with an SIL should also have a PWT. More consideration needs to be put into this train of thought.

I am feeling good, if you couldn't tell, and I go in tomorrow for blood work.

Later.

—JK

04/08/10 (Thursday), 10:48PM-Jeff

I took Brittany to school this morning and then headed to OKC. I had a blood test this morning, and it was pretty good. My counts are good, but my potassium wants to drop down a little. They want me to increase my dosage back to 2 pills every other day and 1 pill in the middle. It kind of reminds me of the summer I had a tractor with a smashed fuel line. When you went up the hill, the fuel was shut down to a small dribble, but when you went down the hill, the tractor ran fine. It took a while before we figured that one out. My white blood cell counts are good, and everything else looked fine. I was in and out of there in 15 minutes. The results from the tests were phoned to us later.

I worked in the office most of the day, with a couple breaks in between. This evening, we went to Anadarko to the Farm Bureau meeting, and we were back home about 9:15 PM.

Later.

—JK

04/10/10 (Saturday), 1:35PM-Jeff

I have been feeling good, and I am finally getting some of my taste buds to work again. We had some more of those fantastic steaks last night, and they were very good.

Later.

—JK

04/12/10 (Monday), 12:14PM-Jeff

We had a nice weekend here at the Krehbiel homestead. No softball games, and everything seems to be going fine. Uncle Elmer (Dad's brother) and Aunt Mildred came by this weekend, and it was good to see them.

I seem to be getting along pretty good. I don't feel as tired, and I led worship service yesterday morning. We had church dinner and then came home.

It is a little cloudy and damp today, but no rain. Brittany is supposed to play softball this afternoon in Arapaho.

The farm show starts this Thursday and runs through Saturday.

I hope we have some good luck there.

Later.

—JK

04/15/10 (Thursday), 10:36PM-Jeff

Tuesday and Wednesday of this week, we sat [set] up the booths for the farm show in OKC. Today was the first day of the farm show. It was a beautiful day, and we had a few people at the show. I was worn out when I got home. A two-hour nap helped, and supper was very good.

Karen finished tax season this evening, and she was very glad to put another tax season behind her.

I have been feeling pretty good, but the farm show takes it out of me.

Later.

—JK

04/17/10 (Saturday), 11:37AM-Karen

Jeff and Wayne went to the OKC farm show yesterday and worked the booth, visiting with farmers, who are prospective irrigation customers. It's also fun to see our agricultural friends who come to look around. Britt and I came over midafternoon to go eat with our district T-L sales rep and his wife. It was good to see them again.

After a relatively relaxing evening and morning, we are headed back to the farm show. We will be in the booth some, work in the Wheat Commission booth a little, and probably make a round to see the other booths.

It was really good to get past the 15th and its tax deadlines. I look forward to a slower spring pace in the office and the gear-up for harvest in about 6 weeks. Talk is Britt may drive something for harvest this year. I think she'll really enjoy that, but I'm hesitant to let her leave the kitchen. She's always been a big help.

I still can't express how much I appreciate each of you taking time out of your own busy schedules to read about our lives so you can interpret how Jeff feels and what prayer needs we have. We continue to have God's wonderful peace as a resident of our lives. I have said many, many times, I don't know how nonbelievers would cope in a similar situation, because we draw on that peace so extensively to get us through each challenge. I guess that search for peace causes unbelievers to search in so many destructive places for something to fill the void in their lives. As a Christian, I know that void can only be filled with peace that comes through claiming Christ as my personal Savior.

Krehbiel's Krew has met and raised their goal from $1,000 to $1,500 and are only $150 from the newest goal of $2,000. We're so honored by the generosity of our friends and family, as well as these kind-hearted agronomists running on Jeff's behalf.

Have a great weekend.

04/20/10 (Tuesday), 10:23PM-Jeff

Yesterday I went to OKC and had an MRI. We took Brittany by school on the way to OKC. Everything went okay, and we stopped in El Reno and had a fried onion burger at Sid's. We still haven't heard the results from the MRI, but we look forward to a good report.

David Bailey came yesterday afternoon, and we worked on some paperwork. Once again, I think we are even for a few days.

This morning, we had a Wheat Commission meeting in Clinton. It started at nine and went until lunchtime. We ate lunch at Montana Mike's, and then I went to Atwoods for a little while. We had a good commission meeting this morning and got to talk about the changes that are happening in the wheat industry.

Later.

—JK

04/21/10 (Wednesday), 1:34PM-Karen

Dr. Keefer's nurse assistant called a few minutes ago about Jeff's MRI results. She read through the radiologist's notes and summarized them for me.

The "rim" visible on the MRI is a combination of scarring from the surgery, possibly cancer cells that weren't removed during the surgery and dead cells that were leftover from the cancer. The "rim" still appears to be shrinking; however, it appears to be more intense than the last MRI. The nurse said Dr. Keefer will have the radiation group review the MRI to get their expertise on whether the increase in intensity is scarring from the radiation. (The nurse used the term *necrosis*.) She thinks it's radiation related.

I confirmed radiation was stopped in December (four months ago). She said the radiation continues to provide results as far out as six months.

This is the nurse practitioner Dr. Keefer said knows almost everything he does. We believe this to be a compliment to Tammy, not a slam toward Keefer!

Jeff's next appointment is Monday at 9:00 AM. We'll get to compare this MRI with the last one. Not that we're expert radiologists, and we might see something they didn't, but rather to keep us informed.

Pray this new intensity is a good thing, that it's visible proof of the healing we're continually asking our Heavenly Father to provide.

I spoke with my earthly father yesterday. I needed to know where, close to Granite, to purchase an inch and a quarter plastic conduit. He willingly gave me all info he had. The first place he called in Mangum confirmed they had the conduit, and Dad called me back, told me where they were located, and gave me visual tips on how to get there. After I made a phone call, I found out our hired men were much closer to Hobart, so I called back and asked for more information. This time, to take less phone calls, Dad gave me the phone number, and I called them, confirmed they had what we needed, and then called our employee to give him the directions and the store name. Now, my dad didn't even hesitate to give what I asked for, which leads me to Matthew

7:11 (NIV): *"If ye then, being evil, know how to give good gifts unto your children, how much more shall your Father which is in heaven give good things to them that ask him?"*

In no way do I intend to imply my father is evil or directions to find plastic conduit qualify as a "good" gift—on the contrary, since I know my earthly Christian father would grant Jeff's healing if it was in his power, then how much more does my

Heavenly Father want to provide that same healing? I believe the only circumstance under which it would not be granted would be because it would interfere with His long-term will.

> This is the confidence we have in approaching God: that if we ask anything according to his will, he hears us. And if we know that he hears us-whatever we ask-we know that we have what we asked of him.
>
> 1 John 5:14–15 (NIV)

We can know if we ask our Heavenly Father for any good gift (Jeff's health), he'll give it, as long as it's within his will. I have struggled a little with how to know if what we ask is in God's will. My understanding may change tomorrow when I learn something new, but at this point in my spiritual growth, I know God will provide Jeff's healing as long as providing healing doesn't interfere with His will and His desire that not one should spiritually perish.

> Even so it is not the will of your Father who is in heaven that one of these little ones should perish.
>
> Matthew 18:14 (KJV)

Keep praying with me that this situation will be a witness to others of God's faithfulness, love, and provision for those He loves.

04/25/10 (Sunday), 4:19PM-Karen

On Friday morning, Jeff and I made a fairly quick trip to Fort Worth to meet a trade group of wheat industry executives from Nigeria. Most of their group works with flour milling companies, and a few were with an instant noodle company. The group has hosted the Texas Wheat Growers and Ken Davis. Ken and Jeff were in the US Wheat trade team that visited four African countries in early 2009. It was good to see wheat friends we only see a few times a year. We stayed in Fort Worth on Friday night, and after lunch Saturday with Jeff's cousin Monty and his wife Cindy, we headed back to Oklahoma.

First thing this morning, we turned on the OKC marathon to watch some of the coverage before church and used the DVR to catch up on the events after church. It was definitely more personal this year, since Krehbiel's Krew, the five OSU agricultural professors, were running in honor of Jeff. The Krew finished the marathon with a fantastic time of 3 hours, 43 minutes, and 15 seconds, and were fifth in their division. The government division had several relay teams with very official-sounding names. Assuming the team names were accurate, the Plant and Soil Scientists finished ahead of both the Secret Service and the Drug Enforcement officers. Way to go, guys!

Dr. David Porter, who left the relay team to participate in the full marathon individually finished with a time of 5:43:12. Impressive! Dr. Porter spearheaded the fundraising for Krehbiel's Krew. In all, the Krew raised $4,405 for the American Cancer Society. They invested so much effort, time, and energy in this marathon.

Jeff will have labs at nine in the morning, followed by a visit with Dr. Keefer at nine thirty. We expect to compare the MRI images from one week ago with the MRI from about seven weeks ago. If all the blood test results are good, Jeff should start month 3 of chemo tomorrow night. He'll take Temodar for five days and then be "off" for twenty-three days. This will be cycle 3 of 6. There is a possibility the dosage will increase to an amount closer to what they typically give, which is double the dosage from last fall. Last cycle, Jeff took close to one and a half times the original dosage, so there is still a little room to increase the dosage to maximize the results.

Thank you to so many prayer warriors who are faithful in petitioning our Heavenly Father on Jeff's behalf. We trust God is working in our lives to produce *good* from this challenge. Please continue to pray for wisdom and knowledge of the physicians and medical personnel, continued peace and patience for our family, as well as continued healing for the patient.

> And we know that all things work together for good to them that love God, to them who are the called according to his purpose.

> Romans 8:28 (KJV)

CHEMO: ROUND 3

04/26/10 (Monday), 9:26PM-Karen

Another answer to prayer—good reports at the oncologist!

Today's lab work shows Jeff's white blood cell counts have held. We reviewed the last two MRI results with Dr. Keefer today, and the report we had last week from the nurse practitioner was accurate. The size of the target area prior to surgery and the corresponding void after surgery are shrinking! The intensity (white area on the MRI) had increased, but both Dr. Keefer and the radiologist believe this increase is a result of the radiation scarring. Dr. Keefer said we can expect the MRI to always have some scarring show up on the images. Keefer will ask Dr. Morrison (Jeff's radiation doc) and Dr. Reynolds (the surgeon) to review the MRIs and give us feedback.

Because the white blood cell counts have held, Dr. Keefer increased the Temodar level for this month's dosage to the full target amount of 360 mg daily for five consecutive days. This is also a positive report. Dr. Keefer believes Jeff's body will tolerate this stronger dosage. But he has a lab scheduled two weeks from today to check Jeff's white blood cell counts.

After we got home from OKC, Jeff went into town to pick up Brittany after school. Later, he rode around with his dad and looked at the crops. Jeff gets tired when he has a big day, so I expect he'll go to bed early. Our idea of early to bed has changed in the last seven months. Early used to be 10:00 PM. Now early is closer eight or eight thirty. He's almost always in bed by nine thirty, and that doesn't count the La-Z-Boy.

Thank you for your time to check on Jeff, and especially for your prayers.

04/27/10 (Tuesday), 11:06PM-Karen

Jeff has been tired and slept a good part of the day today. I was at a client's office and away from home until after I picked Britt up at school. When I came in, Jeff was asleep in the La-Z-Boy and commented he hadn't moved most of the day. I helped him catch up on liquids immediately. He ate a really good supper and will take chemo right before bedtime four more days. I'm not sure if it's the chemo or the anti-nausea pill that causes him to sleep so much during the chemo days—it could be either one. I may have to do a little rereading of the prescription info. Not that I would make any changes, mind you. I yield those decisions to experts.

Please pray for Jeff to have energy and the chemo effects to be balanced somewhere between enough to be effective and just short of too much.

04/29/10 (Thursday), 11:11PM-Karen

Jeff napped quite a bit today and watched a few old westerns on the Encore Western channel. Brittany is sure the plots move way too slow. I think that probably makes them good naptime viewing.

Jeff drove into Hinton to pick up Brittany after school this afternoon. This evening, we had roast, potatoes, and carrots for supper with a wonderful side of family conversation, followed by a little TV. These chemo days are very tiring, and so we really don't plan much. I worked in the office most of the day. It's a real blessing to work from home.

Earlier today, I called Caddo Electric about some electric meters we had turned off when the cattle were pulled off those farms, and Donna Mogg answered the phone. Donna's husband, David, is also taking chemo for treatment of glioblastoma. She and I have never met face-to-face and have only spoken on the phone twice, counting today. But we're both faithful to keep up with each other on CarePages and lift each other in prayer. There's a special bond with this family because of the similarity in our journeys. It was good to visit briefly.

Thanks to each of you for your prayers. Jeff and I have always said we were blessed with so many good friends. Now I realize we just thought we were blessed. Now we know we are! We treasure each friendship. Thanks.

05/03/10 (Monday), 12:28PM-Karen

Jeff took the last of this month's chemo on Friday evening. It really zaps his energy. He spent most of Saturday napping but spent some time with Britt and me in the afternoon. Yesterday it was Jeff's turn to serve as worship leader at church. This is a responsibility Jeff enjoys a great deal. Today he got up when my alarm went off, showered, and cooked breakfast. But when I got back from taking Britt to school, the sleep-infected La-Z-Boy had caught him. Hopefully, he'll be able to rest while Britt is at school and be awake while she's home in the evenings. I don't think we have any after-school activities this week. That's a first in quite while—a rare occurrence.

Thanks so much for the prayers. I know Jeff's healing *is* answered prayer. I want to be sure to give God credit for the healing and the ever-present peace in our home. We are truly blessed.

05/06/10 (Thursday), 10:43PM-Karen

Jeff has a lot more energy this week. Every day he seems to have a little more drive to do things and more energy to get it done. He made breakfast a couple of mornings and took Britt to school the last two mornings. He still has a nap every now and then, but it's nothing like last week during chemo where about all he did was sleep. What a blessing to interact as a family again! Yesterday morning, Jeff went to Wayne and Fern's and hooked up the little trailer to the pickup, and then loaded up our lawnmower and brought it home. Each year, it takes a little more to get it going. He made a list, and I think he and Britt ordered the parts this afternoon in Weatherford. Then we went out to eat. We were in separate vehicles, and he's making a stop or two before he comes home. I figure his evening will be pretty short, and he'll head to bed right away.

End-of-school-year events are in full swing. Britt's calendar is packed full for the next week or two, which means so is ours. Please pray with me that Jeff will have strength to do activities he wants to. We keep praying, and God keeps providing, so we give *Him* credit for the blessings.

Thanks for checking in on Jeff.

05/09/10 (Sunday), 11:10PM-Karen

It has been a few days since I wrote in the blog, so I have several things to catch up on. I feel pretty good. I actually feel better than I have in quite a long time. I am still low on energy, and if I overwork doing things, sometimes it takes me a day to catch up. My La-Z-Boy chair is working to its maximum effeceincy [efficiency]. It has put me to sleep several times over the last few days, and I had another nap just this afternoon. My niece was here for Mother's Day and wanted one of the sleep-infested baby beds. Her daughter is doing well, and Mother and Father are hanging in there.

We had quite a crew at our house last night and today. Glen and Sue Burkhalter, Janice, Larry and Ryan Johnson, Betsy, Jacey [Jasey], and Kelly Groves, and Wayne and Fern Krehbiel were all here for lunch. We ate good, and then the gentlemen seemed to take naps while the women talked about us. We had a good time.

Friday and Saturday were good days, and I especially liked being able to watch the race Saturday night. Jeff Gordon ran well but didn't win. Maybe next time.

Brittany ran the mower some Saturday, but we need to do some work on the mower. It has been ran [run] hard and needs some repair work. I went ahead and let here [her] mow because we were going to have company. Hopefully, we can get this mower fixed up before too long.

Later.

—JK

05/13/10 (Thursday), 11:24PM-Karen

We've had a busy week. Monday Jeff had a blood test. All the numbers were good. The doctor's office called us on Tuesday to confirm the potassium level was also right where it needed to be. Jeff and his dad went on an excursion Tuesday. Jeff got home in time for a quick nap, and then we went to Brittany's FFA banquet. Last night, Wednesday evening, Brittany had youth group, but Jeff and I were at home. I miss our midweek Bible studies. Hopefully, they will resume when we get our new minister, but that will be the middle of summer. Today, Jeff made a trip to Hydro, to the bank in Weatherford, then home, and he and I made a quick trip to Anadarko to take care of some farming business. This evening, we missed a Farm Bureau county meeting to attend Britt's spring vocal concert. High school vocal has been a challenge—not so much vocally, but more as a patience issue.

Jeff's a little congested this evening. We plan on contacting the doctor's office tomorrow to see if he needs to start an antibiotic. I ask you to pray this won't hinder the scheduled treatments or cause any setback to his strength. Things have been as normal as possible after this month's chemo. During the week of chemo, Jeff was almost in hibernation. A couple of days later, it was like he woke up ready to go. He still sleeps quite often during the day, but after he finished this month's chemo, he has wanted to do a lot of things. The beautiful weather has made him want to be out and about. I think he may be overdoing it a little, but I'm trying to keep that comment to myself.

> Now to him who is able to do immeasurably more than all we ask or imagine, according to his power that is at work within us, to him be glory in the church and in Christ Jesus throughout all generations, for ever and ever! Amen.
>
> Ephesians 3:20–21 (NIV)

05/18/10 (Tuesday), 10:21PM-Karen

It has been several days. Sorry to have kept you all in the dark. Our last post told about Jeff being a little congested and a doctor's appointment on Friday. Loren put him on an antibiotic to clear things up. He'll take the antibiotics for ten days. He's still coughing right after he laughs. Good news is he feels good enough to laugh. He's having a really good week. He has had enough energy that he and Brittany are overhauling our mower. They took pictures before they started, and I hope they don't end up with extra parts. I think once school is out, they'll find time to finish that project.

Tonight was Brittany's eighth-grade graduation. I think you will agree with me. We are truly blessed! And not just with the good grades! Not only did God pull her through this year, he let her thrive! He gave her the podium, and she chose to give Him the glory! I'm posting a copy of the speech she wrote. Her presentation was great.

Valedictory Address by Brittany Krehbiel
Hinton Middle School, May 18, 2010

Perseverance—the steady persistence in a course of action in spite of difficulties, obstacles, or discouragement.

Perseverance is a word that means so much to me, especially because if there ever was a year where my grades could have fallen, my attitude could have changed, and my friendships could have been lost, it was this year.

My dad was diagnosed with brain cancer about one month into this school year. The night my dad was diagnosed, I made a decision—a decision to stand up with God's help and every ounce of strength and courage I possessed. This could have been the year things fell through the cracks and no one would have questioned it. Yet here I stand.

I give credit first and foremost to God. My faith has always been there for me, especially through this year. Jeremiah 29:11 says, "For I know the plans I have for you," declares the Lord, "plans to prosper you and not to harm you, plans to give you hope and a future."

My wonderful friends have helped me so much through the hard days. Thanks, guys. My teachers, who have helped me so much and encouraged me daily in ways I never thought possible, and, last but not least, my family. My parents and grandparents, cousins, and aunts and uncles have all helped me through this year in ways unimaginable. I truly am blessed. I love you, Daddy!

Someone once said, "Nobody trips over mountains; it's the small pebble that causes you to stumble. Pass all the pebbles in your path, and you'll find you've crossed the mountain."

According to statistics, two people in this eighth-grade class won't graduate high school. But why should we let statistics *write* our future? We have the ability to *write* statistics! I'm *not* saying there won't be difficult times. I *am* saying that with a great support system made up of faith, friends, and family, as well as perseverance, we can all make it through high school. I challenge each of you to choose to persevere no matter what pebble you must step over, or boulder you must climb.

I will see *all* of you four years from tonight. Thank you.

05/23/10 (Sunday), 4:25PM-Jeff

This morning I didn't go to church. I took my first dose of chemo last night, and then I couldn't go to sleep. My stomach kept causing me problems. When I finally did get to sleep, it was about four thirty. I woke up feeling pretty good, but it was too late to be on time, and Don was lined up to be worship leader. I have slept most of the day so far, and I am getting a little of my strength back. I should get done with my treatments on Wednesday and feel much better on Friday.

It has been a very eventful week or so with Brittany's speech on Tuesday night, and school was out on Wednesday, and Karen and I went to [for] the doctor's appointment on Friday. I have been working on the lawnmower on the other days of the week. It had a lot of things wrong with it, and I spent almost $1,000 on parts and still have a little to go. Maybe after tomorrow we can get it up and running. I need to get it fixed so Brittany can get the yard mowed before this weekend.

This weekend, we are going to have the stone family reunion here at our house. This is Sue and Clarissa's family. There is just the 2 sisters and a brother in Georgia. We have not done this in several years, but we used to do it once a year. If everyone shows up, we could have around 30. I doubt we will have that many. Hopefully, we will have a good time regardless of how many we have.

"For I know the plans I have for you," declares the Lord, "plans to prosper you and not to harm you, plans to give you hope and a future." Jeremiah 29:11

Later.

—JK

06/06/10 (Saturday), 2:33AM-Karen

Jeff took his chemo (Temodar) through Wednesday, the twentysixth of May. Dr. Keefer has mentioned several times that he typically prescribes six months of the Temodar, taking it for five consecutive days a month, then taking twenty-three days off. If that holds, Jeff will have only two more twenty-eight-day time periods left. We will schedule another MRI between the June and July sessions to allow Dr. Keefer and his colleagues to "look" at the surgery site again. Jeff seems a little more active this month, and although I'm not an expert, I believe that's an excellent sign the cancer isn't growing—and that's an answer to prayer.

We've been a busy little family since the last post. Memorial weekend let us play host to both sides of our family. About sixteen members of my mom's family came at varying times on Friday and Saturday, and a few stayed until Sunday. Monday we had Jeff's cousins Monty and Chris and all of their families, as well as Jeff's mom and dad. We absolutely loved having everyone here. Jeff felt pretty good throughout the weekend, and for that, we are thankful.

For the past two weeks, Brittany's had basketball camps during the day on most weekdays and softball on Tuesdays and Thursdays. Tomorrow I have Bible school, and Brittany has two basketball scrimmages as a part of the team basketball camp in Hinton. Sunday is our annual church picnic, so I plan to make something for the potluck dinner, as well as a bucket of homemade vanilla ice cream. Busy, but fun!

If you've been following the progress of the mower, tt was fixed, but has broken down again. Jeff worked on it this morning, and I haven't asked how he got along with the project.

Please know we treasure your friendships and the time you take to check on us.

06/10/10 (Thursday), 12:49AM-Karen

Since the last update, we have shipped our daughter off to Jeff's Aunt Valeta's for a week of Bible school. For several years, Valeta has included Brittany as a granddaughter for the week of Bible school. From the time she gets home, Brittany has been looking forward to the next year. We miss her, but we're glad she has such a fun tradition started with her cousins and one of her "great"-aunts.

We are officially in harvest! We got started cutting on Monday evening, cut a full day yesterday, and had a late start today because of high humidity. Jeff didn't go to the field at all on Monday. He was too weak to exert the effort to go, and we really didn't start until midafternoon. I know he wants to be in the field, but doesn't have the stamina to be out there very long, especially since the prime harvesting days are ninety-eight degrees and windy. He did go to the field Tuesday morning and then crashed in his sleep-infested recliner for most of the afternoon. He then went back out when I took supper to the field and stayed a couple hours. Today he went to the field for a couple hours and came in as I was going out to take supper. He napped in the basement until about nine forty-five and then went straight to bed. We're thankful for each of our employees. A big thanks to Jeff's dad for all his help with the farming.

Jeff's in another "off" week from the chemo. He has a lab and doctor visit scheduled for the twenty-first and should start another five-day chemo cycle.

Thanks for taking time to checkonjeff. I'm thankful for each of your prayers. I ask you to pray that harvest will be safe and weather will allow for full days of harvesting; that Jeff will be patient with his progress and won't push too hard and overdo it during this busy time; and if you have any unallocated prayer time left, pray that I won't get in God's way as He uses our situation for His purpose.

> And we know that all things work together for good to them that love God, to them who are the called according to His purpose.
>
> Romans 8:28 (KJV)

06/17/10 (Thursday), 12:41PM-Karen

Jeff's doing pretty well—and that is my reassurance the cancer isn't growing. We're still in harvest. Jeff has been sharing the combine driving with Wayne. We've only had a couple of days where we cut all day, so that has allowed Jeff to be a part of most of the harvest. We still have three more quarters to cut. Jeff has a doctor's appointment on Monday and should start chemo Monday evening. He'll take chemo as a pill at home five consecutive evenings, and then won't have to take it again until day 28. He should take chemo in June and July. Then the experts will determine where we go from there.

Jeff's strength and energy are both low, so he tires easily. He's learning his limits and often comes in totally exhausted. After an hour or two of napping, he usually feels good again.

I've been preparing meals for our harvest crew. I plan for about ten every time I feed, but I usually have less than a full crew.

Jeff's still working on the mower, putting in time on it every day or two. He's recruited Brittany to help some, and my dad spent part of Tuesday helping. With rains this week, we'll need it again soon.

I better get food to the field.

06/22/10 (Tuesday), 10:20PM-Karen

Jeff met with Dr. Keefer's nurse practitioner Monday morning. Dr. Keefer assures us she knows almost as much as he does. She doesn't make the calls on Jeff's treatment, but every other month, we meet with her instead of Dr. Keefer. She reviews his labs and

makes sure we know the dosage and when to start the chemo. Jeff's lab work was good, so he started chemo Monday evening. He didn't sleep well last night. He woke up about midnight with chills and a low fever. I gave him Tylenol, and the fever broke. He seems to be resting better today. We're learning that every round of chemo wipes him out, and he needs to rest a lot during the day.

Jeff's dad called this afternoon to tell us we were officially through with wheat harvest. It's good that's behind us. We're thankful Wayne helped cut the wheat. In my last update, I said Jeff was helping on the combine. I was wrong—it was the grain cart, but he was able to be a part of the action.

I know no matter the trials here, heaven is my future. I'm thankful for peace, that this isn't really our battle—it's God's. I have to remind myself to leave the burden in God's hands and just be His servant in whatever situation he gives me.

Thanks for checking on us, and thank you so much for your prayers for Jeff. God continues to be faithful with positive answers to those prayers. For those blessings, we are thankful.

06/24/10 (Thursday), 11:13PM-Karen

This morning Jeff started cooking breakfast, as he does quite often. He had the bacon in the pan and butter melting for fried eggs. When I walked in, he was cooking from the comfort of one of our rolling kitchen chairs. Since he's in the middle of a five-day chemo cycle, I assumed he was just tired, so I took over cooking. Once breakfast was ready, I put his plate in front of him. As he salted the eggs, he tipped the shaker on its side very close to the eggs but didn't do much in the way of shaking it. In retrospect, that was probably a sign something was up. I wrote it off as a symptom of extreme fatigue. He started cutting up his eggs, and struggled at this task as well, so I offered to help. He let me cut up his eggs, and then I gave him the fork back. He again struggled with holding the fork; in fact, it slipped from his grip. I again offered to help. I used the fork and gave him a bite

of egg. That's when his eyes glossed over. I was pretty sure he was having a seizure. (Later today, Dr. Keefer confirmed that is what he believes it was.) Of course, I started yelling at Jeff to try to get him to snap out of it. When his eyes closed I yelled a little louder.

About this time, I woke Brittany, and she was almost downstairs. I told her I thought it was a seizure, and he wasn't snapping out of it. She called for an ambulance, and I stayed in the chair beside Jeff, trying to talk to him, praying, trying to talk to him, praying. Eventually, Jeff opened his eyes again but wasn't talking at all. I had Britt sit with him, and I went to call AirEvac. While fumbling with my cell phone for the number, I called Jeff's parent's number on speaker phone in my office. I got Fern, quickly told her to send Wayne because Jeff was having a seizure, and the ambulance was on its way. Then I realized my cell phone had no battery. I ran back downstairs, retrieved Jeff's cell phone from his front shirt pocket, and called AirEvac. I sat with Jeff while Brittany got her shoes on and then went and got dressed. In between doing these things, I was in Jeff's face saying "grip this hand" and other tests I have seen the doctors do to test his motor skills. They seemed fine, but he still wasn't talking.

Wayne arrived first. Then Fern arrived. Soon the ambulance and a couple of Hinton fire and rescue guys were here. All this happened within probably thirty minutes; it just seemed like hours. A few minutes and a couple of phone calls later, AirEvac arrived and landed east of the house. Somewhere in there, Phillip Paxton, deputy sheriff also arrived. Little Dog was going nuts. Britt found his carrier and caged him on the back porch. They buckled Jeff on the ambulance gurney, then unbuckled him, moved him to the AirEvac board, and then put him back on the gurney, buckled him in, and wheeled him out to the helicopter. Britt and I followed in the car. When we arrived at Mercy, Jeff was in the ER. They'd already done a CT scan. That image didn't show any bleeding in his brain, so that's definitely a good thing. This ruled out stroke. They had an IV going and soon took him for an MRI. We were told in the ER that the tumor site was *not*

larger than the last MRI (4/19). However, once Jeff was admitted and assigned a room, he saw Dr. Keefer. After we discussed the events of the day and a little about the MRIs, Jeff asked Dr. Keefer, "So does that mean it's growing?" To which Dr. Keefer replied, "Yes." He later said it could be scarring from the radiation. He said he would contact Dr. Reynolds, Jeff's surgeon from last September, and have him compare the MRIs from today and April to determine if Jeff needs another surgery. In either case, Dr. Keefer has stopped this chemo cycle. His words were "We'll save your bone marrow." We're waiting for an opinion from Dr. Reynolds and hope to learn something tomorrow. Jeff's in better spirits and is carrying on conversations much better this evening.

Although today's circumstances were unexpected, I know God knew about them before the beginning of time. He knew the dates, the time, and the outcome of each step of this journey. He knew Jeff would have cancer, he knew that on June 24 he would take a helicopter ride to Mercy Hospital, and he knew the chemo would stop; and I know that he knows the same things and even more than I will ever fathom about our tomorrows. It reminds me of an old song[4]:

Many things about tomorrow, I don't seem to understand, But I know who holds tomorrow, And I know he holds my hand.

Thanks to all of you and to every prayer warrior petitioning God on our behalf.

06/25/10 (Friday), 6:48PM-Karen

Dr. Keefer made it by this afternoon and changed all of Jeff's meds to pill form from IV. He wants to make sure Jeff handles the switch to pill form steroids well, so Jeff's here for at least another night. Dr. Keefer still wants Dr. Reynolds, the surgeon, and Dr. Morrison, the radiation doctor, to review the MRI, but doesn't believe the fact that they haven't reported back would keep Jeff in the hospital. Jeff took a shower this afternoon and is thinking much straighter compared to yesterday afternoon. Obviously, he's looking forward to going home, hopefully tomorrow.

06/26/10 (Saturday), 12:03AM-Karen

Dr. Reynolds (surgeon) came by late this evening and stayed quite a while. He discussed with us his opinions about when or if he would recommend a second surgery. Reynolds indicated, just as Dr. Keefer (oncologist) had, that this enlarged area on the MRI could be new cancer growth or necrosis (a death of cells) as a result of the radiation last November/December. Both Keefer and Reynolds have indicated it's extremely difficult to distinguish any visual difference on MRI between these two possibilities. Dr. Reynolds said he was just at a conference that discussed this very issue—distinguishing between glioblastoma cells and necrosis. He said a new imaging procedure called thymidine imaging study has recently been approved for this exact situation. He said he would raise the possibility with Dr. Keefer to use this type of imaging to diagnose the cause of the pressure in Jeff's brain. His summary of this procedure is that an injection is given of a dyed nutrient that would be absorbed by cancer cells but not by dead cells. Then a CT scan is done, and the presentation, or lack of presentation of this dyed nutrient, would allow them to determine if the area is cancer growth or radiation scarring.

The steroids are reducing the swelling and the symptoms are less. Dr. Keefer plans to release Jeff from the hospital sometime on Saturday. However, the MRI results indicate another time of assessment is needed. Dr. Keefer indicated today that there are still several options available. I wish I could sugarcoat this news or keep it from you and glaze over the discussions we had with both the surgeon and the oncologist today, but I feel compelled to share openly with each of you what our family is facing and allow you to pray specifically for these matters.

Several options are now on the table: A different chemo drug? Another surgery? Another round of radiation? A combination? The possibility the enlargement of the area is necrosis? Please pray for wisdom of these two men as they provide us guidance. Please pray we'll have continued peace in this situation, and that God's guidance in our lives will draw others close to Him. I'm daily humbled by friends and family who are truly interested in Jeff's treatment and its success and those petitioning God on our behalf, in Jesus's name. His glory is our purpose.

06/27/10 (Sunday), 3:49PM-Karen

Jeff was released from the hospital about eleven thirty Saturday morning, and by eleven forty-five, we were at Red Lobster. When we got home, I was definitely ready for a shower and clean clothes. Jeff was just ready for a nap. He napped for a while in the afternoon, watched a little TV, and then took another nap in the evening, so he would be rested before actually going to bed. As far as I know, he rested well during the night. At least no one woke him every hour or two to take his blood pressure, ask if he had been to the restroom, or if he needed anything. I sure don't want to be a complainer, just making the point. It's good to be home. No matter what brand of bed you have, if it's in your home, it's better than anything the hospital could ever have.

A neighbor stopped by with his lawnmower yesterday afternoon and mowed the yard. It's interesting how things work out when people view their things as God's things, and they're willing to use them wherever and on whoever's yard God directs. We continue to count the blessings, and every time we count, there are more things, more people on our list.

This morning, Jeff got up and around and made it to church. Today was our interim pastor's last Sunday. It was good to be with our church family for this occasion. Of course, it really wouldn't have mattered who was preaching—it was Sunday, and Jeff would want to be there. What a blessing to me to have a husband with that as one of his priorities!

Brittany is at church camp this week. She was asked and has agreed to give the evening devotions every night in the girls' dorm. She sees this as a tremendous opportunity. I know she would appreciate your prayers that she'll be an encouragement to other Christian girls and a witness to those without Christ.

While Britt is at camp, the taxi will be a little less occupied, and I plan to catch up on office work. Tomorrow we'll schedule a follow-up visit with Dr. Keefer. Jeff's next appointment was not scheduled until the nineteenth of July, which would coincide with the next chemo round. Now, we will need to discuss the best plan of treatment. Dr. Keefer is recommending we consult with MD Anderson in Houston. We've heard many good things from several different directions about the care there. We have trusted Dr. Keefer for about ten months now. I had wanted to ask if he thought we would have better results with another doctor. I was really struggling with how to ask and not insult him. (Blessing alert!) Without my prompting, Dr. Keefer offered the fact that if it was him at this stage, he believed he would go to Houston. We will discuss that option this week.

Please pray that we'll know God's will about the next step. Through trust that God's in control, I've given up on having to know the next destination. I'm happy with God's direction in where to put my foot today once it's picked up. Thanks for your prayers and your encouragement.

"For I know the plans I have for you," declares the Lord,
"plans to prosper you and not to harm you, plans to give

you hope and a future. Then you will call upon me and come and pray to me, and I will listen to you. You will seek me and find me when you seek me with all your heart. I will be found by you," declares the Lord, "and will bring you back from captivity."

Jeremiah 29:11–14 (NIV)

06/29/10 (Tuesday), 12:29AM-Karen

This morning I called Dr. Keefer's office. They have contacted MD Anderson in Houston. We're waiting to hear from Houston about scheduling an initial visit. Please pray God will direct the scheduling and provide the right personnel.

Our new minister and his wife arrived in Hydro this evening. What a blessing to have them here—Bob and Linda Sprunger, Oklahoma's newest citizens! Jeff and I went for a few minutes while the church helped unload their moving van.

Thanks for the prayers. I continue to be humbled by the emotional support and encouragement we are receiving. Seems everywhere we go, someone asks how Jeff is or says they're keeping up on CarePages. I can't express how much it means to me to know we aren't alone, that others are truly compassionate and want to offer encouragement.

I'm optimistic about treatment possibilities at MD Anderson, but, I know ultimately any healing will come from God. Most certainly, He who created has the ultimate power to repair!

06/29/10 (Tuesday), 9:54PM-Karen

Jeff's appetite is definitely back full strength, thanks to the steroids. He cooked breakfast and supper. He spent a little time in his office, and then this afternoon, he drove into Hydro to get a much-needed haircut (his hair was actually curly prior to the trim).

We did get a call from MD Anderson today. Dr. Keefer in OKC had referred us to a Dr. Wienberg, a neurosurgeon. They asked lots of preliminary questions but mostly wanted to know if we wanted a consultation with the surgeon or with the nonsurgical options. I didn't know enough to even answer that question. If Keefer referred us to the surgeon, then maybe that was who we should see? The lady we spoke with was going to speak with Dr. Wienberg to see whom he wanted us to see first. We've heard only good things about Houston. I wish we knew a timeframe so we could plan other things so that they won't interfere. But we can always rearrange things if we need to.

07/01/10 (Thursday), 6:23PM-Karen

Jeff has an appointment at 8:00 a.m. Wednesday at MD Anderson. All the arrangements have been made. Once again, it appears God's timing is far superior to anything we would've asked for. All the pieces seem to be sliding into place. We just need to collect all Jeff's MRI images and some paperwork before we go. Jeff will meet with Dr. Puduvalli, and if he believes a neurosurgeon is needed, Dr. Jeffrey Wienberg has agreed to take Jeff on as a patient.

We got our baby girl (she's fourteen) back from church camp today. Just like I remember my first day after church camp—she spent hers catching up on sleep! I believe she had a good time and enjoyed seeing those once-a-year friends and making a few new ones. For the most part, she was a counselor for the girls' dorm, although she had enough fun. You would think the whole camp must have revolved around her! I know she needed and enjoyed the break.

I will send more details on our trip to Houston when I know them. Keep up the prayers and give God credit for the answers!

MD Anderson
Cancer Center

07/02/10 (Friday), 10:24PM-Karen

We are again overwhelmed with being the recipient of generosity! A local couple cashed in rewards points and gave us two round-trip tickets to Houston. What a tremendous gift! This is just the most recent act of generosity, and they were willing to give God credit for directing their actions. Again, we are truly blessed.

I spent a large part of the day rounding up medical records to take with us—mostly the MRIs but also some records I have in folders here at home. I haven't tackled the seven-page patient history yet. I scanned through it quickly and believe it to be easy enough. Hopefully, I will find time over the weekend to get it completed and out of the way so I won't dread it.

Jeff and Brittany went with Wayne to use GPS to plot out a couple of pivots today. It took longer than they had hoped, but they didn't have any major trouble. Jeff gets frustrated easily and has a little trouble with concentration. Both symptoms could easily be a result of the steroids. This evening he caught a nap before and another after supper.

Our new minister will take over the pulpit on Sunday, Brittany will play the offertory, I teach an SS class, our church is in charge of the service at the nursing home before church—and as the wife of the senior deacon, I will get the elements ready for communion. Looks like a very active Sunday to start a busy week. Please pray for God's peace to shine out of every little detail of our week.

Thanks for your prayers, especially that God will cause the medical experts to see clearly what treatment will be beneficial for Jeff.

In all thy ways acknowledge Him and He shall direct thy paths.

Proverbs 3:6 (KJV)

07/07/10 (Wednesday), 10:59PM-Karen

After a thirty-minute weather delay in Oklahoma City, Jeff and I arrived in Houston Tuesday evening. This morning, we met first with registration, where they dotted all the *i*'s and crossed all the *t*'s as far as paperwork. Then we went back to the waiting room. Next he went for blood pressure and a weigh-in, then met with the nurse of the oncologist, then with a resident supervised by the oncologist, and, finally, with the oncologist, Dr. Puduvalli. He had reviewed all the MRIs we brought and the clinic notes from all the doctors in OKC. He discussed each MRI with us, starting with the original in September of 2009 and moving forward to the latest from two weeks ago. He mentioned the excellent job that Jeff's surgeon at Mercy in OKC had done in September, as evidenced by the post-surgery MRI. His comments about the last MRI confirmed that the swelling and pressure that Jeff's experiencing is new growth of the cancer. Given these facts, he wanted one of their neurosurgeons to review the MRI and notes and give a surgical opinion.

The nurse for Dr. Puduvalli took our cell phone numbers and turned us loose for the day. We were to stay in Houston until we heard from her. Dr. Puduvalli was going to contact the neurosurgery department. His plan was to have someone review Jeff's case today if possible, or tomorrow. By now, it was noon, and we went to the food court. I had made my selection and paid out. Jeff was still choosing when my cell phone rang. It was the nurse telling us Dr. Prabhu, the neurosurgeon, could meet with us *now*. I went backward through the food court line and found Jeff. He was literally opening his mouth to order his food. I stopped him, and we went back upstairs to the Brain and Spine Center to meet with Dr. Prabhu. He pulled up the MRIs and used them as reference when he explained the surgical possibility.

Similar to the description we received in September, Dr. Prabhu said that surgery would remove the bulk of the tumor, which increases the effectiveness of the post-surgery chemo. One concern we discussed involved possible surgical damage to the left temple, the area affected by Jeff's tumor, which controls speech. MD Anderson has the ability to perform surgery under anesthesia but then "wake" the patient and have them speak. This surgical option, along with an MRI in the surgery suite, allow the surgical team to check their progress, and allows for a more precise surgery, which lets them be more protective of the speech functions, which include word choice, understanding, and the like.

Bottom line, we were given three options: Do nothing, use chemo only, or undergo a second surgery and then start a chemo treatment. Dr. Prabhu stated that if we chose the surgery option, then the obvious reasoning would be the sooner the surgery can be done, the better. Once again, it appears that God has timing superior to anything I could even ask for: They checked his schedule. He had an opening for surgery on Tuesday. God has once again opened the doors in an awesome way. Once the surgery route was the treatment plan, the nurses started arranging the blood tests, EKG, and other presurgery testing. Jeff had some tests this afternoon, he'll have some on Monday, and then he'll have surgery on Tuesday.

After surgery, he'll spend one night in ICU, then three to four days in the hospital in Houston, and then he should be able to go home. He would follow up with the neurosurgeon and oncologist in two weeks.

And so Jeff will have surgery in Houston on Tuesday, five hundred miles from home. If I have said it once, I have said it a hundred times: "I don't know how people go through anything of this nature without a personal relationship with Christ." Please don't get me wrong, having a Savior doesn't miraculously make everything rosy. There are times, I just simply cry. It's hard to draw a circle around the events we are experiencing, to take it all in and process the reality.

I'm confident Jeff's cancer is as close to fully documented as cancer can be. What a perfect time for a miracle!

Now unto him that is able to do exceeding abundantly above all that we ask or think, according to the power that worketh in us, Unto him be glory in the church by Christ Jesus throughout all ages, world without end. Amen.

Ephesians 3:20–21 (KJV)

I keep asking (praying), as I know many of you are that God will grant a miracle of total healing. I yield that healing only to the Truth of scripture that *"we know that all things work together for good to them that love God, to them who are the called according to his purpose"* (Romans 8:28, KJV).

So, if healing isn't God's will, he has an even better plan.

Thank you for your prayers. Pray where God leads you.

07/12/10 (Monday), 6:25AM-Karen

Wow, I should catch up on several days of activity. Jeff and I traveled home on an earlier flight than scheduled on Thursday. E-tickets—what a way to go! We were easily able to change our afternoon flight to a midmorning flight and were able to eat lunch Thursday at one of Jeff's favs—On the Border. Then we were headed home from OKC for a few days. I was able to work some in the office on Friday and Saturday and finished up some billing for our irrigation business. My knowledge of the parts is growing, but I still have to have a lot of input from Jeff and his dad.

For those of you following the mower project, Brittany mowed last Tuesday with our mower! And it looked good when she was done.

Saturday evening, the church deacons and our new pastor had a time of prayer for Jeff in our home. James 5:14 (KJV) says if anyone is sick, they should call for the elders, "and the prayer offered in faith will make the sick person well; the Lord will raise him up."Our church had a prayer service for Jeff Sunday evening. We're taking that for what's promised.

Jeff, Brittany, and I along with my sister, Janice, headed for Houston on Sunday. Janice is planning to stay with us until later in the week.

What a blessing! We had many offers from people willing to make the trip to spend time with us before or during surgery. I discouraged most of them. It's such a long trip to make to sit for a few hours and head back home. In case you didn't know, prayer is a *perfect* gift, and it's effective from wherever you are, not just in Houston!

Today's packed with doctor's visits and testing. We start at eight in the Brain and Spine Center, and Jeff will have a couple of MRIs before the end of the day. Please pray for our patience as we move through these appointments.

Our day of travel yesterday was draining. Along with your faithful prayers for Jeff, I ask for prayer for me. My Christian heritage taught me my role in our family would be one of submission to my husband, to follow his lead and provide a supporting role—or as it's worded in the creation account, to be a "helpmate." Providing care for Jeff through parts of the last year has meant I've had to temporarily pick up some tasks and aspects of Jeff's role as head of our family. Some of my accountant-type

skills kick in, and I control those aspects a little too long. That leads to conflict. Please pray that I can be strong enough to pick up the slack when my husband isn't able and gracious enough to relinquish that control at the right moment.

One of my favorite verses has become Jeremiah 29:11(NIV): *"For I know the plans I have for you" declares the Lord, "plans to prosper you and not to harm you, plans to give you hope and a future."* Then verse 12 goes on to say, *"Then you will call upon me and come and pray to me, and I will listen to you."*

Thanks for your prayers. I know God is listening.

> And the Lord God said, It is not good that the man
> should be alone; I will make him an help meet for him.

> Genesis 2:18 (KJV)

07/12/10 (Monday), 9:45PM-Karen

Jeff reports for surgery at 5:15 a.m. tomorrow. Surgery should begin within an hour and a half later and last about six hours. This morning Jeff met with a neuropsychologist. They asked a series of questions and gave Jeff a pencil-and-paper test. There was a variety of questions asked. They will compare Jeff's scores with other forty-six-year-old men of similar education. This process is done to set a baseline for his cognitive skills. Then after surgery, he'll undergo the same or a similar set of tests that will yield a score to be compared to today's baseline numbers.

After the cognitive testing, they gave Jeff some fiducial markers, which are stick-on markers to be left on until surgery. These were in place for the MRI. This gives the surgeon more precision to line up the skull with today's images. Jeff was given a traditional MRI, an MRI with contrast, and a special MRI in which Jeff spoke into a microphone. We were told that in combination with the contrast medium, different areas, such as the speech area, of the brain "light up" when they are being used.

This should give the surgeon an increased ability to protect Jeff's speech and motor functions.

After the MRIs, Jeff met with one of the four anesthesiologists at MD Anderson who administer sedation for this special type of surgery called an awake cranial. MD Anderson performs over 150 of these awake brain surgeries a year. This lady explained the surgery from the anesthetist's view. They will sedate Jeff, open the layers, and expose the brain. Then they will wake Jeff enough to answer some simple questions. From Jeff's responses, the surgeon will determine which areas of Jeff's brain control his speech and motor functions to a very precise level so they can avoid any further damage to these areas.

Jeff's brother Randy, along with Wayne and Fern, arrived safely a few minutes ago. Thanks for your prayers for our safety as we traveled to Houston. Once again, God has provided. I'm learning to see the blessings, learning that if you give God control of any situation right from the start, it's easier to see his handiwork. If we retain (or think we retain) control of something and God provides the same blessing, it's easily written off as coincidence, medical or science. If we acknowledge it's in God's hands up front, it's easy to see the blessing and his control, his peace as the situation unfolds. From the start, we have known beating brain cancer was out of our hands. We have placed this battle in God's hands. We have trusted God to open the treatment doors—and over and over, his timing has proved to be more than we could ask or think (Ephesians 3:20). So again tonight, I have to remind myself to place Jeff's care in God's hands. I ask Him to guide the surgeon's hand, to intervene as needed with the staffing and provide the physical healing Jeff needs, and, most importantly, that God receive glory from this situation—that others will see the peace, love, and provision He provides for those who trust Him, which is a physical parallel of the spiritual peace, love, and provision He provides for those who put their trust in Him. Now to Him be honor and glory.

07/13/10 (Tuesday), 2:45PM-Karen

Jeff's out of surgery and in a recovery room. It will be another thirty minutes before they will let me in to see him. Dr. Prabu met with most of the family who was here after he completed the surgery. He was somewhat disappointed at Jeff's responsiveness and willingness to participate in their flashcard speech testing during the awake portion of the surgery. He said Jeff carried on a conversation with them but was uncooperative with the interactive portion of the surgery. In spite of that, Dr. Prabu believes they were successful in removing the tumor. I say tumor and not cancer because he said what they removed appeared to be scarring or necrosis. The pathologists should have a definite answer by the end of the week.

There is some concern with whether or not there was damage to his speech areas. They want to keep a close eye on his speech and may suggest a speech pathologist for some speech therapy.

Overall, a definite praise. Thank you for your prayers, and I will post more this evening after I have had a chance to speak with Jeff.

In all things, give thanks!

In every thing give thanks: for this is the will of God in
Christ Jesus concerning you.

1 Thessalonians 5:18 (KJV)

07/13/10 (Tuesday), 11:13PM-Karen

Jeff was still a little groggy from the sedation this evening and was
having some pain. They were able to give him pain meds, and he
quickly went back to sleep. He has had a clear liquid diet today, and
from their comments, I expect he'll soon get to eat anything that sounds
good to him.

Jeff seemed to be speaking pretty well tonight. He struggled to complete
some of his sentences, but Dr. Prabu warned us that when we met with him
right after surgery, there would most likely be some temporary speech issues
in the first day or so after surgery, because of the trauma of the surgery. A
little time should tell how short-term these symptoms are.

Jeff's motor skills seem to be fine. He was picking up a tea glass
and using a straw to get a drink and then placing the glass back on the
bedside table by himself. Sounds simple maybe, but it was definitely
encouraging to see all the skills that are still okay. He was even scooting
himself up in the bed. Of course, the beds in Houston aren't any longer
than the ones in OKC. Unfortunately, they all seem to be about ten
inches too short for maximum comfort.

We are optimistic the mass removed was scar tissue and not cancer
growth. We won't know the results of the pathology reports until later
in the week, possibly on Friday.

Jeff's brother, Randy, is staying at the hospital with him tonight.
Everyone else came back to the hotel to rest. Hopefully, Jeff will sleep
well so Randy will get some rest too.

My update this evening reminds me a little of the old hymn "Count
Your Many Blessings." Tonight the concept of naming the blessings one
by one is a little more real. We are truly blessed in so many ways. Please
continue to pray that God will provide complete healing for Jeff and
use this for His Glory.

07/14/10 (Wednesday), 8:02PM-Karen

When I arrived this morning, Jeff was standing up, and they had most of the bandages off of his head. Overall, he's doing exceptionally well. He's visiting and in good spirits. They've changed his diet from clear liquids to anything he wants. For a farm boy, that's definitely a good thing. He was up multiple times today and walked several circles around the nurses' station. This evening, he had a post-op MRI. I suspect Dr. Prabhu will review it with us tomorrow during his rounds.

Jeff's parents and Randy left after lunch to go back home. I know they were glad they came. I was glad Jeff was having such a good day to visit with them before they left. The surgeon is planning toward letting Jeff go home on Friday.

As Jeff's mom, Fern, and I were leaving the hotel this morning, Leroy Meriwether overheard Fern in the lobby, and I quietly hummed a chorus of "It's a Small World After All." Leroy is from Hinton, and he's here for treatment as well. He stopped by Jeff's room this afternoon, and he and Jeff had a good visit. Jeff does well visiting if there aren't *any* other distractions.

My sister Janice, Brittany, and I have met several patient families in the waiting rooms here. Every family has a heartwrenching story. My heart goes out to them, the families with small children and grandchildren undergoing cancer treatment. I spoke with Donna Mogg from Binger (fifteen miles from Hinton) before we left home. Her husband is surviving the same variety of cancer as Jeff. She put it in perspective: "Of every group of people you see, you know at least one of them is battling cancer."

I'm very thankful Jeff's recovering so well tonight. Truly, we're blessed.

07/15/10 (Thursday), 10:06PM-Karen

Jeff had another good day. He walked to the next patient area and made a loop through, mostly for a change in scenery. They have him taking three to five walks a day and sitting up four to six hours so that he doesn't just lie in bed. He called and ordered his lunch and supper today. They are set up in a room service format instead of a bulk cafeteria served at a certain time determined by your location. This room service format allows the patient or a family member to call and order what they will eat. Their standard is less-than-forty-five-minute delivery.

To best explain Jeff's status today, it hinges on focus. He does pretty good formulating sentences and carrying on a conversation *if* all other distractions are eliminated. The more distractions there are, the harder he has to work to put his thoughts into words and stay focused. Some of this is expected to be caused by the surgery. Any long-term issues will be discovered overtime.

We expect Jeff to be discharged from the hospital Friday morning. I do not expect to be on the road until about 11:00 AM. We've been told to take a break and let Jeff stretch every two hours or so. Please pray Jeff will tolerate the travel home well.

> But my God shall supply all your need according to his riches in glory by Christ Jesus.
>
> Philippians 4:19 (KJV)

> Do not be like them, for your Father knows what you need before you ask him
>
> Matthew 6:8 (NIV)

> Now to Him who is able to do exceeding abundantly above all that we ask or think, according to the power that worketh in us, unto him be glory in the church by Christ Jesus throughout all ages, world without end.
>
> Ephesians 3:20–21 (KJV)

I'm constantly reminded of our blessings. God is truly supplying our need according to *His* unlimited riches, which is more than we could even ask or think of.

07/17/10 (Saturday), 9:18PM-Karen

We are home! Jeff's doing incredibly well. Before we left MD Anderson, Jeff went to their volunteer barbershop. He had them shave the rest of his head. The surgeon only needed the area around the incision shaved, which left his hair kind of lopsided. He wasn't Jeff's barber, but it looks pretty good. The stitches look clean. He has to keep them dry until tomorrow; then he can get them wet in the shower. With a shaved head, he won't need much shampoo.

He got up this morning and cooked some sausage. We were out of every other breakfast staple, so late morning, we all went to Weatherford to the grocery store. Jeff rode the little electric scooter until the battery ran down. He barely made it to the front of the store, but he was able to enjoy a task we have always done together. Since Jeff enjoys cooking and eating, he naturally enjoys selecting the food as well. They sent him home from the hospital with instructions to sit up four to six hours a day and to take four to five walks. I think the trip to Weatherford knocked out several of both. Of course, he was ready for a nap when we got home.

While Jeff was in the hospital in OKC the last of June, they put him back on steroids to control the swelling. They were giving him 4 mg four times a day for a total of 16 mg a day. While Jeff was in MD Anderson, they increased that dosage to 6 mg, every six hours for a total of 24 mg a day. When he was released from the hospital, they dropped that dosage to 8 mg a day, with a schedule to taper to 0 by the time he goes back. We have been told several times since last September these steroids are *not* the type athletes want to take. This type of steroid is known for destroying muscle, increasing irritability, decreasing the quality and quantity of sleep, and increasing appetite. We are all glad the dosage is going down.

I mentioned in an earlier post we would know the results of the pathology report yesterday. With all the activity of getting home, we didn't call in to find out. We hope to have the pathology results on Monday. Jeff will go back on the twenty-eighth to have the stitches removed.

Again, the generosity of our neighbors has overwhelmed me. We were ready to leave for Houston when the air conditioner in my Yukon went out. The generosity of others loaned us an unbelievable vehicle for the trip. With Jeff sick, we were behind on working our farm ground. Several area farmers and businessmen have made a big dent in the groundwork and on the application of chemical for another field. Another neighbor family fed and watered our dogs while we were away. What a blessing! In an earlier post, I mentioned the mowed lawn and the airline tickets. These men and women who have been so generous didn't act in order to receive praise; they acted because they truly care. I don't even have the ability to count the number of people who have spent their time, their most precious resource, to pray and to ask others to pray on our behalf. I know that God providing for Jeff's health in a wonderful way is an answer to those prayers. So tonight all I can do is thank my Father in Heaven for His generosity and His provision and send an inadequate "thank you" to each person who has been willing to be used by God to provide for our family in our time of need. To each of you who have helped us, I trust God will richly bless you.

07/19/10 (Monday), 5:15PM-Jeff

I realize it has been a long time since I have written in the blog. I have not been in the mood, and it has been hard for me to type for a very long time. I can type a little, and usually, I have to do it twice to get it correct.

First of all, thank you for getting your prayers in for me. I feel pretty good, but it is a slow process. Keep praying, and whatever happens will be with God's hand.

I am going to keep this short for now. Keep praying.

—JK

07/21/10 (Wednesday), 3:40PM-Karen

Pathology report from Jeff's surgery shows no *live* cancer cells, only necrosis from the radiation. "To God be the glory, great things He hath done!"

07/25/10 (Sunday), 12:07AM-Karen

Thanks for all the posts, comments, phone calls, and cards, and especially for all the prayers. I know Jeff has been on countless prayer lists for a little over ten months now. Please pass on our thanks and make sure God gets the credit for the answer to our prayers that came this week with the report of "no live cancer cells."

We've been celebrating, so to speak, since we got the pathology results on Wednesday, which also marked our twentieth wedding anniversary! It was a very busy day. Jeff had a Wheat Commission meeting in OKC that morning. A longtime friend of Jeff's before our wedding, and mine since the wedding, was in the States for a family vacation. We met his family and a few other friends for supper Wednesday evening. By Thursday morning, Jeff was ready for some catch-up naps.

This coming Wednesday will be the last day for Jeff to take any of the steroids. Jeff has three appointments scheduled in Houston on Wednesday. The first is with the surgeon, Dr. Prabhu, to remove the stitches, the second is a post-op evaluation of his cognitive testing, and the last appointment will be with Dr. Puduvalli. We should get an explanation of their recommended short-term and long-term treatment plans.

Today, Brittany and I traveled to Granite to attend a memorial service for a family friend. We left Jeff home alone. I believe all of us needed a break from the 24/7 togetherness the events of the last month have mandated.

We continue to give God the credit and glory for the healing Jeff has experienced. Please pray that along with us, others will be drawn closer to Christ as a result of our journey, and that we will "be ready to give an answer."

> But sanctify the Lord God in your hearts: and be ready always to give an answer to every man that asketh you a reason of the hope that is in you with meekness and fear:
>
> 1 Peter 3:15 (KJV)

07/28/10 (Wednesday), 11:23AM-Karen

This morning at MD Anderson, Jeff met with Dr. Prabhu, the surgeon and his assistant and a couple of students. The assistant removed the stitches, and then Dr. Prabhu visited with us. He showed us the Before and After MRI images. They're confident the surgery was a success. They visited with Jeff and asked a lot of follow-up questions. Jeff only took pain meds the first couple of days. I'm convinced a lot of the pain was caused by the trip home from Houston.

Next Jeff met with the cognitive testing group to reevaluate his speech and memory ability. The new assessment will be compared with the pre-op numbers to determine the extent of the changes. Finally, Jeff met with Dr. Puduvalli.

Today was the last day of steroids. Brittany and I have noticed the welcome changes of reduced irritability and appetite. Along with discontinuing steroids from Jeff's current medications, the Pepcid prescribed to protect his stomach lining from the steroids was also discontinued. Jeff's down to taking two drugs: Keppra, the antiseizure medication (for prevention) and potassium, and he only takes them once a day.

07/28/10 (Wednesday), 9:45PM-Karen

Good reports with both the surgeon and the oncologist today. Surgeon turned Jeff loose. The oncologist is giving Jeff three to four weeks off and will continue the chemo schedule for about six more cycles. Because the pathology report didn't show live cancer cells, the Temodar is considered to be effective. The typical treatment by Dr. Puduvalli is twelve cycles of Temodar. Since Jeff was in cycle 5 prior to the last surgery, he can expect the remaining cycles. Jeff will have another MRI before he starts the chemo, to compare and confirm the surgical progress and then an MRI every two months for a while. Dr. Puduvalli confirmed the excellent news: the pathology report showed no *live* cancer cells.

He again discussed how visually impossible it is to distinguish between new growth and necrosis, and how drastically different our approach to Jeff's treatment is since we know the cancer isn't growing. Given the blessings God has poured on us, I expect today's cognitive testing to reflect the improvement that I have seen/heard in Jeff's speech since the surgery.

Thanks for all your prayers. God has answered, and we are thankful. Praise God from whom all blessings flow.

08/02/10 (Monday), 11:45PM-Karen

Jeff talked on the phone some today to a couple of our irrigation customers. He was able to talk one guy into fixing something on his pivot. He napped most of the morning, and after lunch, he napped most of the afternoon. Because he's coming off of the steroids, food doesn't taste quite as good and doesn't sound near as appealing to him as they did while he was on steroids. This is probably not all bad, because he can shed a few of the steroid pounds, but I still want him to keep up his strength. This still is not the time to worry about what the bathroom scales say.

On Saturday, Jeff went to a deacons' breakfast in Weatherford. When he came home, he fell asleep in his recliner and stayed there until lunchtime. Then he napped again for an hour or two before we loaded in the car and headed to Mangum to my aunt and uncle's home for a cookout with about twenty family members on my dad's side. Shortly after supper, we headed back home. It doesn't sound like a whole lot, but it was too much. Jeff slept most of Sunday and has slept most of today as well. We will have to do a better job of planning so we don't overdo things.

Brittany has started daily practices for fall fast-pitch softball. Today she had both a morning practice and an evening practice. She'll be involved in both junior high and high school sports this year. So it looks like the taxi will be busy and the lawn chairs will get a workout.

Our focus now is getting Jeff's strength and stamina back. It appears there aren't any shortcuts to that goal. It will take some time. That's where the patience you've been praying for will be of good use. Jeff wants to be a part of everything, and we want to include him in all the activities that are going on, but he can't do it all—*yet*. We're so thankful for the good pathology report and look forward to the oncologist's prescription for "time off" from treatment.

Thanks for the continued prayers. I am humbled by the number of people who keep up with Jeff's progress. People have told us we're on their church prayer list. We've received cards from several churches. The church family of one man Jeff serves on a board with sent an afghan. The note attached says that they passed it around at their church and everyone prayed for Jeff as they held the afghan. It's a truly special gift to remind us not only of those who are praying for Jeff but also to give God credit for the answers to prayers.

It's my prayer that God will continue to use our situation to bring honor and glory to himself, that others will be drawn to *Him* by the peace *He* gives us, or by the comfort *He* surrounds us with, or by the joy *He* gives in the midst of trials…I could go on, but I will stop there. I'm trying to keep my eyes open so I don't miss any of the blessings God gives us or miss any opportunity to share with those around us our story of how God sustains us. Pray that I will know when to open my mouth and speak and when I should keep it shut. (Maybe that is where patience and wisdom will come in handy.)

> If any of you lacks wisdom, he should ask God, who
> gives generously to all without finding fault, and it will
> be given to him.

> James 1:5 (NIV)

08/05/10 (Thursday), 7:09AM-Karen

Good morning to all. I think Jeff's staying in one place longer at night, so I tend to think he's sleeping a little better, although when I ask him, he still doesn't think he sleeps well at night. He was up and dressed by six this morning, and now at seven, he's napping in his chair. His appetite has continued to decrease, and I'm trying to push liquids, especially with the Oklahoma heat.

Yesterday Jeff made a trip to his parents' just about a mile as the crow flies. Wayne needed Fern to meet him with a part. Jeff went to help get the right part. When he got back home, his only comment was "I overdid it." And then he headed straight for his recliner. Today the Oklahoma Wheat Commission is having a monthly meeting in Stillwater (home of Oklahoma State, for those who don't know). I called yesterday and cancelled the room reservation. It was obvious he would not be able to make this month's meeting. Jeff takes this board member role very seriously. He gets discouraged when he can't be at the meetings, or participate like he would have a year or so ago. The same is true for his Farm Bureau Board and serving as a deacon at our church. A special thank-you to those picking up the slack while he's out of "commission."

Britt will start school in one week. It's so hard to believe our little girl will be a freshman. In other ways, it seems she's so grown up I find myself wishing she had a driver's license already to eliminate some of my taxi mom duties. I do treasure the times when she and I are in the car. We get to visit and get a break from the cares of the day. She's such a great kid. What a blessing!

We have notice of Jeff's next appointments at MD Anderson. He'll have blood work on August 31, followed by a 10:00 p.m. MRI, then meet with Dr. Puduvalli at 8:30 a.m. on the first. Flying was so much easier on him than the long drive. I've already made the flight, motel, and car rental reservations. I'm getting a little better at my travel agency duties.

Thanks for your continued prayer.

08/06/10 (Friday), 2:58PM-Karen

Since our last update, Jeff has been sleeping much more and running an occasional fever and needs Tylenol occasionally to keep it down. He's not cooperative with taking food or liquids, and he hasn't been very alert. This morning we went to Hydro to see the PA. She sent him to Weatherford for labs. Right now, she's concerned with dehydration, build up of the antiseizure medication, or a thyroid imbalance triggered by the variety of meds he has taken in the last year. We are waiting for test results.

Please make this a matter of prayer.

08/06/10 (Friday), 8:38PM-Karen

We received a call from the doctor's office late this afternoon. Today's results look good. The thyroid level was in the center of the normal range. A little infection appeared in the testing, so Jeff will take an antibiotic twice a day for ten days. We won't have results on the specific blood test that will show whether Jeff has built up an excess of the antiseizure meds (Keppra) until next week sometime. This morning, Jeff had not taken the Keppra before the doctor's appointment, and she told me not to give it to him. Thankfully, Jeff seems to be more alert this afternoon. He's still having trouble with conversations, mostly with choosing the word he wants; but he's definitely more alert. I keep trusting in the truth of Romans 8:28 (KJV) that *"all things work together for good to them that love the Lord, to them that are the called according to His purpose."* This is another one of those "things" I know is part of a greater good. A good I/we may not understand—and often don't understand. I'm reminded of a line from a song. "Many things about tomorrow I don't seem to understand, but I know who holds the tomorrow and I know He holds my hand."

Seizures after
Necrosis Surgery

08/07/10 (Saturday), 2:40AM-Karen

Late Friday evening before we headed to bed, we asked Jeff if we could
delete the show we just watched from the DVR. He couldn't answer.
He tried several times, but his answer each time was gibberish. The
sounds weren't even words. I called the PA, and she sent us to the ER
in Weatherford. She called and told them we were on our way. As part
of his evaluation, they took him for a CT scan and two chest x-rays.
Because Jeff was confused and disoriented, they asked if I wanted to
go with them in case he had trouble. Jeff made it through the CT scan
fine and then moved to the next room for the x-rays, but right after she
took the X-rays, Jeff had a seizure. They now have him sedated, and his
blood pressure and fever are both coming back down. I ask for prayers
that the medical personnel will be able to determine the cause of this
latest setback. Thanks for your concern, and especially for your prayers.

08/07/10 (Saturday), 9:15PM-Karen

Jeff has rested pretty well today. He saw Lauren Binder, PA, this
morning. She was confident his speech would return and he should
be able to go home tomorrow. He was on a liquid diet for breakfast
and lunch, but this afternoon, Dr. Stutzman, the doctor whom Lauren
works with, came by and saw Jeff. She upgraded his dietary orders to a
regular diet, so Jeff got solid foods for supper. I know he was happy to
have that luxury back.

Jeff still has problems putting together coherent responses when
people ask him questions. Everyone who has seen him says his speech
will improve. From what I have gathered from the doctors who have

explained the seizure to me, the best way I can describe the effect on the brain to you is (my words, not theirs) it was an electrical brainstorm that temporarily shut down and garbled all the brain's electrical impulses, causing a drop in service to the communications area. They say it's common for seizure patients to have brief memory loss that covers the time of the seizure, so I expect he won't remember most of the last day. I'm reminded of the scripture in Psalm 139:14 (KJV): *"I will praise you, for I am fearfully and wonderfully made; marvelous are your works, and my soul knows very well."*

The farther my family travels this path, the more I marvel at the resilience God created in the human body. I'm convinced all healing is at the command of my Heavenly Father, the creator of the universe.

A year or two ago, my dad made a CD from a 33LP (that reference will be lost on younger readers) that my Aunt Betty made when I was a kid. One song I really enjoyed this week talks about recognizing that no matter what we do for Christ there is always more we can do. Part of the lyrics are as follows:

> But I don't tell it enough, I don't pray enough.
> I don't love my neighbor as I should enough.

The chorus plays in my head often: "Lord, I need you again today."[5]

I'm prayerfully optimistic Jeff's speech will be restored quickly. This afternoon, he knows more names and is sitting up some watching the Food Network. I can't wait till our breakfast chef is home again.

08/08/10 (Sunday), 1:22PM-Karen

Jeff was dismissed from the hospital with the question "Do you want to go before or after lunch?" Bet you can guess what he chose. We came home. I fixed fried pork minute steaks, mashed potatoes, and a little gravy. It's good to be home again.

Jeff's walking and eating well. His speech is still a little sluggish. Short answers he does well. If his comments get much longer, he loses his thoughts easily and sometimes doesn't make sense at all. Keep praying and trusting that all these aspects will continue to improve as he's home.

Jeff was put back on blood pressure meds before he was dismissed. They said his BP had been consistently high while he was in the hospital. He's to finish the antibiotic that he started on Friday, resume the antiseizure med and the potassium, as the lab in the ER showed his potassium was a little low.

The PA intends to speak with Jeff's medical team in Houston possibly as early as Monday. I'm sure Houston will want a copy of the x-rays and the CT scan. There is some question about fluid in the area of the surgeries.

08/10/10 (Tuesday), 7:02AM-Karen

Jeff's up, eating and taking liquids better than he did last week. He's walking on his own, but his balance isn't too good. He's still having trouble with focus and communications. Monday evening, he rode with me to Weatherford, and we stopped by Sonic for a burger, not just because I'm a fan, but also so that he wouldn't have to get in and out of the car. When I talk to him, he seems to understand what I tell him but seems to have trouble putting sentences together to respond. Last week he didn't have any trouble running the remotes to watch TV. This week, he's pushing the wrong buttons and having trouble with the sound system. Yesterday the hospital called, and I wasn't home. Brittany and Kim were here, but they would only talk to Jeff. Now he can't tell me what they needed. I'll have to track that call down today. Yesterday he told me his phone was broken, but it appears to be fine. Maybe it was another issue with running electronics.

I'm prayerful this is just confusion left from the seizure and that he'll quickly lose the sluggishness he's experiencing. Most of all, I'm praying God will continue to protect his mind and his memories through this time.

I have contacted MD Anderson through their website. They received my message, but I haven't yet heard from the medical personnel. I plan to call today and request a callback from Dr. Puduvalli's nurse. I would like to have guidance from the oncologist on what he wants to do now. Does this weekend's events change the plan for starting chemo in September? Does Jeff need immediate treatment? I'm not sure what steps to take to make sure he gets the best care, other than to ask God to continue to guide this process. (Insert sound effect: I'm humming a verse of the old hymn "Trust and Obey.")

Please pray not only for Jeff's healing but also that I can be patient with the man I love. In fact, while you are at it, pray that I will have an abundant harvest of the fruit of the Spirit. Galatians 5:22–23 (NIV) says, *"But the fruit of the Spirit is love, joy, peace, patience, kindness, goodness, faithfulness, gentleness, and self control."*

PS: Britt's school starts in two days. Please pass the fruit!

08/10/10 (Tuesday), 9:45PM-Karen

I received a call from the local doctor's office today about the Keppra level. Keppra is the antiseizure medication Jeff's been taking all along. When he was released from the hospital midJuly, the dosage was dropped from two 500 mg pills a day to one 500 mg pill. He was also to taper off the Decadron steroid. After I got the Keppra blood level results (1.0, and I was told that was low), I called the nurse for Dr. Puduvalli and asked for someone to call me so that I could review the situation and ask for the oncologist's opinion. Dr. Puduvalli increased the Keppra back to two 500 mg pills a day and put Jeff back on the Decadron. The nurse was confident we would see a marked improvement in Jeff's speech and a decrease in his sleepiness by tomorrow afternoon/ evening.

I was away today at a client's office. Brittany stayed with Jeff this morning until she had to leave for her first fast-pitch softball game. Wayne stayed about four hours this afternoon, and then Fern stayed about an hour until I got back home. Jeff's terribly weak, and I couldn't stand the thought of leaving him home alone. I didn't quite get done at the client's today but should be able to finish up tomorrow morning while Britt is home. Then I shouldn't have to be away from the house for any extended period of time for a while.

I have shared before how thankful I have been during the last year for the Sunday school and Bible school teachers who pushed me to memorize scripture. Often scripture pops into my consciousness, usually at the perfect time to be relevant to my situation. Sometimes I have to consult the Concordance to locate the reference, but the scriptures, as I remember them (or as God brings them to my mind), are almost always complete verses. I guess I always knew in theory how important it was to memorize scripture. Now I know how calming it is to have instant access to the Truth.

Along those same lines, I often find myself humming or singing a song. Growing up, music always had a major role in our home. Apparently, the story indicates I would bop in my high chair to Herb Alpert & the Tijuana Brass. I grew up singing along with whatever my older brothers and my sister liked. So as each of them found a secular style they liked, I learned the songs and sang along. At least until Phillip asked me one day, "Who sings this?"

To which I promptly gave the correct answer. His response was "Then let them sing it!" Despite that discouragement, I learned to sing along with John Denver, Waylon, Willie, and a whole group of Outlaws. Then as Janice started choosing the albums, I sang with Billy Joel and the Captain & Tennille. And there was a year or two I would rather forget when Mom liked Slim Whitman and Freddie Fender. By the time I was in college, Reba McIntyre, George Strait, and Garth Brooks were the popular country artists. But despite the changes in secular music, *every* Sunday, I was exposed to the same "old" hymns. Sing two or three every Sunday morning, two or three more on Sunday evening, throw in another one or two on Wednesday evening, and overtime, I have memorized a lot of them—one of the benefits of being a preacher's kid, I guess. So it shouldn't surprise me that I catch myself humming the tunes or singing the words. Recently, though, I have developed a real enjoyment of them. Most of them are a complete sermon, with verse 1 discussing the concept of being lost in sin or the past, verse 2 or 3 usually covering salvation, or the present, and the last verse often speaking of *"what a day that will be!"*—looking forward as believers in Christ to our future in heaven. I marvel at the trials the writers must have gone through to write them. The hymns seem richer and more relevant than ever during this last year. The hymns haven't changed, but maybe I have?

Thanks for the prayers, and thanks for letting me reminisce.

08/11/10 (Wednesday), 9:10AM-Karen

We are seeing improvement in both Jeff's speech ability and frequency. When asked, Jeff said he slept all night! What a blessing. Then he asked what was for breakfast.

Thanks for the prayers!

08/12/10 (Thursday), 11:15AM-Karen

During Jeff's weekend stay at the hospital, the PA came into the room on Saturday while he was sleeping. She is convinced he has sleep apnea. She set up an appointment to have Jeff tested. We had a minor phone message mishap with the call from the scheduler. The lady spoke with Jeff; however, he doesn't remember that conversation at all. I'm now up to speed, and Jeff's scheduled for a sleep study tonight in Weatherford. Pray they get an accurate evaluation of his sleep.

One of Jeff's college roommates, Scott Skidmore, came by to see Jeff yesterday evening. Jeff was able not just to call him by name, but he accurately called Scott by his nickname. I believe they both enjoyed the visit. Jeff has maintained a close relationship with several friends from college. The Gardner, Skidmore and Krehbiel families have been spending New Year's Eve together for nineteen years. Ringing in the year 2010 would have been year 20, but Jeff was in the hospital, and the group decided they didn't want to get together without him. The first year we celebrated together was December 1990. That year the Skidmores had their first child, the Gardners got married, and so did Jeff and I. Some friendships aren't damaged by miles and days. We always pick up right where we left off.

Brittany started back to school today. She's always ready to see her friends, not so ready for the studying and the homework. She has softball games today. My little girl is growing up. She's such fun to have around. I know God has big plans for her. She seems to be coping with Jeff's medical situation very well. As I'm sure it is with anyone living with a family member who has a serious illness, she and I both have our moments when the burdens seem to be too much. Usually, we snap back quickly and move forward. I often have to remind myself this isn't my battle. I gave it to God—in fact, it was never mine; it was always His. That definitely takes the pressure off. When the battle is God's—and I'm only helping God as His earthly hands—then suddenly, the load isn't too heavy.

> Come unto me, all ye that labour and are heavy laden, and I will give you rest. Take my yoke upon you, and learn of me; for I am meek and lowly in heart: and ye shall find rest unto your souls. For my yoke is easy, and my burden is light.
>
> Matthew 11:28–30 (KJV)

Trusting God to maintain the truth of Romans 8:28 (KJV) that *"all things work together for good to them that love the Lord, to those who are the called according to His purpose"*—that is, giving the burden to God, trusting that He has it all under control and knowing that I don't, can't, and won't ever be able to lighten the load, solve the problem, or cure the cancer on my own. That makes it His battle. So now that I don't own the battle, I'm able to see my job description (obey), and I'm free to do my job (Christian) to the best of my God-given ability. And oh, the peace that's mine when I *trust and obey*.

Thanks for the prayers. Have a great day.

08/16/10 (Tuesday), 11:35PM-Karen

Off to a busy start this week. Britt had softball in Minco on Monday and two home games this evening, one junior high game with Fort Cobb and a high school game with Hennessey. This morning, Jeff and I had an errand to run in El Reno, and then we came home through

Anadarko for another errand. We were only home a couple of hours and then we left for Britt's games in Hinton. I wasn't sure whether Jeff would want to go with me this evening, but he did! We were able to park next to the fence for both games. I'm thankful we live in a small community. Everyone is more than accommodating to allow Jeff to watch the games from the air-conditioned car instead of in the heat, which he wouldn't be able to do. By the time we got back home, he was tired. A plate of Spanish rice, a little baseball on TV, and now he's ready for bed.

I got a call today from the local doctor's office. She has the sleep study results, and Jeff has sleep apnea. The sleep clinic will call to schedule a follow-up appointment to fit Jeff with a sleep machine. This situation could be part of the sleep-infested condition that was being blamed on the La-Z-Boy, along with the meds and treatment that Jeff has had over the last year.

Yesterday, the nurse practitioner from Dr. Puduvalli's office in Houston, called and left a message on my phone to decrease Jeff's evening steroid pill to half of the dosage that he has been taking for the last week or so. He'll will take 4 mg in the mornings and only 2 mg in the evenings for the next week. Then he'll cut the morning pill in half for a week and then stair-step on down if all goes well. I'm to make sure the drop in steroids doesn't trigger any side effects.

Monday was Jeff's parent's fifty-eighth wedding anniversary. Britt reminded me on Saturday of a popular country song that says, They called them crazy when they started out Said seventeen's too young to know what loves about They've been together fifty-eight years now That's crazy.[6]

The point of the song is that when people believe in something, they follow through, even when other people say they are crazy. We heard it on the way to school Monday morning; it was a very appropriate reminder. When Jeff and I got married, my sister cross-stitched a short line from a song that was popular then, and this sums it up: "I come from a long line of love." We really do come from a long line of love—fifty-eight years for the Krehbiels and fifty-three years for my parents next month. Now ain't *that* crazy?

Better go catch some sleep of my own. Thanks for checking on us, and most of all, thanks for the prayers. God still answers!

Jesus Christ is the same yesterday and today and forever

Hebrews 13:8 (NIV)

08/21/10 (Saturday), 11:36PM-Karen

Hydro Fair Weekend: Brittany had school on Friday and softball games on Thursday and Friday evenings, we didn't try to make it to the fair until tonight. I went at about four and helped with the cake judging before the cake auction, and then I came home, and we all went back. Jeff was feeling good today, and he went from about seven thirty until about nine thirty. What a fun time to see people! For our little communities—Hydro this weekend and Hinton next weekend—the fairs are a homecoming of sorts. This is an experience people who have moved away want to share with their children. For most of the people from Hydro, it's a whole lot of community service (hard work) focused in three days a year. The cake auction usually sells between twenty-five to thirty cakes and other donated items and raises about $15,000, which is used to fund fair premiums the following year. The fair is truly an experience that could be right out of a Norman Rockwell painting. My first visit to the Hydro Fair was the year Jeff and I got married. It has grown a little since then, but it's still a one-of- a-kind experience.

I'm thankful Jeff's doing well this week. His speech is good most of the time, unless he's tired. Then I notice a little trouble. Jeff accurately explained it to someone this evening by saying, "Sometimes I run out of words."

I have noticed an improvement from the steroid side effects since they cut the evening dosage in half. The plan is to taper the steroids off over a three- to four-week schedule. As mentioned before, the steroids are prescribed to decrease cranial swelling, but the side effects also increase irritability and increase appetite.

We're just ten days away from our next trip to MD Anderson. Tentatively, they plan to restart Jeff on the chemo drug Temodar at that visit. This is not for treatment of new cancer growth but is really more of a continuation of the treatment started in March. We're expecting six more cycles. Jeff will also have another MRI at that visit. I've never claimed to be a physician or a radiologist, but I find myself predicting the test results, based on my knowledge of Jeff's level of activity and his interaction with others in conversations. I expect the MRI to show positive results since last month.

Thanks for the prayers! I know God is listening, and I believe the results we are seeing are direct results of God's participation in Jeff's healing process. Keep up the prayers and keep giving God the credit/ glory for his handiwork.

> In everything give thanks: for this is the will of God in
> Christ Jesus concerning you.
>
> 1 Thessalonians 5:18 (KJV)

08/24/10 (Tuesday), 11:36PM-Karen

I keep telling you Jeff's doing pretty good or Jeff had a pretty good day. I have decided I will tell you about his day. You decide.

Today Jeff cooked fried eggs and a hamburger patty for his breakfast; then for lunch, he cooked tenderized pork cutlet, corn, and baked potatoes. He went with me to Okarche to Brittany's softball games this evening. The weather was very nice, and we sat in lawn chairs for both games. After her games, we went to Eischen's for chicken. While we were there, he recognized two men he knew that I don't believe I'd ever met before. One he worked with at the sheep barn at OSU during college. The other was the father of a guy he showed sheep with in high school. When we got home, he decided he would take his shower tonight. Now he's watching a little TV.

Now how did he do? You may think as I did that the hamburger patty for breakfast was a little out of the ordinary. What you don't know is that the hamburger was what was left in the package he used last night to make spaghetti while Britt and I were at a softball game, so he fried it this morning. It may have tasted good last night, I don't know, but either way, he knew it would spoil if it wasn't cooked. As for recognizing people he hadn't seen in a long time—he gets bonus points for this. I have been around him twenty-plus years, and I still haven't met everyone he knows. I suspect I never will. Going places with a Krehbiel is always an adventure. We always run into somebody they know. I quietly enjoyed today's moment, thrilled Jeff passed today's pop quiz with flying colors.

Yesterday the temperature was about 110 degrees. So Jeff didn't go to the games. The temp for today's game was about 75 degrees. Perfect for softball. We had a brief rain shower this morning, and it was cloudy almost all day. The clouds cleared this evening in time for a beautiful rainbow in the eastern sky and a gorgeous sunset in the west. It made the trip home from Okarche a very pleasant drive.

At this point, I have to confess: I see sunsets with new eyes these days. For the first nineteen years of our marriage, our home didn't have very many windows, so we didn't see many sunsets. Since we moved last year, our current home has lots of windows to the west, and we're able to enjoy the sunsets. Now comes the question: Were the sunsets pretty before last year? In theory, I know the sky didn't just all of a sudden take on beauty. I had noticed sunsets before, but somehow they seem more vivid now, more vibrant, like God paints each one just for me to enjoy. It's as though the sunsets could have been black and white until this year, when God suddenly turned on the color. Now I know the color isn't any different than it was a hundred years ago when cowboys rode into the sunset. I tend to think that just as the words to the "old" hymns are more meaningful to me during this journey, so are the sunsets, so is scripture, so are ties with family and friends.

My sister tells the story of a fifth-grade field trip with her science teacher, who apparently was frustrated she was seeing beautiful things and the students weren't. Her comment stuck with Janice, and ultimately with me, because of the humorous value in it: "We came on this field trip to have 'fun'—now look at the yucca plant." So what is it that lets some people enjoy things others miss? Is it age? Life experiences? Wisdom? New windows? Or just perspective? I see with new eyes, and for that I'm thankful.

The heavens declare the glory of God; and the firmament sheweth his handywork.

Psalm 19:1 (KJV)

193

Thanks for your prayers. God has given more than I could have asked for in the way of Jeff's medical progress. Keep giving Him the credit.

> Now unto him that is able to do exceeding abundantly
> above all we ask or think according to the power that
> worketh in us, unto Him be glory in the church by Christ
> Jesus throughout all ages, world without end. Amen.

> Ephesians 3:20–21 (KJV)

08/31/10 (Tuesday), 10:13PM-Karen

We traveled light to Houston this time. No checked luggage and only one small carry-on bag. It sure was nice not to have to wait at the luggage carousel. Jeff had another "good" week. He has cooked some, gone to some softball games, church on Sunday, eye doctor, more softball, and, last Wednesday, spent a second night at the sleep clinic.

Jeff hasn't slept as much during the days this week as maybe he did the last few. He's sleeping well at night, though. He usually catches a nap in the morning—one in the afternoon and another after supper. I have definitely noticed he's alert more hours during the day. What a blessing. Now that he's on steroids again, things taste "normal" again. I anticipate the oncologist will give us a plan tomorrow to finish tapering the steroids.

September 1 last year was the first day Jeff mentioned the headaches, and that's when he started the trend toward sleeping all the time and, ultimately, the glioblastoma diagnosis and reality. One year.

At the airport this morning, we ran into two men Jeff recognized—one an irrigation customer, the other, Paul Blair, a former OSU football player, with a God-given story to tell of how God turned his life around. It was an encouragement to visit with him. He and a gentleman from his church prayed with us right there in the airport. Sometimes being willing to visit with someone is a gift God uses to bless someone. Which leads me to today's food for thought. In telling Jeff's story, I mentioned that although cancer is not a choice we would have made, we trust God that it was/is the best choice to make *all things work together for good to them that love the Lord.* Then Jeff said, "You don't know. We might have." I'm not sure what Jeff was thinking about when he made that comment. I still hold to my statement. On a human level, I can't think of any reason why I would have ever chosen this path. But I've been thinking...

When Brittany was little, she had to have five separate shots in one day to get her ready for school. As a parent, I hated that she needed to go though that pain, but I didn't doubt for one minute it was the best decision. I tried my best to prepare her, held her and moved forward with the decision. I can see a little bit of a correlation with our situation. God knew from the foundation of the world what we would face. He has prepared us for each step, has sent family and friends to be His arms when we needed hugs, and I hold to the truth that He knows what role Jeff's having cancer will play in the big picture of *"all things"* working together for good.

So now the food for thought: How willing am I to submit to the decisions of my Heavenly Father in the interaction of *"all things working together for good"*? Am I willing to accept *this* journey as part of His plan for the greater good? I should follow Brittany's example: she never even questioned whether I was right to subject her to the torture of five shots in one day. She trusted my judgment. I should be as trusting and confident in my Heavenly Father.

> And we know that all things work together for good to them that love the Lord, to them that are the called according to His purpose.
>
> Romans 8:28 (KJV)

> Verily I say unto you, Except you be converted and become as little children, you shall not enter the kingdom of Heaven.
>
> Matthew 18:3 (KJV)

Please keep Jeff on your prayer lists. Pray that the doctors would have wisdom as they treat Jeff [no change] and that I will grow in my "childlike" faith.

YEAR 2

09/02/10 (Thursday), 11:43AM-Karen

We have received a new plan of treatment for Jeff. The MRI from late Tuesday showed some inflammation or irritation of the brain cells around the area where the cancer was removed a year ago and the necrosis was removed in July. Dr. Puduvalli showed us the MRI from July and compared it with the MRI from Tuesday. The most recent MRI shows some intensity that wasn't there in July's post op MRI. This necrosis, or buildup of dead cells, is a direct result of the radiation Jeff finished last November. We were told early on the radiation could still provide benefits as long as six months after the end of the treatments, and in Jeff's case, it appears that may have been a very conservative guess, as we are now close to nine months after the last radiation treatment. Dr. Puduvalli explained that if we didn't know whether this was necrosis or new cancer growth, they would have to find out for sure, which would mean a surgery. Since we have a very recent pathology report from July that indicated the issue is necrosis and not new cancer growth, they can move forward with treatment, confident it is in fact necrosis. Dr. Puduvalli consulted with a radiation oncologist in Houston to get his professional opinion. He agreed the chain of events indicate this is necrosis, not new cancer growth.

The buildup and recession of the necrosis following radiation was described to me as a bell curve, kind of a hill. Immediately following the radiation, the necrosis starts building up, peaks, and then starts to diminish and be absorbed by the body. In Jeff's case, the buildup of necrosis caused too much pressure and had to be removed (fairly common). Tuesday's MRI would seem to indicate that July's surgery was not at the top of the bell curve, at the end of the buildup of the necrosis, but still in the uphill portion, with indications that more necrosis will still occur. At this point, because the area of the brain affected is speech, motor skills, and memory, Dr. Puduvalli didn't recommend a wait-and- see approach but, rather, an aggressive plan to *stop* the effects of the radiation and resulting necrosis in an effort to protect the brain.

He explained there are a couple of treatment methods to calm the intensity or irritation of the tissue in Jeff's left temple. One was using a hyperbaric oxygen chamber, which came with risk of damage to the eardrums and the lungs. – this option was *not* recommended because Dr. Puduvalli believed the risk outweighs the benefit. A better option is to use the drug Avastin to stop the effects of radiation and stop the necrosis. Avastin is a tumorstarving therapy drug that has been used to treat other cancers but only received FDA approval in 2009 for use in treating brain cancer. Typically, it's used only to treat regrowth of cancer. In Jeff's case, Avastin was selected for his continuing chemo regimen based on its known side effect of stopping/reducing the necrosis. The dosage will be a little bit different than it would be if it was treating a tumor, where treatments were done every two weeks. Jeff will get the Avastin every three weeks and is scheduled to get only three treatments. Avastin is an infusiontype drug given in an IV. It will take about an hour and a half to get a treatment. Jeff's oncologist in OKC, Dr. Keefer, will oversee the administration of the Avastin, and we will only have to go to Houston every six weeks.

We finished Jeff's appointments at MD Anderson a couple hours early yesterday and were able to change our flight to leave earlier. It was nice not to have to spend the extra two hours in the airport. We arrived home in time for me to finish up some cooking and host our church ladies last night for their monthly meal. Jeff rode to town with his dad to go to the men's meal at the parsonage.

Today Brittany has softball, and we have a family friend stopping by to visit. Jeff will start the Avastin tomorrow.

Thank you for your continued prayers. I'm humbled that you invest a portion of your prayer time in our family. We are choosing to see the switch to Avastin as a blessing—given in God's timing, to work *all* things together for good and to bring honor and glory to *Him*.

09/10/10 (Friday), 12:48AM-Karen

There seems to be daily reminders that Jeff's battle with cancer started almost a year ago. Yesterday was the one-year mark in our home, Thursday was Jeff's forty-seventh birthday, Saturday will be the Caddo County Farm Bureau annual meeting. I went alone last year because Jeff wasn't feeling well. I'm hopeful the weather will be nice so we can make an appearance this year.

Jeff seems to be tolerating Avastin well. It has not made him sick at all. He's cooking breakfast most mornings and cooked tacos for supper tonight. He even had his laptop out yesterday and today—a sign he has time on his hands and wants something to do. He has cabin fever and is always ready to "go" anytime I have errands to run.

I'm noticing Jeff's appetite and irritability increasing as a side effect of the steroids. Dr. Puduvalli wants to keep him on 4 mg a day of Decadron while he takes the Avastin treatments. I'm trying to remain calm during this storm. As I have asked before, please pray that I'll have patience during this time. Jeff will go back to OKC for the second treatment in two weeks and will go to Houston in five weeks for an MRI and updated blood work.

We got some nice rain showers yesterday out of the latest tropical storm. We've been very dry, so the moisture will help the wheat that we will be sowing before long.

Thanks for the prayers for our family. God continues to provide.

09/11/10 (Saturday), 12:58AM-Karen

Jeff had another pretty good day today. We went to Hydro to get him a haircut late this afternoon. Then we came home and picked up Brittany and headed to Watonga to watch football. Since Brittany is a freshman this year, and Hinton has a very young team, several of her classmates get to play. It's fun to sit with friends and watch our kids play ball; whether it's softball, football, or basketball—our family enjoys the games. Our team did not win tonight but put out a good effort. We weren't able to stay till the end as Jeff always likes to do. He was getting tired, so we left about nine thirty.

Jeff still isn't allowed to drive. This is definitely a topic of debate at our house these days. As we have been told, the state of Oklahoma won't allow someone to drive for six months after they have had a seizure. Jeff's last one was on August 6, so he'll have a while to wait. So much of our independence is tied to our ability to drive (or should I say our legal right?). Keep up the prayers for patience.

I considered keeping this a private treasure, but have decided to share.

Last summer, before we closed on the purchase of our home, as we were packing and planning and considering the debt load of purchasing our first home and more farmland, I began to find pennies. At first they arrived slowly, then more frequently. I have heard it said Bill Gates loses money if he uses his time to stop to pick up a dollar on the street. My picking up pennies should explain a lot. Now I have to tell you that I've always picked up money that I find. This picking up pennies thing didn't suddenly start last summer. To me it was always money, no matter how small. As I was packing, shuffling our things around and putting them in boxes, I would find a penny every now and then. Sometimes I found them in parking lots, on the ground, lots of different places. I finally decided I would accept each one with a thankful heart and as a sign: God was sending me pennies to reassure me He was in charge of *"all things"* (Romans 8:28, NIV). If he could send me pennies, He would be faithful and provide the dollars as they were needed, and since *"the cattle on a thousand hills"* are His (Psalms 50:10), he would certainly provide for the needs of His children. Even what money we "think" is ours is really His, and He alone is in charge of our finances. When we turn it over to Him, He will provide. So it wasn't long until I let Jeff in on my little secret and started giving him each penny I found with a verbal reminder God is going to take care of us (Matthew 6:25–30). Just a reminder, this is also the time frame when we found out Jeff had cancer, so each penny I found began to represent God's provision, not only for our finances, but also for Jeff's health. At some point last fall, Brittany's class was collecting pennies for a fund-raising project of some kind. So for several days, she was searching for pennies—only pennies. When her project was over, she gave up on hunting pennies. One day I found a penny and tried to give it to her. She said, "We are through with that project. I don't need them anymore." It was time for me as a parent to give my child an object lesson about spiritual things. I let her in on my secret. After we discussed me finding pennies, she suggested we should give those pennies back to God by putting them in the offering plate at church as a response to His faithfulness to us. Wow! She got it, all right. Sometimes I teach, and sometimes I'm the student in these little object lessons.

That same day, she and I were headed to Kohl's in Yukon for a last-minute clothing purchase for a vocal concert. While we were there, Britt needed to visit the restroom. All of a sudden, she came out of the restroom with the biggest grin on her face. She held out her hand, and she had twelve pennies in her palm. She said "Mom, I found them in the stall in the bathroom, and I washed them! They were just lying on the toilet paper dispenser." So timely. God reinforced the object lesson in a phenomenal way. One penny might have done the trick, but twelve really opened not only her eyes but mine as well.

Since then, we have been finding pennies, nickels, dimes, and quarters in some of the strangest places and in the funniest ways. My mother-in-law even unknowingly participated in this special game of hide-and-seek God's been playing with us. She brought in a rusty quarter one evening. All she said was "Here, I found this on your driveway."

It would be easy to write all of this coin finding off as coincidence. The more you look for pennies, the more you would naturally find, but I "know"—it's a God thing! Once, while Jeff and I were in Houston, I found a dime on top of my purse. I tried to justify how that happened, but I had a hard time writing that one off.

So what prompted me to share this story with you after a year? Britt came in my office this afternoon and told me that when she was walking to Ag class today, she found a penny on the ground. Then she was walking and kicked a second coin up from the dirt. She found a quarter somewhere else, and another penny was lying in the middle of the only empty seat when she got on the school bus on the way to the softball field. If I have it right, she found coins four separate times today—each one a reminder that our battles aren't our own. They are God's, and He'll provide the resources—whether financial or health related—that will enable us to complete the tasks He has for us. I believe God has planned things he wants each of us to do. It's more of that *"all things work together for good"* concept of Romans 8:28 (KJV). Now if I truly believe he has a plan for my life—and I do—then shouldn't

I trust Him to provide the "little" things I need to accomplish the tasks?

Thanks for the prayers. God is faithful.

> For every beast of the forest is mine, and the cattle upon a thousand hills.
>
> Psalm 50:10 (KJV)

> Therefore I say unto you, Take no thought for your life, what ye shall eat, or what ye shall drink; nor yet for your body, what ye shall put on. Is not the life more than meat, and the body than raiment? Behold the fowls of the air: for they sow not, neither do they reap, nor gather into barns; yet your heavenly Father feedeth them. Are ye not much better than they? Which of you by taking thought can add one cubit unto his stature? And why take ye thought for raiment? Consider the lilies of the field, how they grow; they toil not, neither do they spin: And yet I say unto you, That even Solomon in all his glory was not arrayed like one of these. Wherefore, if God so clothe the grass of the field, which today is, and tomorrow is cast into the oven, shall he not much more clothe you, O ye of little faith?
>
> Matthew 6:25–30 (KJV)

09/12/10 (Sunday), 11:24PM-Karen

Saturday morning, I drove Jeff to Weatherford for a seven o'clock deacons' breakfast. Then I hit Wal-Mart to pick up a few items. I left thinking I should arrive at that time of day more often when there are a lot less people in line. Later, after I woke up good, I decided that probably wasn't going to be a reality. Generally, I would rather sleep in than go to Wal-Mart.

After Jeff's deacons' meeting, we came home for an hour or so and then headed to OKC. The Oklahoma Wheat Growers were serving bread as a part of the Septemberfest events on the lawn of the Governor's Mansion. We were there to help for about three hours. The event was open from 10:00 AM to 4:00 PM, so we weren't there for the whole day, but hopefully, we were a little extra help for a few hours. Brittany has always enjoyed helping with this event.

After just a couple hours at home, we drove to Salyer Lake east of Binger for the Caddo County Farm Bureau Annual Convention. For a few years, this event has been in a picnic format, with a youth fishing derby, the business meeting, a free meal, and some entertainment, this year a local bluegrass group. I think a month or so ago, I wrote on Jeff's page about enjoying all types of music. I don't remember mentioning bluegrass, but it should have been on the list as well. The group was really good, and the meal was excellent. But after the meal, Jeff was tired, so we headed back home.

This morning, of course, we had church and then a church dinner. It was good to visit with our church family. This afternoon, at home, Jeff watched some football. I had to laugh. I was in the other room. Jeff was the only one in the living room, and all of a sudden, I heard him yelling at the referees that some play should have had a flag. It has been a long time since Jeff talked to the TV. You may laugh, but I see that as a major improvement in his health. Not once but several times he disagreed with the calls. He's enjoying sports again, and that's a blessing.

Jeff's brother called this evening, and they visited quite a while. There was a time when Jeff really didn't want to talk on the phone much at all, but today they visited for quite a while, so I see that as an improvement in Jeff's focus and conversation skills.

I'm hopeful/prayerful this will be a calm week. The number of you faithful to visit Jeff's page and take an interest in our activities remains overwhelming.

09/15/10 (Wednesday), 10:21PM-Karen

Britt had softball games in Apache on Monday, Binger on Tuesday, and then had youth tonight. Jeff went with me to both games and went with his dad to Stillwater today to a meeting and to pick up some seed wheat. I believe Jeff has had a better week this week than he has had in quite some time. I believe the Avastin is working and calming the irritation around the surgery site, but my honorary doctorate certificate in medicine seems to be lost in the mail. Really, I'm relying on what Dr. Puduvalli told us, that we should see an improvement with the first dose. I believe we are.

God is answering our prayers. I want to make sure He gets the credit for the healing as it comes.

09/18/10 (Saturday), 11:26PM-Karen

Jeff's gaining stamina this week. Friday morning, after I took Brittany to school, I pulled into the yard, and Jeff was on the riding lawnmower. Jeff had aired up the flat tire and was mowing a little. He stayed out longer than I thought he should have, but I had to smile. It was nice to see him getting to do something he wanted to do.

Wednesday I came down with a "bug," and the medical advice I was given on Thursday was to avoid Jeff. That may sound funny, but our PA suspected what I had was viral and would be gone in a day or so. Her main concern was Jeff's immune system. It has taken so many hits this past year with the chemo, and possibly with the Avastin, that she wanted to protect him as much as possible. I checked into the guestroom upstairs for a night and kept my distance for about twenty-four hours to get past being contagious. The PA seems to be right in her diagnosis because I feel much better.

Jeff has slept two nights with his CPAP machine. He said he slept through both nights without waking up. I believe that will be very beneficial in Jeff's overall health—to get a good night's sleep every night.

Friday, September 24, Jeff will go to OKC for the second treatment of Avastin. We are seeing definite improvements in Jeff since the first treatment over two weeks ago. Please continue to keep the medical staff and technicians in your prayers as they evaluate and plan Jeff's future treatment. We are so blessed to have access to such wonderful doctors, nurses and PAs, and their staff, and a host of friends praying.

Brittany Remembers:
Walking Down the Aisle

In our church, we have a tradition of putting a birthday offering in a little wooden piggybank—like church—the week of your birthday. In 2010, my birthday fell on a Sunday, so I was going to put my birthday money in on my actual birthday, September, 19. Dad's birthday was ten days before mine. However, Dad didn't feel well the Sunday he would have put his offering in and was going to put his offering in with mine. Dad and I both ran the sound system at church and stayed in the back during the worship service. When it came time for us to put our birthday offering in, Dad linked arms with me and basically marched us to the front of the church!

We were a fourth of the way down the aisle when it hit me. My dad would never walk me down the aisle to meet my husband. A hundred different thoughts ran through my head. Who would the man I marry be? How soon would I get married? How much time did I have left with Dad? Would I walk down the aisle alone? Did I already know my future husband and Dad got to meet him? Every part of me knew he would not live to see my wedding. I fought to hold back tears; after all, I was only putting in a birthday offering, not getting married. The day I turned fifteen, my Heavenly Father let my daddy walk me down the aisle to put in a simple birthday offering, which prepared me for the day when he wouldn't be there to walk me down the aisle to meet my husband.

09/21/10 (Tuesday), 9:14PM-Karen

Jeff's having another good week, and for that, we are thankful. He'll get the second treatment of Avastin on Friday. He seems to be more active this week. He has filled the lawnmower with gas and has mowed a little on the yard. This may be an ongoing project. He has also taken out the toilet in our bathroom. It had developed a "wobble" sometime during the last year. So for a while, we'll have to use the bathroom at the other end of the house until we get this one put back. Jeff got it out fine and discovered the problem. Now it seems to be a little intimidating how to repair the problem. I have my own list of priorities, and this project is now at the top of the list, even above mowing the yard. I think he enjoys having a "project" or two he can tinker with. Perhaps prayer for my patience is still in order.

Our little girl turned fifteen on Sunday. To celebrate a little early, Jeff cooked steaks on the grill Saturday evening. Jeff had missed the opportunity to put his birthday money in the week before, so he and Brittany both took their birthday offering to the front together on Sunday. That brought lots of smiles. Celebrating the milestones of our lives now seems to bring a special thankfulness, that Jeff's sharing each one with us.

Brittany's softball team will start playoffs on Thursday, hosting the first round against Geary. Go Comets! Brittany is a freshman, but in Hinton, the freshmen "play up" with the high school team. Jeff and I have really enjoyed watching the advanced speed and skill of the high school games.

The church youth have resumed their Wednesday-evening meal and lessons. Brittany and I will cook for this week's meal. It seems we jump from one event to another. Other moms have told me high school will go by very fast. Maybe we'll sleep in the Saturday after she graduates in three years and eight months. Wow, that doesn't sound like very long!

Thanks for the prayers for the whole family.

09/25/10 (Saturday), 11:57AM-Karen

Another week has gone by. Time doesn't really have "wings" that it can fly, but we certainly use the flapping of the arms to keep track (unless you have a digital clock). Since my last post, Jeff met with the Oklahoma Agricultural Leadership Program alumni in Hydro on Wednesday evening to plan the stop for OALP class XV when they come to our area in October. At the same time, Brittany and I were hosting the youth meal at the church. Thursday Britt's team played in the first round of softball playoffs. They eliminated Geary 19–1 and 12–0.

Friday Jeff's appointment was scheduled for ten forty-five, but it was almost twelve before they started the infusion of the Avastin. There was a slight delay, in part because the infusion room was full and partly because our insurance had not paid for Jeff's first treatment. Since the first treatment was only three weeks ago, the clinic wanted to make sure there wasn't a problem before they gave the second treatment. Thankfully, all questions were worked out, and Jeff did get the treatment. We have a high one-time deductible each year, and then the insurance has covered everything else. What a blessing when it all works correctly, or, even better, when you don't need it at all. Once again, I see God's handiwork years earlier in the selection of our primary insurance company as one way he has protected us—financially—from a potentially devastating side effect of Jeff's cancer. And as a reminder, three years to the day prior to the date of Jeff's first surgery, we signed a supplemental cancer policy that pays us directly based on a preset chart of treatments and payments. Again, God at work prior to the moment.

This is when I'm reminded that God's timing and his carefully orchestrated plan are absolutely perfect. Once you believe that God created the world, that he knows the end results of *all* things, then you're free to believe that having all resources at his disposal, he gives us everything we need to complete the tasks he gives us (Jeremiah 29:11). In my personal walk with God, I'm at a place where (some days this is still just a theory) I can believe that Jeff's cancer intertwines perfectly with God's "perfect" plan, that He has had our whole lives to prepare us for this time, that He truly has the whole world at his command, that He knew every detail of our lives before the foundation of the world— including our choices, whether good or bad, *and* He has made every adjustment needed (because of our choices) to allow His plan to remain perfect. And at this point anyway, I believe His perfect plan is to allow everyone every opportunity to have a relationship with Him. He wants to have a relationship with only those who choose to have a relationship with Him. No one will be able to stand before Him with an excuse, because He'll have already given *every* opportunity.

Because of His perfect nature, he cannot tolerate sin. To have a relationship with God, we have to be sin-free. We need atonement for the sin that comes with choice. Jesus Christ was the only perfect atonement for our sin (John 3:16). Once we accept that substitute payment for our sin, then we are free (clean) to have that personal relationship with God. Part of that relationship with God is submitting to being a part of his perfect plan to reach everyone. I have to remind myself that once I have made my choice, I should daily submit to the direction of the Holy Spirit so I can be used of God to reach others, so they can choose God.

If you have read to this point, and you are asking yourself, "How does she take something so simple as updating us on how Jeff's doing and turn it into a full-blown sermon with the optional altar call at the end," look up Romans 1:16.

Friday evening, my niece treated a few of us to tickets to the bull riding and vocal performance by Josh Turner. For a bassloving family like mine, it was quite a treat! We got home late last night and are taking things easy today. Jeff and a hired hand finished mowing the yard this week so he can have guilt-free rest today. (At this point, we are just ignoring the lack of a working toilet in the bathroom!)

Jeff's feeling well, no sickness with the Avastin. We've decided the Benadryl they dispense with the Avastin may be causing some sleepiness, but we can live with that.

For God so loved the world, that he gave his only begotten Son, that whosoever believeth in him should not perish, but have everlasting life.

John 3:16 (KJV)

For I am not ashamed of the gospel of Christ: for it is the power of God unto salvation to every one that believeth; to the Jew first, and also to the Greek.

Romans 1:16 (KJV)

09/30/10 (Thursday), 11:12PM-Karen

Sunday we all went to Sunday school and church and slipped out without much visiting afterward to head to Oklahoma City to help the Oklahoma Wheat Commission with the Wheatheart Baking Contest. It's always fun to see our wheat friends. While I was unwrapping bread before it went to the judges, my fifth grade teacher and 4-H leader, Mrs. Pietz, came up to visit. She had heard our names mentioned in the introductions. It took me a while to place her. Growing up in a small town gives you a lifetime connection with classmates, teachers, and townspeople. You can always strike up a conversation and pick up right where you left off—even if it has been thirty-three years!

After the contest, we ate a very late lunch with friends and then headed back to Hydro for church.

Monday and Tuesday evenings, Britt's team had scrimmages in Hinton for the regional games that started today. We were excited that Hinton was able to host the games, so we didn't have very far to drive. Wednesdays are always busy. Britt had softball practice after school, an hour off, and then her piano lesson. Then it was time to head to church for youth group activities.

Jeff seems to be gaining strength and mental clarity. He played a little on the laptop this week. One day he worked about ten of the easy Sudoku puzzles and caught up on several weeks of the local newspapers.

We had developed a pretty good stack, and someone needed to go through them and clip the articles about the softball team and Brittany being voted class president. Jeff agreed and got through the project in one afternoon. Today he went to the grain bins to check on a semi load of wheat headed east. He came home in an hour or two and said he needed a nap before we went to the softball games. Britt's team lost the first game to Fairview and won the second game against Hennessey. They will play the loser of Fairview and Healdton tomorrow at twelve thirty. We took a canopy, and even though the breeze was cool, the shade was nice.

Yesterday a nurse from the cancer center in OKC called to let us know Jeff's last lab results showed his potassium level to be a little low at 3.1, and that they want that level to be no lower than 3.5. So they increased his potassium intake to twice a day instead of only once. I suspect Jeff will get an energy boost when the increase takes effect.

The steroids are still causing some side effects, and we are anxiously awaiting once again the possibility of tapering off after his next Avastin treatment in two weeks.

Thanks for letting me journal our days. I trust that from Jeff's participation, or nonparticipation, you can decide how his progress is this week. In case you can't, I think he's gaining every day.

Thank you for checking in on us. I continue to be humbled that over a year later, so many of you are still keeping up with us. It's a blessing to know you are praying for our family and that God's still answering your/our prayers.

10/07/10 (Thursday), 11:05AM-Karen

Jeff's feeling better and is mowing the yard some this morning! I know he wants something to do, and he's enjoying the lack of wind and the warm sunshine—nice fall weather. I believe he's gaining on his verbal skills and is able to carry on longer conversations without getting distracted. He can remember things pretty well if I ask him a direct question, but for him to take a phone message and remember to tell me something just doesn't happen.

Brittany's softball team lost in the regional tournament last week on Friday, and she started after school basketball practices this week. We've quickly transitioned between sports and already have our lives planned through February or March—in theory anyway.

Jeff will get his third round of Avastin next week. The appointment is scheduled for Friday, the fifteenth, but Jeff wants it moved to accommodate some fun Ag Leadership things that would conflict if his treatment is on Friday. I'm waiting for word from Houston from Dr. Puduvalli, then I will coordinate with OKC and Dr. Keefer's office.

As Jeff gains strength, he's drawn back to the leadership roles he has on several boards. Since he hasn't been cleared to drive, this continually presents a challenge, as you can imagine.

Please keep our family in your prayers. I know God has it all worked out. I'm just His servant. I know in His timing He'll provide what I need to complete the tasks he gives me—for His glory, not mine.

I can do all things through Christ which strengtheneth me.

Philippians 4:13 (NIV)

Now unto him that is able to do exceeding abundantly above all that we ask or think, according to the power that worketh in us, Unto him be glory in the church by Christ Jesus throughout all ages, world without end. Amen.

Ephesians 3:20–21 (KJV)

10/12/10 (Tuesday), 11:08PM-Karen

Saturday my sister, niece, and great-niece, as well as my mom and dad, came for a visit. Way too short on the visit part, but we've been planning to get together for a special day for a while, and I was glad they came. Sunday morning, Dad, Janice, and I gave a special number at church. We sang "Earthbound Eagle," which Dad wrote about fourteen to fifteen years ago. I honestly believe we have more fun hunting a song to sing than actually performing.

Sunday evening we received a brief rain shower and a little lightning. I say "a little," but it packed a powerful punch: *"The heavens declare the Glory of the Lord"* (Psalm 19:1). We are still in the discovery stage of what was damaged. So far, the list of damaged electronics includes five telephones, a TV, a printer, the Internet modem, a garage door opener, the peaks unit for the hot water heater, and a breaker for the spare bedroom. All lives and data are safe, and the rest can be replaced. Prayerfully, the list won't grow anymore. Earlier in the evening, we were watching TV, and lightning struck an oil field tank battery a couple of miles west of us. Best we could tell from our view that the fire burned for at least a couple of hours. I really don't know how long it burned; I finally quit watching it and went to bed. We sure needed the rain.

Yesterday, I spoke with our contact at MD Anderson, and we mutually agreed the time frame the oncologist had in mind was not the time frame used to set up Jeff's next visit. As it stands now, the appointments for the nineteenth and twentieth of October are being moved to November 2 and 3. The later date will allow the MRI to reflect the complete post-Avastin picture. Dr. Puduvalli wanted to see Jeff and assess the situation at the end of the second treatment, just prior to the third treatment (that would be tomorrow—and that isn't possible) so they will move the appointments to the end of the third treatment cycle, three weeks after this week's Avastin infusion. I'm waiting for confirmation that the appointments are moved before I reschedule with the airline, hotel, and rental car. I checked online this evening (after we got our Internet running again), and the MRI had been rescheduled, but not the appointment with Dr. Puduvalli. I will keep checking back until all the appointments have been moved.

Jeff's been having another good week. He's restless and wants to get out of the house and drive. I try to take him on all my errands, so he gets out some. We have plans for making the five- gallon freezer of ice cream for an Oklahoma Ag Leadership Program lunch on Friday. That should liven things up a bit.

Brittany competed in an FFA contest today and came home with third place. I'm proud of her—not just for the fact that she excels but proud she does her best. She keeps it pulled together even though this situation has to be hard on her. God has blessed us with one terrific kid! I better go spend a little time with her before bedtime.

We are thankful God protected us through the storm. I heard a song this week, and I keep playing the words in my head. One line of the song says, "Sometimes He calms the storm and sometimes he calms me." That has been thought-provoking, considering the lightning, and the cancer. God's peace is much more than I could even ask for. Ephesians 3:20–21 (KJV) says, *"Now unto him that is able to do exceeding abundantly above all that we ask or think, according to the power that worketh in us, Unto him be glory in the church by Christ Jesus throughout all ages, world without end. Amen."* And for that—God's peace that surpasses understanding—for that, I am truly, truly thankful! *"In everything give thanks: for this is the will of God in Christ Jesus concerning you"* (1 Thessalonians 5:18, KJV).

Thanks for your prayers for Jeff. God continues to provide the healing!

10/22/10 (Friday), 11:12PM-Karen

We are enjoying a Rangers game via TV this evening. Britt and Jeff a little more than me. I can enjoy them, but it takes a lot of focus; I always think of something else I could/should be doing.

We got the MD Anderson appointments moved to the first week in November. Jeff will have an MRI and lab work and see Dr. Puduvalli. He's also scheduled for a round of cognitive testing to compare with July's presurgery and postsurgery results. I just confirmed with Jeff: since he had his first surgery in September of 2009, he hasn't had any sickness from the cancer or from the treatments. What a blessing! We are prayerfully awaiting the oncologist's plan. We haven't had any hint of what treatment is planned/scheduled. We are cautiously optimistic that this might be the last treatment for a while. None of the doctors have spoken any such notion, but we were told Puduvalli only prescribes three Avastin treatments for necrosis. After that, we'll see.

Wednesday, Jeff had a Wheat Commission meeting in Stillwater, so he and I went up on Tuesday evening. It was great to see some of our wheat friends. Even going the night before, by Wednesday evening, he was exhausted. He caught a nap on the way home, and another after we got home. But after a full day, he still went with us to church on Wednesday evening.

We have started a study in Romans. Two weeks later, we have covered seventeen verses. I think the speed will pick up a little as we go. We haven't had Wednesday evening Bible study since our last minister retired. It's good to get back at it. There is a closeness experienced within the group that studies the Bible together. It is not the Sunday morning crowd, or even the crowd that attends on Sunday evenings, but a smaller, hungrier group (Hebrews 5:11–14). Over the years, I have been encouraged by this group. I have sat in awe of the biblical knowledge of our older members and their faithfulness to study and continuing hunger to learn more. The group has changed over the years; some members have gone on—graduated, so to speak—and others have joined us. I'm blessed and encouraged every week we meet. I truly miss it when meat isn't on the menu. That reminds me of an old Wendy's commercial: "Where's the Beef?"

Brittany was out of school Thursday and Friday for fall break. She had a dentist appointment on Thursday and basketball practice today. So much for the "break" part. As for the "fall" part, we enjoyed a nice rain last night and today. We are a couple hundred acres shy of having the wheat sowed, and the rain was definitely needed. Since we are in the irrigation business, and since I have accounting ties, I once tried to put a dollar value on an inch of rain in our community. I asked Jeff for an average cost to pump an inch of water on an acre, then took that value times the number of acres of crop land in our community. Bottom line: timely rains add to the production of our crops, and that's priceless. It's time to hum a verse of "There Shall Be Showers of Blessings."

I often run into some of you in various places. It's always an encouragement to know so many people are still keeping up with us.

Many times, the comments are followed by "We are praying for Jeff" or "Jeff's on our church prayer list." We'll never be able to express how much we appreciate your faithfulness to pray and to remind God we need His help. Next time you pray, please offer thanks for the peace that God is in control and this is His battle, not ours.

10/28/10 (Thursday), 5:52PM-Karen

Friday, Jeff and I went to Minneapolis for the US Wheat fall board meetings. Jeff had meetings scheduled all day Saturday, Sunday, and Monday; and we returned home on Tuesday. Jeff struggled with the walk between terminals in Chicago when we had to change planes, so when we arrived in Minneapolis, he agreed to request a wheelchair. Good thing, too, because he needed to conserve his energy when he could. He made all the scheduled meetings on Saturday but was only able to attend the morning sessions on Sunday and Monday. Both of those days, he returned to the hotel room after lunch and absolutely crashed for a few hours. The restaurants were fairly close, two to three blocks away, so we usually would walk to the restaurant. After a meal, however, he would be too weak to walk back to the hotel, so we would take a taxi. It really wasn't too bad; the area taxis had a flat downtown rate, and Jeff just had to conserve his energy when he could.

As we have been planning, Jeff will return to Houston next week for an MRI and cognitive testing, and we will meet with Dr. Puduvalli, and we should get a glimpse of what the next stage of treatment will be. We are hoping/praying it will be wait-and-see, get an MRI every couple of months and just be cancer-free for a while.

Our home seems to have plenty of stress lately. Things like Jeff not driving, Brittany not driving, limited patience, and limited physical strength each have their own challenges. Please pray that the fruit of the Spirit will be produced in abundance so others (even those we live with) will see Christlike qualities in us.

But the fruit of the Spirit is love, joy, peace, patience, kindness, goodness, faithfulness, gentleness and selfcontrol. Against such things there is no law.

Galatians 5:22–23 (NIV)

Thank you so much for all the prayers. God is faithful. I know he won't let us down now.

11/01/10 (Monday), 10:35PM-Karen

Quite often, our day takes us places that weren't our original destination. Today was one of those days. Today's events haven't unfolded as we planned, but I hold to the promise *"all things work together for good to them that love the Lord"* (Romans 8:28, KJV). For several weeks, we planned to be in Houston tonight for Jeff to have an MRI tomorrow morning and see Dr. Puduvalli at MD Anderson on Wednesday. However, those plans have changed, and the appointments are being rescheduled.

I struggle with how to write tactfully and yet give you an open, honest update. Issues of a digestive nature are generally a guarded topic, so I will try to phrase it politely. Over the weekend, Jeff developed some bleeding, which has turned out to be signs of a digestive complication of some kind. One of the side effects of Avastin we were cautioned about is a thinning of the walls of the digestive tract and the possibility the colon or intestines could be easily perforated. Given that information, I've been very adamant this issue couldn't be ignored. This afternoon Jeff finally agreed to see Lauren Binder (our God-sent personal medical provider). Upon her referral, Jeff saw Dr. Jimmie Jackson, a general surgeon in Weatherford. He didn't elaborate much today but prescribed an antibiotic and scheduled a follow-up tomorrow. We aren't sure as to extent of the situation, but he believes the trip to Houston should be postponed until this matter can be resolved.

I'm glad God's on our side. He continues to pull strings for us and get access where we could easily hit roadblocks. Jeff wasn't scheduled for either visit today. I'm thankful both Lauren and Dr. Jackson were able to fit Jeff in their schedules. In case you were thinking the whole world is cold and uncaring, think again. There are still some kind, compassionate, caring people who haven't forgotten why they do what they do. Come to think of it, there are a lot people with these qualities reading this update. You give up your valuable time to check on us. Thank you for the prayers, I know God is faithful to listen, and I trust Him to guide our path, one day at a time, one step at a time.

> "For I know the plans I have for you," declares the Lord, "plans to prosper you and not to harm you, plans to give you hope and a future."

Jeremiah 29:11

As I was writing this update, I caught myself singing one line of a song: "To guide my footsteps." It was "God Walks the Dark Hills." If you've heard it before, maybe it'll give you something to hum.

11/06/10 (Saturday), 11:56PM-Karen

Jeff saw Dr. Jackson again Tuesday. He believed the digestive issue I spoke of on Monday would be resolved with an antibiotic. Monday and Tuesday, Jeff's blood pressure was quite high, so Wednesday, Lauren Binder, PA, doubled Jeff's medicine and gave me instructions to monitor his BP and call her in a week.

On Friday, Jeff had a scheduled appointment with Dr. Keefer, the oncologist in OKC, as a follow-up at the end of the third Avastin treatment. Jeff had routine blood work and then saw Brenda James, the nurse practitioner for Dr. Keefer. Usually, Jeff's appointments alternate between Brenda and Dr. Keefer. I explained the week's events and the cancellation of appointments in Houston and that they were rescheduled for December 21 and 22. Since Jeff's last MRI was August 31, she and Dr. Keefer agreed that was too long to wait for another MRI. We were sent to the scheduling desk with orders for an MRI as soon as it could be scheduled. The scheduler said they were an MRI short that day, so she wasn't sure how quick they would get Jeff in. When she hung up the phone, she said, "Now! They will work you in now." This was certainly a blessing from God; Jeff could have the MRI on Friday and not have to wait or make another trip to OKC. Since the last MRI was at MD Anderson, the new MRI will be sent there for comparison. I expect to hear from Houston and/or Keefer's office midweek with the results and revised treatment plan.

Tuesday the high school girls had a basketball scrimmage in Hinton. Each year the team changes a little, but in our small town, many of the girls play both softball and basketball, so we know most of the faces in the home crowd. This year should be fun—Britt will be on both the junior and high school teams.

Britt has basketball practice most afternoons until about five, but on Wednesday she has piano practice for thirty minutes and church in the evening. I should get used to the busyness. I suspect our calendar will be full until she graduates.

Last night Brittany and I went to the last Hinton football game. This has really been a tough year for their team. Win or lose, it's important to have fans in the stands to encourage the kids. Britt's in some classes with upperclassmen, so she knows more players than I do. Still, I know enough that it's fun to watch. We worked the first half in the booster club hamburger line, so our focus on the game was limited, but we watched the last half from the stands.

Jeff spent most of the day in front of the TV—first watching our OSU Cowboys win, then watching the Sooners lose. He's as happy for one event as the other.

I started reading a book about prayer time for the busy woman. If I find time to finish the book, I'll give you my opinion.

We're having a beautiful fall. The gradual change in temperature produces beautiful foliage. As we drove yesterday, I couldn't help but notice the trees and the vast array of greens, yellows, and oranges topped with a clear blue sky. I'm glad God put color in the world. His plan of salvation didn't require color, so it appears

He put it there "just for *me*?" Our Wednesday evening Bible study is focusing on Paul's letter to the Romans. As we drove, I was reminded of the verses that discuss people are without an excuse because all nature points to God.

> For since the creation of the world God's invisible qualities—his eternal power and divine nature—have been clearly seen, being understood from what has been made, so that people are without excuse.
>
> Romans 1:20 (NIV)

11/13/10 (Saturday), 7:25PM-Karen

Brittany had basketball games on Tuesday in Hinton (a big win) and Thursday at Amber-Pocasset (a loss). I went to both games, but Jeff didn't feel up to going. He's been in a battle with blood pressure the last couple of weeks, and I believe he's more tired than usual. I understand this is an issue attributable to the Avastin.

Wednesday Jeff went with Wayne and Chris Lee (a cousin) to Wayne's stepmother's funeral. Grandma Mary passed away at the age of 101. The funeral was in Inola, so it was early evening when they got home—too late to go to church with us.

After a full day of activity on Wednesday, Jeff slept a lot on Thursday. He did go to Hinton with me for the high school Veteran's Day program. Since Britt's in vocal, it was a double treat for us: we were able to honor veterans and hear the choir. Britt was excited about the song selections. The band played one verse of "The Star Spangled Banner," and then the vocal group sang the second verse. (Etiquette question: Once seated after the band finished the first verse, is it proper to stand for the second verse?) They also sang the second verse of "God Bless America." Both have excellent words and should be sung more often. The band played a medley of armed services anthems. As each song was played, the veterans of that branch stood. The American Legion had a presentation on folding the flag and what each fold represents.

There was a video of Red Skelton's Pledge of Allegiance. Boys State delegates spoke, and Girls State delegates were recognized. It was a very good program. Good job, Hinton High School!

On Thursday, I called OKC to check on last Friday's MRI. There was a delay because Jeff's MRI ended up in some lady's medical file, with her name on his images; and that lady's MRI ended up in Jeff's medical records with Jeff's name on it. I had to smile a little. Apparently, that isn't a breach of the HIPPA privacy regulations because the medical information released didn't include the patient's name. The radiology department remedied the situation—shipped Jeff's MRI to Houston, probably on Thursday. The radiologist in OKC, without reviewing Jeff's history, believed he had suffered a stroke, because of what he saw on the MRI. Brenda James, NP, reassured the radiologist that Jeff's wife was very good to catch the symptoms, and she would have caught stroke symptoms. (I wasn't sure whether to take that as a compliment or a gentle nudge that there might be a page or two of notes where I had called with questions—I chose to take it as a compliment!) Brenda caught the radiologist up to date with enough of Jeff's history to confirm what he was seeing on the MRI were effects of Avastin, not a stroke. She also relayed that it appeared the hole from surgery had healed. She made sure I understood it was a good report.

So the MRI should be in Houston. I expect to hear from Dr. Puduvalli and Dr. Keefer what the plan is going forward. We are prayerfully hopeful Jeff won't need any further treatment, and quarterly MRIs will keep an eye on the former cancer site. This would be great news. I hope our family can enjoy some time "off" from time-and-energy-consuming treatments. Don't get me wrong, I'm very thankful we're blessed with research and medical knowledge. God's been very generous to us. I'm looking forward to Thanksgiving and Christmas with anticipation. I think Jeff would agree "Home for Christmas!" would be a definite improvement over last year's three-week, semi-isolated, anti-vacation at Mercy.

Thank you so much for your prayers. I'm humbled by the blessings God has showered on us: family, friends, neighbors, church family, provision, peace, and our salvation. This year especially, I am thankful for Jeff's restored health. Even though Jeff's path to recovery may be long and may not even result in a full recovery, I'm thankful for the ability to enjoy the blessings along the way. As I type, I'm humming "Count Your Many Blessings." Sometimes it's good to "name them one by one."

> Shout for joy to the Lord, all the earth. Worship the Lord with gladness; come before him with joyful songs. Know that the Lord is God. It is he who made us, and we are his; we are his people, the sheep of his pasture. Enter his gates with thanksgiving and his courts with praise; give thanks to him and praise his name. For the Lord is good and his love endures forever; his faithfulness continues through all generations.

> Psalm 100 (NIV)

I'll let you know as soon as I hear from Houston. (Just like the lunar missions, we don't want to hear from Houston Mission Control that there is a problem.)

11/15/10 (Monday), 11:00PM-Karen

We've been monitoring Jeff's blood pressure for several weeks. On Friday I faxed the doctor's office in Hydro a listing for the week. This morning they called and wanted to make sure our BP monitor was accurate. It was. So Lauren Binder, PA, has changed Jeff's BP medicine. She expects to see improvement in a few days. We're to continue monitoring the readings daily. We're prayerfully hopeful this change will lower Jeff's BP and restore a little more of his energy.

The doctor's appointment turned into a two-and-a-half-hour trip because I ran errands in Weatherford, and we took advantage of the opportunity to eat out before his appointment. By the time we got home, Jeff was ready for some serious time in his sleep infested La-Z-Boy.

Jeff had a couple of visitors this afternoon. This evening he opted to stay home while I went to Britt's basketball games. The scoreboard didn't reflect the score we had hoped for, but I enjoyed about three hours of visit with friends.

We're still waiting for MRI results from Houston. I'll probably call tomorrow and follow up with our contact nurse.

I always close with a thank-you for your prayers. I want you to know it isn't just a habit. I'm grateful for the investment you make in our well-being. As you invest in prayer for us, I believe you can "own" the blessings of the healing and provision God supplies.

> On him we have set our hope that he'll continue to deliver us, as you help us by your prayers. Then many will give thanks on our behalf for the gracious favor granted us in answer to the prayers of many.

> 2 Corinthians 1:10b–11 (NIV)

11/19/10 (Friday), 5:56PM-Karen

Still haven't heard from Houston. I received a call Tuesday (I think; they all run together) from OKC and learned the MRI disc had *not* left the state. For all that has progressed with lightning speed, I'm trying not to get irritated at this minor issue. As soon as I know anything, I'll let everyone in on the results. In the meantime…

Brittany's junior high basketball team is in a tournament at Calumet this week. They played Okarche the first night and lost (that was on Monday's post). They played again last night and won. They play on Saturday for the consolation title. However, Britt won't be playing with them. During Thursday's game, Britt took a hit, landed on the hardwood, and was knocked out. I'm sure it was just a minute or so, but it seemed like an eternity to this mom. I made it out of the stands and down courtside before she moved at all. Big thanks to those who helped, and especially those who prayed in the stands. Who says you can't have prayer in schools?

Once again, it seems God has deemed my prayer within the parameters of His greater plan, and he has allowed my request— protection for my baby girl. Britt seems to be doing well. She had a headache this morning, which I expected. She took some Tylenol before school, and I dropped her off as usual. At some point during the day, Britt learned that OSSA rules say something along the lines of "when a player is removed from play by an official, the player must be cleared for re-entry into the athletic program by a physician." She got in to see Dr. Stutzman in Hydro today. The verdict: concussion. She can't practice or play until the Monday after Thanksgiving. Please pray for her recovery.

Hinton High School will have its first game on Saturday. Friday night, Jeff's cousin's husband's football team is in playoffs, and Britt is excited to go. Jeff and I are enjoying some Oklahoma Farm Bureau convention activities in OKC. Because a lot of walking would be involved, Jeff decided he would like to rent an electric scooter for the weekend. That was a good decision; I wish I had thought of it. Oh wait, I did about two days ago, to which I got a stern "I don't need that." Oh well, he's happier since it's his idea. Either way, I think he's learning he has to conserve his energy.

Jeff's PB is still high, but we're in a holding pattern waiting for it to balance out.

Thank you so much for the time investment to "checkonjeff." I'm humbled at your interest in our lives and thankful for each prayer. I'm confident God will use all these things to work for good to them who love the Lord (that's us!).

Have a blessed weekend.

> And we know that all things work together for good to them that love God, to them who are the called according to his purpose.
>
> Romans 8:28 (KJV)

11/20/10 (Monday), 11:48PM-Karen

Jeff's MRI is in Houston, on Dr. Puduvalli's desk. I expect an updated treatment plan any day. Jeff saw Dr. Keefer today in OKC. His blood work was good, but his BP is still elevated. We should be able to visit with Lauren Binder about the BP dosage/ prescription tomorrow. Dr. Keefer also changed the steroid dosage to taper off over the next month.

Britt seems to be improving and mentions headaches less all the time. She wants to be on the ball court with her teammates but knows doctor's orders are always to be followed.

Thanks for the prayers.

12/01/10 (Wednesday), 9:13AM-Karen

Since my last update, we celebrated Thanksgiving. We have so much to be thankful for. It's a very long list that will have to wait till another post.

I finally got a call from MD Anderson. The MRI taken November 5 shows a significant decrease in the intensity of the edges around the surgery site. That's definitely good news. Since the Avastin seems to be having a positive effect, Dr. Puduvalli wants Jeff to have two more Avastin treatments before he sees him, sometime mid-January. So the appointments scheduled for December in Houston are being postponed. I talked to Dr. Keefer's office in OKC to schedule the Avastin. They don't want to give them until the abscess issue is completely resolved. With Avastin, as with many cancer drugs, healing would be halted as the drug takes effect. That is part of the issue that causes trouble— to kill all the *bad* cells, some *good* cells are sacrificed.

Thanks for all your prayers. Please pray for my patience and wisdom. Too many tasks, not enough time. I need wisdom to know what activities should be cut so there's still time for the important things. The past year has yielded some insight into what's important, but that must be balanced with work and fun. Pray that time issues will be resolved or that I'll at least have patience when they aren't.

I can do all things through Christ which strengtheneth me.

Philippians 4:13 (KJV)

12/05/10 (Sunday), 10:24PM-Karen

To God be the glory.

I wrote a couple weeks ago that Brittany had received a concussion during a junior high girls' basketball game. After sitting on the sidelines for almost two weeks, she was cleared to play on Wednesday. She practiced with the team on Wednesday and Thursday and played in a JH game on Thursday night. She did a great job. She drew several fouls and made five free throws. However, in the fourth quarter, she was knocked around a little. When she fell, she hit her head on the court. She was out—again. Apparently, consecutive head injuries can be quite serious. She's out until sometime after the first of the year. She has quite a few fairly intense headaches. Tylenol and rest seem to be the best medicine. As I sat in church this morning, listening to my baby girl play "Silent Night" for the offertory, I had to choke back the tears. We are so blessed; even with two concussions in the same number of weeks, she had enough focus to play the piano—and beautifully, I might add.

We're still waiting for Jeff to heal completely before scheduling his Avastin treatments. Once he starts the Avastin, all healing in progress would stop.

Please pray for continued healing for both Brittany and Jeff.

Thanks so much for checking on us.

OUR SECOND
CHRISTMAS AT MERCY

12/16/10 (Thursday), 4:08PM-Karen

Hopefully, a brief update as I'm headed out the door to a JH basketball game. Britt still experiences some headaches as a result of the concussions. She has a doctor's appointment Tuesday and an appointment with a physical therapist Monday to see about relaxing the muscles in her neck to help alleviate the headaches.

Jeff's running a low temperature and seems to have a stomach virus. We are pushing fluids on medical advice. Jeff has a second appointment with Dr. Jackson on Monday to follow up on the abscess issue. On Tuesday he's scheduled for an MRI, and Wednesday he has an appointment with Dr. Puduvalli in Houston. It's been six weeks since the last MRI, so it's time for another.

A year ago, we were starting what turned out to be a twenty- one-day nonvacation in a somewhat isolated room at Mercy. What a year! We have ups and downs, good days and a few bad ones, but through it all, we're so blessed: no matter how bad things may seem, they would definitely be worse without faith in God's plan for our lives, our trust in Jesus Christ as our Savior, and, especially, the daily comfort of knowing the Holy Spirit is with us. God will never leave us or forsake us.

> For he hath said, I will never leave thee, nor forsake thee. So that we may boldly say, The Lord is my helper, and I will not fear what man shall do unto me.
>
> Hebrews 13:5b–6 (NIV)

12/20/10 (Monday), 1:52PM-Karen

As I type this update, Jeff's undergoing a surgical procedure at Mercy to dissolve a large blood clot that is either in his left lung or very close to it. We discovered this in the ER this morning. This forty-five-minute procedure will place clot-dissolving medicine directly on the blood clot. Please pray for the staff and Dr. McCullum as they work on Jeff.

12/20/10 (Monday), 3:01PM-Karen

They finished the procedure, and Jeff's in ICU. They will leave the drip line in for a day or so, then check the progress. He'll be in ICU for at least two days. The doctor said there were a lot of little clots in the left lung, and it was completely blocked. The largest clot is the size of a hotdog. His right lung has some clots. The next twenty-four hours are the most critical.

Thanks for your prayers.

12/21/10 (Tuesday), 1:59AM-Karen

Jeff's in ICU on pain meds, antibiotics, and blood thinners. He seems to be sleeping some, but his rest isn't very peaceful yet.

From the beginning, in September of 1963…well, maybe I won't start at the beginning: Midweek last week, I called the local PA because Jeff had symptoms of a virus (diarrhea and fever). She said she was seeing a lot of cases, and it was going around. She ordered lots of liquids, so Jeff wouldn't dehydrate (sports drinks if he would take them), and rest. We followed those orders. Over the weekend, Jeff seemed to be getting better. He was more alert for longer periods of time, carried on longer conversations, had less fever, etc. But last night and early this morning, his speech seemed slurred. This slur is different from the speech issues of the past year—an occasional difficulty in choosing the right words. With this morning's changes, I contacted the local doctor's office. She wanted him in OKC.

As part of the ER evaluation, they pulled a chest X-ray. That X-ray showed multiple blood clots in Jeff's lungs with one particularly large clot. The left lung was completely blocked, and the right lung had partial blockage. Very quickly, they sent a pulmonologist to pull blood. From there, things moved fast. They moved Jeff from the ER to a surgical room. In the hall outside the procedure room, we met Dr. McCullum. As they often do, the doctor asked how each person is related to the patient. (I'm sure that plays into HIPPA regulations somehow.) Our pastor introduced himself. He headed to the hospital as soon as we started our church prayer chain. Dr. McCullum summarized the procedure of placing a direct line from the groin to the clot and starting a blood thinner drip to dissolve the clot along with an ultrasonic device that helps break up the clots. Then a very nice thing happened: the surgeon suggested our pastor pray with Jeff and the team before the procedure. An occasional refocus on God and His supremacy puts things back in His hands and gives us such sweet peace. Placing the line only took about forty- five minutes. They kept Jeff awake to monitor his vitals and verbal feedback.

Once the line was placed, they moved Jeff to ICU. They'll monitor the progress of the clot busting once or twice a day and will remove the med line when they believe it has been effective.

A urologist, Dr. Charles McWilliams, came by about 9:00 p.m.to evaluate a sporadic lower abdominal pain. It is excruciating for about thirty seconds and then eases off until the next round. He decided the source of Jeff's pain is bladder spasms. He ordered pain meds and an ice pack.

Since Jeff's been in ICU, he has seen his oncologist, a urologist, and a pulmonologist, and he's scheduled to see a neurologist in the morning. Even though he sees specialists for a variety of issues, I know my Heavenly Father is the ultimate special*ist* with authority to provide for our every need.

Matthew 21:22 (NIV) says *"If you believe, you will receive whatever you ask for in prayer."* For now, we wait and pray.

12/21/10 (Tuesday), 8:45AM-Karen

I stayed with Jeff in ICU last night. There were the usual wakeups for meds and blood testing, but this morning, we woke to a seizure. That was about an hour ago. They haven't gotten him to wake up from that yet. I remember after his seizure in August, he went through an extended time of this heavy breathing and unconsciousness. I don't remember it being this long, but it could've been. There's more testing ordered this morning. They took an ultrasound of his chest to measure the blood clots and ordered a CT of his head and abdomen to confirm there isn't any internal bleeding from the blood thinners. Thank you for the prayers. I can't imagine going through this time without the peace God gives. It's beyond explanation.

12/21/10 (Tuesday), 5:11PM-Karen

Jeff went back to the cath lab about an hour ago. Dr. McCullum checked the progress of the clot busters. He said the smaller clots were clearing up some, but the larger (hot dog) clot still needed the drip meds. He discontinued the ultrasonic portion of the treatment but will keep the drip on the larger clot. He hoped he would be able to remove the sheath line with meds but wasn't comfortable with that yet. They'll recheck the progress tomorrow.

Dr. McCullum said there is a large clot at Jeff's knee. Judging from his hand motions, I estimate it's about a five- to eight-inch clot. He said the IV clot busters would decrease the size of the knee clot. He wants to consult with Dr. Keefer about whether they should put in a filter to catch the clot should it break away and become mobile. This isn't something he wants to do unless it's absolutely necessary.

Earlier today, the CT scan showed no change from the scan before the seizure. That's good news. Jeff's still in a sedated state although it's a post effect of the seizure and not drug-induced. He's not speaking yet, but he responds to requests to wiggle his toes and squeeze hands.

Jeff's brother, Randy, has agreed to stay tonight so I can go home for a good night's sleep. There are so many doctors and specialists in and out; I want someone here to get updates and results.

Thanks for the concern, calls, cards, and especially the petitions to our Heavenly Father on our behalf. I'm humbled by the number of concerned people wanting to keep up with Jeff's progress. We're so blessed with many friends and family and the overwhelming peace that God is providing during this time.

12/22/10 (Wednesday), 6:19PM-Karen

Jeff's pretty alert today. The tubes and wire bother him, and he tries to take them off. He's having some confusion about where he is and what year it is, but at other times, he answers coherently. He seems to know who *he* is.

Jeff's on his way back from the cath lab. Today's check showed more clots in the left lung, but the right lung is clean. Dr. McCullum removed the ultrasonic treatment yesterday but is restarting that option in an effort to dissolve more clots. They will recheck Jeff's progress tomorrow.

Drs. McCullum and Keefer consulted and recommend inserting a Greenfield IVC filter in Jeff's inferior vena cava (IVC) to protect his heart and lungs. By inserting the filter, they can decrease the blood thinners while still obtaining the desired effect of less risk from clots.

Placing the filter should only take about forty-five minutes. Because it will be placed where the drip line is currently located, the procedure will be done after they believe the clots are completely clear.

I believe they're adjusting the dosage of clot buster meds in both the sheath and his PICC line.

12/23/10 (Thursday), 12:36PM-Karen

Jeff's cousin, Chris, stayed last night. When Britt and I came back this morning, Jeff was still trying to remove the oxygen tubing from his nose and the monitor for the blood oxygen level from his finger. The ICU staff makes everyone leave from six thirty to seven thirty in the morning and the evening so they can complete reports and change shifts. When Britt and I came in at seven thirty, the nurse was taping the monitor back on his finger, and a few minutes later, we discovered he had removed the oxygen as well.

About nine, he had a brief seizure. It didn't seem near as severe as Tuesday's, but each one has its own recovery to bring him back to where he was before the seizure. They are again increasing the antiseizure meds.

The side effect of that is sleep seems to increase in direct proportion to the Keppra. He seems to have regained the reflexes in both feet and can squeeze your hand but falls back asleep almost instantly. I'm learning far more than I thought I would ever want to know.

They have ordered a CT scan to compare with the last scans. The EKOS machine is still being used to ultrasonically break up the clots through the sheath line.

I want to thank each of you for your prayers and for sharing our needs with your own prayer chains. I'm still convinced God's plan will turn this trial into a blessing in some way. I struggle with wanting things *my* way—Jeff healed and at home. I continually have to remind myself to yield to a bigger, better plan that may take us through the valley of the shadow instead of around it as most humans would probably choose, trusting he has a reason I may never comprehend.

Jeremiah 29:11 (NIV) has been a favorite verse for us this year. It reads, *"For I know the plans I have for you," declares the* Lord, *"plans to prosper you and not to harm you, plans to give you hope and a future."*

We tend to focus on just verse 11. The preceding verses discuss the trials the exiles faced in Babylon. The following verses discuss seeking God and finding Him, praying, those prayers being heard, and the restoration that follows. I trust I'm not taking the verses too far out of context to claim for myself: That God knows the plans he has for the Krehbiel family, plans to prosper the Krehbiels and not to harm us, plans to give Jeff, Karen, and Brittany hope and a future. And to put the three parts together, the trial first with an understanding that God knows the plans he has for us, and that the trial will cause us to seek and find Him. I'm convinced that by going through this trial, I seek and find a little more often. My goal should be to abide in Him—keeping the communication lines of prayer open and in constant use.

This Christmas we celebrate the gift of not only the Christ child in a manger but also our Savior on the cross and the joy of an empty tomb. By accepting that gift, we can know our future is secure, with that comes a wonderful, indescribable peace. Christ truly brought *joy to the world.*

12/23/10 (Thursday), 8:06PM-Karen

About two this afternoon, Jeff was taken back to the cath lab to check the blood clot-busting progress. The size of the clots was down—not as much as they wanted, but down. Jeff had been on the clot-busting drip for three days, and Dr. McCullum said that's about the maximum time frame for that type of treatment with high-dosage thinners and ultrasonic treatment. So they discontinued both. He's now on a blood thinner. But as Dr. McCullum discussed with me on Tuesday and Wednesday afternoons, they placed a Greenfield filter in Jeff's abdomen. This should stop any clots from getting into vital organs.

Dr. Grode, the pulmonologist that replaced Dr. Nehme (who is now on vacation), is making most of the calls about Jeff's care. They hope to treat the remaining clots with medication and blood thinners.

Dr. Keefer stopped by this evening. His participation in Jeff's health care this week has been limited to consultation. He starts a week of vacation tomorrow and mentioned his expectation that we could still be here next Friday when he returns. Please pray with me that God will provide a speedy recovery and that Jeff will be home soon.

> Now unto him that is able to do exceeding abundantly above all that we ask or think, according to the power that worketh in us, Unto him be glory in the church by Christ Jesus throughout all ages, world without end. Amen.

> Eph 3:20-21

12/25/10 (Christmas Day), 12:59PM-Karen

Merry Christmas. With Christ in our Christmas, we have a joy that isn't determined by health, wealth, or social status. We are adopted children of the Creator with full family rights—what more do we need?

Jeff's more alert today. Randy stayed last night. When Britt and I arrived this morning, Jeff was sitting up drinking a Pepsi. He stayed awake about twenty minutes and participated in our conversations more than yesterday. Dr. McCullum came by a few minutes ago. He really didn't have anything new for us; he said he just popped in to pester Jeff. I asked how much follow-up they would have on the blood clots. The answer I got was that they are through "looking" at the clots. They will allow his body to absorb what's left. He said the clots *aren't* keeping Jeff in ICU. He said he would make sure Jeff's chart reflects that. So now I have a new question: What condition *is* keeping him in ICU? Maybe Jeff will gain strength and be able to get up and move around some in the next few days.

Thanks for all your prayers. We wish you each a very merry *Christ*mas! Don't forget to invite Jesus to His birthday parties!

12/25/10 (Saturday), 9:15PM-Karen

Jeff has improved quite a bit today. Dr. Grode left orders to transfer him to a step-down unit. We're waiting for transport. We've known for about seven hours he would move sometime today. We were told we were waiting for a room to open up. Jeff's appetite is almost nonexistent, but he's had a little liquid and half a dish of pudding today. Maybe tomorrow his appetite will return.

Today the Burkhalter family took over an ICU waiting room for our family Christmas. At one time, I think these rooms were available like hotel rooms; now they're more like private waiting rooms. Anyway, we had a five-foot sub, chips, dip, lots of snacks, and candies. The food was good, but most of all, it was good to see everyone. They were able to see Jeff two at a time then gave him a break before more came back. Jeff and I are watching *Elf* this evening. I looked for *It's a Wonderful Life* but didn't find it.

Tomorrow we have plans to share the afternoon with the Krehbiels. The weather has been much better this year than last year's record snow in the metro that stopped drivers from much travel at all.

12/27/10 (Monday), 3:36PM-Karen

Jeff's sleeping a lot today. He wakes up, looks around, and then falls back asleep. When I wake him for a meal, he takes a couple bites, pushes the rest away, and goes back to sleep. Dr. Kaplan, the neurologist, concerned with any aftereffects of the seizures, doesn't believe this is a side effect of the Keppra (antiseizure med). He discussed changing the Keppra to a different antiseizure med but said they all have some side effects, and at least Keppra doesn't interact with any other meds Jeff's taking. He did question whether Jeff was using his sleep apnea machine at night. He wants to give it another day or so and make sure Jeff sleeps well at night before he changes the meds.

There is discussion about having Jeff sit in a chair for a while and trying to get him to walk a little in the room. To my knowledge, he hasn't gotten out of bed at all while he has been here. As much as he's sleeping, that may prove to be the equivalent of sleepwalking. I'm glad to see him move some. He was getting pressure sores from lying so long in the same position. He hasn't moved much, especially during the time that he had the drip line in with clot busters.

The abscess from November is still causing problems. A wound specialist has been by this afternoon to assess the open sore. He suggested a treatment that should jumpstart the healing. I just spoke with a dietician about his suppressed appetite. She suggested a few foods to try that have high protein content. They are suggesting milkshakes if Jeff would eat/drink them. He does like milkshakes, so I'll give that a try right away.

I need a few hours in my office to finish up some end-of-the- year issues. Jeff's dad has volunteered to sit with Jeff this evening and stay through the night. It's hard to leave and hard to stay. I'm torn with how to best use my time. I wear many hats: my wife hat says "Stay and supervise Jeff's care," but my mom hat says "It's Christmas break, and Brittany needs to spend time with Mom doing something other than sitting in the hospital." The accountant hat is now screaming "You're short on continuing education hours for the year!" I'm trying to lean not on my own understanding but acknowledge God in all my ways so that He'll direct my path. I've seen other ladies—some from church, some friends, and some family—successfully juggle the demands of a sick loved one and their ongoing responsibilities of being a mom, wife, daughter, Sunday school teacher, business owner, employee, etc. Many have struggled down this path before. I'm sure I won't be the last person this internal conflict affects. Prayerfully, I trust God will use *my* experience to help others.

I'm grateful to each of you for investing your time to read these updates and especially for the time you spend in prayer for our family.

> In all thy ways acknowledge him, and he shall direct thy paths.
>
> Proverbs 3:6 (KJV)

12/28/10 (Tuesday), 11:09PM-Karen

Wayne stayed last night and all day today with Jeff, which allowed me to spend some much-needed time in my office. When Britt and I arrived this evening, Jeff was awake. He had several visitors today. I was sorry I missed them but was glad they were able to pop in and see Jeff.

They changed his bed to one that is a little...nicer? It should reduce the risk of bed sores. We brought a chocolate chip milkshake in hopes that it would sound or taste good enough that Jeff would drink it. I think he did pretty good, maybe a fourth of the milkshake. I know that doesn't sound like much, but it is, compared to what he's eaten since he arrived last week.

Dr. Grode ordered a test of the thickness of Jeff's blood to check the effectiveness of the blood thinners. That reminds me of a Thanksgiving or Christmas at my sister's house several years ago.

Jeff and my oldest brother were discussing the proper viscosity of gravy in comparison with the standardized motor oil weights. We often laugh about how much fun they had. I think they had the whole family laughing before the conversation moved on to another topic. I can't help but think a few months ago, Jeff would have discussed with the doctor the proper viscosity of human blood. I miss his humor and quick wit.

As a matter of prayer: Over the last couple days, Jeff's responses to questions are sometimes inaccurate. This is a symptom that he has experienced some in the past year. He sometimes responds with a phrase that doesn't fit as a response to the question asked. He seems to do fairly well with "yes" or "no" answers but has trouble with longer answers. The frequency seems to have increased since he has been in the hospital this time, but the neurologist doesn't believe it was caused by seizures. Please pray that the doctors will have wisdom to find the cause of the increase and minimize or eliminate the effects.

On a positive note, Jeff seems to be able to recall names of his visitors immediately when he sees them. Thanks for the encouraging calls, notes, and messages and our special thanks to all of you who are so faithful to pray.

12/29/10 (Wednesday), 6:09AM-Karen

Jeff's Cowboys are playing in San Antonio, and he can't keep his eyes open long enough to watch the game. (OSU won!)

They took a chest x-ray this morning. The results show his lungs are clear. He's on oxygen while he's awake and his CPAP machine at night. A doctor from physician services came by today to disconnect the IV and remove the catheter. They got Jeff up for a few minutes today, and it took all the energy he had stored up. Hopefully, taking away the fluid today will increase his appetite tomorrow. I have tried to push fluids and food, but when he closes his mouth, there isn't much I can do.

I won't sugarcoat it. In black and white, it looks like he had a good day, but today has been rough. His thinking isn't clear, and his memory seems limited. Those changes are hard to see no matter how temporary I hope they are.

I have typed it enough; you are each probably tired of reading it: I know God has a plan for us. If my prayers for Jeff's complete healing aren't being answered in my timeframe, I know God has a reason. I know the Creator of the Universe would not allow us to suffer physically or emotionally if it didn't serve a purpose. After all, who am *I* to question God? Please pray God will give me enough strength that I can draw others to Him. After all, if I can't handle this trial as a Christian with the support of the Holy Spirit and within His will, with the full resources of my Creator, what hope is there for nonbelievers?

> Pray also for me, that whenever I open my mouth, words may be given me so that I will fearlessly make known the mystery of the gospel, for which I am an ambassador in chains. Pray that I may declare it fearlessly, as I should.

> Ephesians 6:19–20 (NIV)

> Let your light so shine before men, that they may see your good works, and glorify your Father which is in heaven.

> Matthew 5:16 (KJV)

01/02/11 (Sunday), 1:52PM-Karen

2011—that's *so* hard to believe. Time flies not just when you are having fun, but I think it appears to fly by faster as we notice more things around us.

My last update was last Wednesday. Jeff had a report that his lungs are clear. Since then, the physical therapists have worked to get Jeff out of bed a little more each day. They put Jeff in a specialty bed that prevents bed sores in immobile patients. His appetite is increasing at a pace so slow it's hard to see the progress—a definite matter of prayer since the nurses and doctors are threatening a feeding tube if he doesn't start eating more volume. That sounds funny to those of you who know Jeff personally. His appetite has always been fine!

Jeff still experiences some confusion as to *where* he is. Randy, may have discovered part of the problem. When Jeff became ill this last time, we were planning to keep appointments at MD Anderson. Instead we ended up at Mercy in OKC. Jeff has asked me several days, "Are we going home tonight?" He asked his dad several times, "Can you take me home to Oklahoma?" He hasn't answered the nurse's question—"Do you know where you are?"— correctly since he's been in the hospital this time. One day he looked at me and asked, "Is this our house?" He seems to forget things when he sleeps, and he sleeps a lot. This is definitely a matter for prayer.

Brittany goes back to school this week. With that comes the return of basketball games and after-school practices. She goes and watches even though she's still on the injured list because of the concussions. As Jeff's wife, I want to oversee every detail of his care and be there every time a doctor stops by. As a mom, I want to be there for Brittany as she returns to a student's life that continues to move forward even though Dad's in the hospital.

I have had a few volunteers to stay with Jeff at night. Although this goes against my "wife" instincts, I've agreed. Jeff's brother and dad have stayed multiple nights. Chris, Jeff's cousin, stayed two nights and will stay again tonight. This seems to keep home life closer to normal and gives me time in the evenings to run the dishwasher and do laundry. One friend came and washed dishes and a few loads of laundry, and her husband hauled off our trash. Friendship—what a blessing! I wonder if we would know and appreciate the blessings God gives us without the turmoil that makes us appreciate them. That kind of sounds a little bit like "Which came first, the chicken or the egg?"

Thank you to each of you who are holding us up in prayer. I know God is answering your prayers and strengthening us. That reminds me of a Bible passage:

> So Joshua fought the Amalekites as Moses had ordered, and Moses, Aaron and Hur went to the top of the hill. As long as Moses held up his hands, the Israelites were winning, but whenever he lowered his hands, the Amalekites were winning. When Moses' hands grew tired, they took a stone and put it under him and he sat on it. Aaron and Hur held his hands up— one on one side, one on the other—so that

his hands remained steady till sunset. So Joshua overcame the Amalekite army with the sword.

Exodus 17:10–13 (NIV)

01/05/11 (Wednesday), 12:07AM-Karen

Brittany's Christmas break is over. She returned to school today. The basketball teams played at Calumet tonight. Randy's staying with Jeff, so I was able to go to both games. The girls won; the boys lost. It was a nice three hour-distraction from health care.

Since Wednesday, Dr. Grode has discussed with me his plan for Jeff's care. He said that the blood clots and seizures seem to be under control. Jeff could go home. But because he isn't eating well, he's extremely weak and will definitely have to have rehab to increase his physical strength before he'll be able to go home. He suggested an LTAC (long-term acute care) hospital. All five of these facilities in Oklahoma are in OKC. Because I had never heard of an LTAC, I called Loren Binder, PA, for her opinion. She discussed the situation with me and indicated that Jeff might be able to get the needed care on an extended basis at the hospital in Weatherford. That would definitely be closer and more convenient.

I want to be sure his care won't be compromised for my convenience. When I spoke with Dr. Grode, I was encouraged it might work out. He also says Jeff may stay a couple of days in the rehab wing at Mercy before he's transferred. I will post as I learn more about the long-term plan; for now, Jeff's still in intermediate care at Mercy.

I haven't said much about the initial diagnosis of Jeff's blood clots. If you have been following our story for very long, you know we seem to "catch" things that could have easily gone unnoticed. I want to be very clear: I believe God is in control and that the virus and resulting fever that led us to the ER were symptoms God used to get Jeff to the care he needed—yet another twist to our already-blessed story. God has provided every step of the way, and I believe Jeff's rehab days will be the same: God will provide everything we need emotionally, spiritually, and, especially for Jeff, physically.

But my God shall supply all your need according to his riches in glory by Christ Jesus.

Philippians 4:19 (KJV)

In Matthew 7:11, the Bible compares our Heavenly Father giving us gifts (providing for our care?) with our earthly fathers giving us gifts.

If ye then, being evil, know how to give good gifts unto your children, how much more shall your Father which is in heaven give good things to them that ask him?

Matthew 7:11 (KJV)

I know that either of our fathers, mine or Jeff's, would, if it was within their power, immediately restore Jeff's health. I have to believe our Heavenly Father loves us even more and wants to restore Jeff's health. Because he hasn't done that on my time schedule, it only means there is a greater plan that would be negatively impacted by an immediate healing, and there is more he wants to accomplish through this situation. That may be in our lives or in the lives of someone close to us or someone reading about us. I may someday know what that purpose is, and I may never know. I just need to trust my Heavenly Father to make some choices *for* me and accept His timing as perfect.

Thanks for your prayers for my family.

01/05/11 (Wednesday), 2:10PM-Karen

We received confirmation that Jeff will move to Weatherford tomorrow, where he'll get physical therapy as well as medical care. I'm excited Jeff will be closer to home, and our family activities will be a small step closer to some kind of normal. Please pray that the transport process will go smoothly.

PHYSICAL THERAPY

01/06/11 (Thursday), 7:31PM-Karen

Jeff was transferred from Mercy to Weatherford Regional Hospital today. Mercy was an hour away; Weatherford is only fifteen miles from home and will be much more convenient. I don't believe his care will suffer any because of this change. In fact, I think he'll get more physical therapy in Weatherford daily than he received the whole time he was at Mercy. His rehab was not our priority while we were there. We were definitely more concerned with blood clots and seizures. With both of those under control, his energy can now be focused on physical rehab, and prayerfully, his appetite and nutritional level will increase as well.

From the start of a new segment of our journey, the road again looks long and impassable. But as before, I know God won't leave us stranded on the side of the road but will walk with us each step of the way.

I hope to be able to update with a progress report soon. Until then, please pray that the therapists and nurses will create an encouraging environment to challenge Jeff physically.

Thanks for your encouragement and thanks for the prayers.

01/08/11 (Saturday), 3:41PM-Karen

Some of Jeff's prescriptions cause him to sleep, and at least one makes him jittery. The neurologist that Jeff saw at Mercy assured me that the antiseizure med was not causing Jeff's sleepiness, but I'm not convinced. Prior to the latest hospital stays, Jeff was taking 500 mg of Keppra twice a day (1000 mg daily). After the two seizures the week of Christmas, the dosage was increased to 1500 mg twice a day (3000 mg daily). Prior to his year-end complications, Jeff would fall asleep about an hour after he took the Keppra. The only other drugs he was taking were a pill for blood pressure and a potassium pill. So in my unlicensed opinion, the full dose of Keppra is causing the extra sleepiness.

As for appetite, it seems to be improving. He's getting pretty good at opening the eight-ounce cartons of milk and polishes off a couple a day. He seemed to be thirsty yesterday evening and willingly drank two glasses of tea between the fifteen bites of supper the doctor wants him to have of each meal. That is still a major battle, but we are seeing improvement.

This morning, for the first time, Jeff asked to get up to go to the restroom. While he was out of bed, the staff gave him a shower. That had to feel good. His last shower was while he was still at home (that was last year—just a few weeks, but based on the changing of the calendar, it was nonetheless, last year). Waterless shower caps and Redi-Bath products are still inferior to running water. My sister's family has a hilarious memory of my nephew wanting a "washoff" instead of a bath. A lot of the humor comes from the fact that it was a public request and the resulting humiliation my sister experienced. Sorry, Ryan, the washoff only works on a limited basis.

Our church family and numerous friends have asked, "Is there anything I can do to help you?" In looking toward our long-term plans, I have to admit, I need help. Alone, I can't keep all the juggled objects in the air at the same time. When I focus my time on Jeff, our businesses and Brittany are cheated. On the other hand, focusing on family or business doesn't leave time for Jeff. God has blessed us in many ways. Once again, I trust Him to maintain the aspects of the full life he has provided. This morning I called a friend and asked that she set up a schedule for volunteers to sit with Jeff at the hospital. If Britt and I can stay at home each night, we can put the suitcases in the closet and begin to find a "normal" that will allow for time at home. I estimate I could have about six hours to do office work each day. With God's blessing, I can stay current with bookwork for all three of our businesses and keep the financial aspect of our lives somewhat stable. That would still leave some time each day for us to spend with Jeff.

But for that schedule to work, I'm asking for help from our friends. If you are willing to sit with Jeff, let me know.

Thank you for being a part of the prayer network that supports our family during this time. I trust my Heavenly Father to repay the debt I owe each of you for your thoughtfulness and your prayer.

While I was typing this update, Jeff asked to get out of bed and go for a ride in a wheelchair. We made it down two hallways before he was ready to go back to bed. Things are improving daily!

> Now unto him that is able to do exceeding abundantly above all that we ask or think, according to the power that worketh in us, Unto him be glory in the church by Christ Jesus throughout all ages, world without end. Amen.

> Ephesians 3:20–21 (KJV)

01/12/11 (Wednesday), 11:31PM-Karen

Jeff's making progress, but at times it seems very slow. Physical therapy comes to the hospital each weekday. He sits up a minimum of fifteen minutes in a chair during each meal, and he has done a little weight lifting. I think they were probably one- pound weights, and he lifted them while he was in the bed, from his side toward the ceiling, 20 reps each side, knee lifts on the side of the bed, 20 each knee. And he stood beside his bed for a short time. His strength is very limited, and he seems to be weaker in his right side. He's a little hard-headed (nothing new there) and wants everything *now*. He doesn't yet see the value of the therapy and just wants back in bed.

Britt and I have been home each night. That provided some much-needed rest for me, and I suspect Britt is benefiting from sleep in her own bed as well. It's hard to proceed with our activities while Jeff's in the hospital, but every morning, like clockwork, God turns the earth to reveal the sun, and we start another day.

Many thanks to those who have sacrificed their evenings to sit with Jeff so that Britt and I can spend a few hours in our home instead of the hospital. The dishes are all clean this evening, and we are closing in on the laundry!

A brief update on Brittany: When the constant headaches subsided over Christmas, she contemplated a review of her medical status, hoping she would be cleared to play again. She ran up the stairs at home one day and quickly decided that since the headaches returned, even though temporarily, she's still not ready to return to practice and play. Thanks for the prayer on her behalf.

Please continue to pray that I will have wisdom to make good decisions concerning Jeff's medical care.

01/15/11 (Saturday), 10:52PM-Karen

Wednesday Jeff walked with a walker to the door of his hospital room and back to bed. Thursday he progressed even more, making it to the nurses' station and back to his room. Friday he walked the length of one hallway, rode a ways in the wheelchair, and then walked again, making it back to his bed. I'm thrilled with the progress! Lauren Binder wanted Jeff to sit up for at least fifteen minutes during each meal. This evening, he sat in the chair for about forty minutes to eat the carried-in Chinese buffet takeout.

That was a win on two levels—he's eating better, and he sat up for a nice long time.

Thank you to all the friends who sat with Jeff, called, sent cards, and offered prayers—especially the prayers.

Last Sunday, Lauren spoke with me about moving Jeff to a different swing bed that would have speech therapy as well as occupational therapy and physical therapy. The first part of the week, we worked in that direction. Thursday morning, she called to tell me she had contacted Jim Thorpe Rehab at Clinton, and they were sending someone to the hospital to evaluate Jeff to see if he would be able to tolerate their level of therapy. Jim Thorpe called me Thursday afternoon to review Jeff's situation; they were working with our insurance company to negotiate a daily rate. Friday morning, someone from Jim Thorpe called me to tell me they accepted Jeff, had the insurance worked out, and are planning to move him on Monday.

When Jeff was moved to Weatherford, the plan was to get him strong enough to be admitted to Jim Thorpe. The estimate I was told was three weeks at Weatherford and then move to Jim Thorpe. Apparently, Jim Thorpe had empty beds this week and is willing to accept Jeff "early." What a blessing! Since his first surgery in September 2009, Jeff has had some aphasia—trouble selecting the correct words to express his thoughts. Speech therapy will help him handle this type of situation by finding another word or talking us through guessing the words that he's having trouble choosing. I'm optimistic this will be a big benefit.

I was told there is a possibility Jeff had a mini-stroke during the time he had blood clots and seizures. He does have a visible weakness on his right side when he stands and during physical therapy. I believe we're already seeing improvement in his balance and strength because of the physical therapy. I'm somewhat discouraged that he doesn't receive physical therapy on weekends—only what he does at our prompting. I tend to think that is less than trained professionals could get out of him if they were here on Saturday. I'm still waiting for Jeff to decide it's to his benefit to be aggressive with the physical therapy—that it will only make him stronger.

Jeff's relocation to Clinton will mean a longer commute for us, but I believe it's vital to his recovery to have the three types of therapy in a positive environment.

You have been so faithful to keep Jeff (and our family) in your prayers that by this point, I probably don't even need to ask you to pray. I know you are already doing that. But I do have a favor to ask: as you think and talk about Jeff's progress with others, please give the credit to God for the blessings he's giving our family. I know He's answered our prayers (yours and mine), and He's providing the healing Jeff needs. As you pray, tell God "thank you!"

> O give thanks unto the Lord; call upon his name: make
> known his deeds among the people.

> Psalm 105:1 (KJV)

In every thing give thanks: for this is the will of God in
Christ Jesus concerning you.

1 Thessalonians 5:18 (KJV)

01/18/11 (Tuesday), 9:45PM-Karen

On Monday, Jeff was transferred to Jim Thorpe Rehab in Clinton.
Since he's able to sit up, I took him in our Yukon instead of having an
ambulance take him. He's been evaluated by the therapists and has
started all three types of therapy—speech, occupational, and physical.
His appetite has increased, although I believe he's still receiving an
appetite stimulant. Today for lunch, I took him a double cheeseburger
and onion rings. He ate all of the burger, a couple onion rings, *and* part
of the pork chop, mashed potatoes, and gravy that the hospital was
serving, along with a glass of milk.

On Tuesdays, the JT therapists and doctors have a staff meeting to
determine the therapy plan and staffing needs for the coming week.
Jeff's need for each type of therapy will be reevaluated each Monday.
I'm still learning procedures. It looks like Jeff will have therapy in the
morning, break for a couple hours at lunchtime, then have another
session or two in the afternoon. They have therapy every day except
Sunday. I keep running into folks with good things to say. I'm confident
that we'll see progress each week.

Again, thanks for taking time from your busy schedules to
checkonjeff and for the prayer investment you are making in our family.

01/24/11 (Monday), 11:44PM-Karen

Hinton was in the Caddo County Tournament last week. The girls won
consolation champ. Thursday was a "snow" day, but we really only had
ice. A quarter inch of ice is as slick on top as any other thickness would
be, and even though it was gone from the main roads by about noon,
no school. The weathermen predicted we would have snow on top of the
ice, but that missed us. Britt and I took advantage of the opportunity
for Brittany to see Jeff a few hours that afternoon. Hydro and Corn

Bible Academy teams were also in a basketball tournament last week at Clinton, which made it convenient for several families from church to see Jeff on days their teams played.

Jeff's gaining strength. Although day-to-day progress at this point seems very slow, when I look back at how far he has progressed since I posted last, he has made good progress. He's walking to and from the therapy room for his physical therapy sessions. His appetite seems better, and he's making some food choices about what we should carry in to supplement the cafeteria options. His speech therapy is usually in his own room. Jeff has always had a pretty good sense of humor, and we see a glimpse of that every now and then. He's able to kid a little with the nurses. The abscess is free from signs of infection, and we're still waiting for it to heal.

Dr. Blakeburn has been working to stabilize Jeff's Coumadin dosage to keep his blood clotting numbers at a constant level. The INR, international normalized ratio, is the indexing that reflects the speed at which blood clots. Jeff seems to be sensitive to the Coumadin and too much or too little makes a big swing in the lab results for his INR. When people discuss how "thick" or "thin" a person's blood is, they use the term "thick" to mean it clots faster and the term *thin* to mean it would take longer to clot. One of the doctors at Mercy said normal people (whoever that is) have an INR of 1 or 1.5. That would be too "thick" for Jeff since he has had a problem with clotting. They want his INR to be about 2.5 or 3. One day Jeff's INR was over 6, which means his blood would take way too long to clot should he get hurt, and there would be a high risk of bleeding. Those days when his INR was high, they withheld the Coumadin until the INR level was lower, and then they gave it in a lower dose. All that said, they seem to have the INR leveled out. They have given me pamphlets on risks and warning signs, etc.

All of the staff and the therapists at Jim Thorpe will meet tomorrow to determine their staffing requirements and provide input as to what they believe the patient needs to optimize their care for the coming week. I'm not sure what that will mean to us personally, but I'm expecting feedback from them sometime tomorrow—sort of a midterm report card?

Reading this morning, I came across the following verse:

> Then Samuel took a stone and set it up between Mizpah and Shen. He named it Ebenezer, saying, "Thus far has the Lord helped us."
>
> 1 Samuel 7:12 (NIV)

The naming of the stone "Ebenezer" made me think about the second verse of "Come Thou Fount of Every Blessing," which says, "Here I raise mine Ebenezer..."

After humming that song all day and mulling over the words the writer chose to reflect his thoughts, I think it's appropriate for me to acknowledge that in our lives, in our family, in this situation, *God* has helped us this far! Our battle is not over, but God has helped us *this* far.

I'm also intrigued by the phrase "tune my heart to sing His grace." Sometimes I trip over the words, and sometimes my thoughts don't flow on paper very fluently, but it's my prayer that God will use this situation to His honor and His glory, and that I can be ready with a reply when asked about the reason for our hope.

> But in your hearts set apart Christ as Lord. Always be prepared to give an answer to everyone who asks you to give the reason for the hope that you have.
>
> 1 Peter 3:15 (NIV)

As always, thank you for your prayer and your concern for our family.

01/28/11 (Friday), 11:18AM-Karen

Dr. Blakeburn and the JT staff met on Tuesday afternoon. They agreed that after one more week of therapy, Jeff would be strong enough to come home. Yipee! That week seems to be going by very quickly. I have decided the week is somewhat for me to get the house ready, and not just because Jeff needs to gain strength before they turn him loose. With Jeff's discharge tentatively scheduled for Tuesday, his physical therapist, Susan, came to our house yesterday for a walk-through to measure and evaluate what changes would be beneficial to make maneuvering around the house safer—safer but not necessarily easier so that he still gets some physical activity completing daily tasks. It's a major concern that Jeff will want to sit in his chair or lie in bed and won't be cooperative in activity that would be beneficial.

During yesterday's visit, Susan and I discussed changes we hope will make Jeff's post-hospital environment better. After twenty years of marriage, Jeff and I are changing sides of the bed so he'll be closer to the bathroom and can conserve his energy. I moved Jeff's "sleep-infested" La-Z-Boy recliner closer to the tiled path to minimize his steps to get to both the kitchen and the bedroom/bathroom and make it easier for his walker to roll on the flooring. I got a tip on what kind of showerhead to purchase, so I'm headed to the hardware store this afternoon to make that little change.

Today, Susan returned with a speech therapist, and they brought Jeff to the house on a field trip of sorts to let him help them see areas that might need attention. The choice to include a speech therapist allowed Jeff to have a speech therapy session on the way to the house, and I suspect another session on the way back to the rehab center, assuming all this activity didn't wear Jeff out so he sleeps all the way back.

It's no surprise that "The House the Smiths Built" passed inspection with flying colors! After all, God designed it, and he knew what Jeff would need before the foundation of the world and put things in place to provide for us. What a blessing! Jeff will just need a few items, and our case manager is working with insurance and a durable medical equipment company to get a wheelchair, walker, shower chair, and toilet extender.

Now comes the hard part—realizing that when I bring my husband home, at least for now, he's handicapped. Somehow this is different from getting a handicapped placard to use the primo parking at Wal-Mart to conserve Jeff's energy while he was weak from the chemo and radiation and the recovery period that followed—that always seemed temporary. Or sitting in the car at Brittany's softball games, that too seemed temporary, like we did that this year, because Jeff was too weak to be out in the wind and heat. But moving the furniture—silly, but somehow that seems more permanent. It seems a constant challenge to remind myself not to look at the big picture—after all, I have never been given authority to make adjustments to the big picture anyway. I suspect I would be better off to focus on today, and the tasks that God gives me today—going to the hardware store to get a handheld showerhead!

Please continue to pray for us as we transition from hospital to home. For a while at least, we will have some home health care workers in and out of the house. This will be another opportunity for God to use us, for us to tell our story, for God to get the credit for the peace he provides in our lives. Please pray that we are helpful to His plan and not a hindrance. Please pray for my patience to increase. I want to be a Godly wife—especially now. Pray for wisdom that God will continue to guide our decisions for our farm, our irrigation business, our family, and Jeff's continuing medical care.

> In all thy ways acknowledge Him, and he shall direct
> thy paths.
>
> Proverbs 3:6 (KJV)

And, please pray that in the midst of this continuing storm Brittany will thrive, and through that, God will be glorified.

HOME HEALTH

02/01/11 (Tuesday), 6:32PM-Karen

Home again, home again. Jiggety jog. No clue where that saying came from, but my dad would always say that as we pulled into the yard when I was a kid. I couldn't help but repeat the phrase while bringing Jeff home yesterday. It's good to have Jeff home, and we are so blessed we are warm and dry, given the extreme weather outside. School was cancelled for today in anticipation of a snowstorm, and we have already gotten the call that there will be no school tomorrow either. I was somewhat caught up on deadlines, so I didn't work at all today—unless you count cooking, which I don't. It was good to have home-cooked meals after so many days of eating away from home.

Home healthcare will start as soon as weather permits their visits. The nurse assigned has been good about calling to make sure I'm okay taking over the nursing activities until they can get here. So far, I'm okay.

We are humbled to have so many of you checking on us.

02/06/11 (Sunday), 11:23PM-Karen

We went to the ER Wednesday evening for a blood test. His blood counts seemed to be in the target range, but his liver enzymes were very high. The ER doctor wanted us to follow up with Lauren on Thursday. I called on Thursday and scheduled an appointment for early afternoon. Before we left home, Lauren called, and we were able to discuss Jeff's lab results over the phone, thus avoiding a trip to town in the extreme cold weather. Lauren reviewed Jeff's current list of meds to find which one might be causing the liver enzymes to be so elevated. Turns out one of the blood pressure meds had side effects that might be accounting for the elevated enzymes and the colon bleeding issues. She stopped that medication and doubled the other blood pressure medicine. Tomorrow's lab should give us an idea of whether that was the problem if the enzyme level shows a decrease.

Home health physical therapy came to evaluate Jeff on Friday. By then, our snow-drift-packed road was opened up (thanks to all who helped). It looks like physical therapy will start next week. The extreme weather this past week seems to have put a one-week gap in Jeff's therapy regimen. Even though the PT therapist from Jim Thorpe went over the exercise that Jeff should do on the days he doesn't have a therapist coming to the house, Jeff's showing some stubbornness in not wanting me to help. At this point, I'm tired of the constant friction of trying to coax him into doing the therapy and his resistance.

Weather seems to be the cause for not receiving the prescribed armed shower chair. But after holding out as long as we could, I got Jeff in the shower on Friday. As expected, he seemed to feel a lot better afterward. On Saturday, Hinton had home basketball games. When I told Jeff I really wanted to go and was going to ask someone to come and sit with him while I was gone, he thought if we used the wheelchair instead of the walker, he could go with me, and he did. He made it through the girls' game and was ready to go eat. We chose Mexican. Britt stayed for the boys' game, which went into overtime, and then we picked her up and headed back home. Girls won, boys lost.

For this morning only, our church swapped Sunday school and the church service, which put the church service first. Jeff went with us! What a blessing he felt good enough and wanted to go. Again, we used the wheelchair to minimize his walking. I still think he got in quite a bit today. We had Jeff's parents for lunch today. Since Jeff and I left right after church and Brittany stayed for Sunday school, I asked Wayne and Fern if they would bring her home—which they did. I used a roast lunch to bribe them into bringing Britt home. Just kidding. They have been very helpful in getting her from point A to B and back again.

This week looks like it will be another busy one. Britt's teams have games I want to watch, I need to spend a few days before the tenth at a client's office, helping with bookkeeping, and I have a board meeting in Anadarko Wednesday. Helping Jeff with just about everything is very time consuming. I feel a constant battle for my time. He's very weak, and every task seems to take about three times as long as it should and that doesn't leave much time for work. Please pray that our scheduling will work out. Pray that Jeff will gain strength and stamina to be able to go with me on some of my taxi runs so that we won't need anyone to sit with him while I'm gone. As I have asked before, please pray that I will have patience and peace. I struggle with whether I can handle my customary tax load this year. This could be a great time for God to shine. Please pray that I don't get in the way. Pray that God will guide my decision making so that I will have peace in that area as well.

So many people have been generous with cooking, cards, and calls. I don't know where to start other than to say "thank you."

02/07/11 (Monday), 7:35PM-Karen

The home health nurse, Tessa, came today and tested Jeff's blood for the INR level. The numbers (1.9) show the blood is clotting quicker than his target that is closer to a 3. She also took a blood sample and took it to the lab in Weatherford. The results are sent to Lauren Binder, PA, in Hydro for her review. Even with the change in Jeff's blood pressure meds, the enzyme level is still elevated, so she has scheduled a CT Scan of Jeff's abdomen tomorrow at 7:00 AM. That is a little early, but that was when it would work for them, and she wanted to have it done before the next wave of snow.

While Jeff was at Mercy over Christmas, he had a PICC line placed. It's sort of a long-term IV that can stay in as long as it's needed. The dressing on that line has to be changed weekly using sterile procedures. The hospital staff will change that dressing tomorrow. Home health is working on a home visit solution of some kind so we don't have to go to the hospital each week for this procedure.

I received a message from the speech therapist wanting to set up a time to evaluate Jeff. I phone-tagged her back but haven't scheduled anything yet.

Jeff and I enjoyed a beautiful sunset this evening during supper. Britt is at another ball game. I hope to get some office/tax work done this evening. Since you are reading this, you know I'm not really working yet...I better get to it.

> Trust in the Lord with all thine heart; and lean not unto thine own understanding. In all thy ways acknowledge him, and he shall direct thy paths.
>
> Proverbs 3:5–6 (KJV)

02/11/11 (Friday), 11:44PM-Karen

Jeff had the CT scan of his abdomen on Tuesday. The results are a fatty liver, which accounted for the elevated enzyme levels, so Lauren readjusted the blood pressure meds back to the same dosage he was taking when he was released from Jim Thorpe Rehab on January 31. The CT also shows a blood clot in his abdomen. Low enough that the filter should catch it should it break loose. Lauren also increased Jeff's Coumadin level by doubling the dose to 4 mg on Tuesday. He took 3 mg on Wednesday and is back to 2 mg for the weekend. The INR level was tested today. It's better, but still not quite on target. The home health nurse will retest on Monday.

Along with a fatty liver and a blood clot, the written report from the CT indicated that Jeff also has pneumonia. I hadn't noticed any coughing or an increase in wheezing. It is a blessing that we have caught it early. He'll have injections (via PICC) for ten days. Again, we are thankful that Jeff has the PICC line, which makes giving the meds and drawing blood for the INR tests easier. Because the liver wasn't the problem with the bleeding that sent us to the ER last week, Lauren has referred Jeff to Dr. Michael Winters (gastroenterology department) at Deaconess Hospital in OKC. Jeff's scheduled for a colonoscopy on Tuesday. Usually, patients on Coumadin are taken off of the anti-clotting drug for this procedure, but given the clot situation, Jeff will stay on the Coumadin. All this means is that if the procedure reveals any issues that need to be resolved, it will require a follow-up visit when Jeff could be off the Coumadin. Basically, it will allow the professionals the information they need to make an educated decision about the risks and benefits.

Home health has sent therapists to perform the initial evaluation for OT (occupational therapy), PT (physical therapy), and ST (speech therapy). The therapists may or may not be the same person who performed the initial evaluation. In all, I think we have seen six or seven different therapists this week, along with nurses who came three times this week. I trust that in a week or so, we will get some type of a schedule worked out so that we can plan our days. To say the least, this week has been a little hectic, especially with a snowstorm Tuesday night that dismissed school on Wednesday.

Jeff did get out with me on Monday and Thursday evenings for ball games. We planned our outings so that we only sat for one game to minimize the stress on Jeff. It was fun to be at the games and nice to be out of the house. I'm glad we pushed for the wheelchair—the ball games wouldn't have even been an option without it.

Please continue to keep Jeff's care in your prayers. Especially, pray for our witness to those who may be in our home two or three hours a week. What an opportunity to share how God has provided for us.

02/22/11 (Tuesday), 11:12PM-Karen

Where to start?

Physical Strength

Jeff has had home health therapy visits, and I think he's gaining a little on physical strength. He went with me to basketball games on Thursday and Saturday. Our ball teams were in district playoff games. Girls and boys won their first games, which earned them a place in the regional tournament, but lost on Saturday, which left them as district runner-up and a lower seed for next week's games. When we take the wheelchair, Jeff doesn't get too tired. Saturday, he watched the girls' game and then went to the car. He said he got in a good nap while I watched the boys' game. Sunday, he went with us to church, and we stayed for the potluck dinner. He napped in the car during Sunday school, and I brought him in for church and the dinner. His endurance is limited. I'm thankful he's willing to ride along and nap in the car so that I can still enjoy some of our old activities. During his physical therapy on Monday, his therapist commented that this was the first time he stood for all of his exercises! What a blessing that he's making some progress.

Lungs

In our last update, I spoke of the abdominal CT scan having signs of pneumonia. Jeff was given a round of the antibiotic Rocephin. This was a daily injection that was mixed with normal saline and then given over a thirty-minute time frame via the PICC line. Again, that PICC line came in handy. Last week, Jeff had a deep cough. Last Friday, the home health nurse listened to Jeff's lungs and heard some "rattles" that she noted in the report to Lauren. Lauren got the fax on Monday and wanted Jeff to be seen at a location that could take an image of his lungs to assess any pneumonia signs. So she sent us to the ER to have the INR level tested, the PICC line removed, and a chest x-ray to evaluate his lungs/pneumonia risks. The ER doctor, Dr. Lamb, said that the lungs are clear, and he did not hear anything unusual in Jeff's breathing.

Blood issues

Jeff's INR (that's interpreted "viscosity" for my brothers!) has been too low; now it's too high. He hasn't had Coumadin in two days in an effort to stabilize the numbers. His white blood cell counts are good, his blood oxygen level is good, but we can't seem to get the INR numbers to stay in the same range long enough to find the Coumadin dosage that will work. Friday, Lauren Binder wrote orders to have the PICC line removed. She's concerned that long-term, the PICC line could be the subject of infection issues. When we were at the hospital to have it removed, Jeff's blood INR was 3.85, so the ER doctor decided to leave the line in until the INR level was a little lower. There was a blood clot in Jeff's abdomen on the CT scan early February, but the chest x-ray shows his lungs are clear of both pneumonia and blood clots. The bottom number of Jeff's blood pressure has been running a little on the high side, so Lauren has again adjusted the blood pressure meds.

Brain MRI

Dr. Keefer's office called last week and set up an MRI for today, followed by an appointment with Dr. Keefer. The MRI seems to be about the same, just some slight variation in the intensity, but nothing Dr. Keefer was worried about. He believes this variance could be caused by the difference in the contrast dye/injection. A good report is always a blessing! Dr. Keefer has changed the Decadron steroid dosage. Jeff has been on 8 mg/day. For the next two weeks, that dosage will be 6 mg/day. The steroids are the cause for lots of frustration, so I'm definitely glad to see them taper off.

Colonoscopy

When we found out Jeff was scheduled for a colonoscopy, everyone told us the prep was the worst part—it was by far! Drinking the gallon of liquid was an almost-impossible task on its own, much less with steroids in the picture. Jeff's easygoing, laid-back personality was nowhere to be found. I set the timer on my phone for ten-minute intervals and brought out a fresh eightounce glass every time the alarm went off. He finished drinking the prep at midnight. As for the colonoscopy, the specialist suggested that Jeff would need another —in about 10 years! A good report!

Family

I got up Monday morning and felt so bad that I called Wayne to come take Brittany to school. I got Jeff a bowl of cereal and his morning pills, and I went back to bed. I slept most of the morning and part of the afternoon until about 2:00 p.m. and then only got up so that I could get Jeff to the ER for his chest x-ray and lab work. Lauren called in an antibiotic prescription for me, and I'm much better today. This has been a tough week. I'm trying to adjust to the added responsibilities of caring for Jeff and juggling our business responsibilities and family time. Some days caring for Jeff is a full-time job. I am little concerned I'm not doing very well with the juggling. It's mid-February, and I haven't even started on tax work yet. I think Brittany is frustrated with the whole situation. She's such a strong kid, but I know it has to be hard to come home from school every day to a house full of geriatric equipment and Dad on steroids.

But I *am* learning (learning a lot—with a lot left to learn) about dependence on God. For that, I'm thankful. When it seems I'm physically exhausted, run out of gas as it were, that's when God draws my attention to a hidden gas can that gives me a boost and gets me back on my way. I know He carefully placed or hid each of these gas cans for me before the foundation of the world, knowing exactly what I would need to get through each situation and what would encourage me at each moment along my journey (Psalm 139:16). Sometimes that gas can is a song or a verse, and occasionally a card in the mail from a friend. Tonight's gas can was Brittany playing a classical version of "It Is Well with My Soul" on the piano, her offertory for the first Sunday in March. What a calming old hymn, composed out of extreme sadness. God knows exactly what I need even before I need it. I think sometimes I get all the way to the point of frustration before I remember to turn it over to Him (1 Corinthians 10:13). Only when I turn it over to Him can I experience His peace for that situation in its fullest measure.

While we were at the ball game Saturday, a lady came up and introduced herself. She had parked by our vehicle (my accounting logo was on the side of my Yukon) and said she had to come find us and introduce herself. I'm glad she did. It's nice to hear that people are following our story and that they are drawn into what God is doing in our lives. They "keep up" with us either through a friend, a family member, the e-mail updates, word of mouth, or church prayer lists. Please pray that God will continue to receive the glory through our story.

Please pray that we'll have the mental and physical strength needed for this journey. Pray that God will get credit for what He is doing in our lives and for the many blessings that he sends our way. Please pray that Jeff will be motivated to get up and move without our prompting. I know activity will lead to more energy, and more energy will lead to more activity. Please pray that our family can remain close during such stressful times, and that we can reflect Christ's kindness—especially to those we live with (1 Timothy 5:8).

Thank you for your faithful prayers.

> All the days ordained for me were written in your book before one of them came to be.
>
> Psalm 139:16b (NIV)

> No temptation has seized you except what is common to man. And God is faithful; he will not let you be tempted beyond what you can bear. But when you are tempted, he will also provide a way out so that you can stand up under it.
>
> 1 Corinthians 10:13 (NIV)

> If anyone does not provide for his relatives, and especially for his immediate family, he has denied the faith and is worse than an unbeliever.
>
> 1 Timothy 5:8 (NIV)

03/06/11 (Sunday), 1:17AM-Karen

Some days Jeff gains a little on strength and endurance, and some days I think he just holds his own. The PICC line was taken out on Tuesday. He saw all the regular therapists this week and the PT supervisor and will see the OT supervisor next week to check his progress/improvement. Jeff was able to do more of his physical therapy standing and less in a sitting position this week. The wound seems to be about the same size. He has finished all the antibiotics prescribed for the bacteria in the wound. I'm hopeful that will accelerate healing. He's still having some bladder issues they're treating with medication. Those issues seem to be one of our biggest battles right now.

Jeff, Britt, and I went to the state basketball playoff games on Thursday and Saturday. On Thursday, Corn Bible Academy girls played at one thirty, and the Hydro boys played at seven. That made for a very long day. He stayed home on Friday but went with us again today. He used the wheelchair for getting around at all the games. For two games, we got him out of the wheelchair, and he sat in a regular chair. The chair didn't have arms, so getting him up after the games was a little bit of a challenge. Thanks to those who lent a hand. At least he had enough drive to want to go with us. He uses his walker to get to the car, and then we use the wheelchair while we are away. Our church had a youth group member on both of these teams. FYI: CBA girls won state!

One of the biggest challenges right now seems to be the massive amount of time Jeff's care takes. We really don't do anything in a hurry anymore, and about everything he wants to do or needs to do requires help. Please pray that God will provide the patience and physical endurance that is required of me.

As I reread this post, things sound a little negative. I wish that wasn't the case. That just seems to be where we are this week.

03/19/11 (Saturday), 1:59AM-Karen

Our lives seem to be moving so fast, so full of activity, and yet to me, they still seem like they are on hold. We seem to have a lot of busyness that occupies our time: therapy visits, softball, tax season, church activities, that list goes on, but it doesn't seem "normal."

Before Jeff's original surgery in September 2009, we were all busy. Jeff had his interests, and I had some of my own, and of course, some activities where we were all involved. Brittany had a busy student schedule, but there were two drivers to get her where she needed to be. Since Jeff's second surgery in July, we have been a one-driver family. I'm blessed to have my in-laws and a few friends as chauffeurs to get Britt to and from her activities.

Jeff has two visits per week from each of the physical, occupational, and speech therapists (total of six) and one or two visits from the home health nurse. I'm glad they are set up to come to our house so we don't have to "go" to their locations. At this point, that much travel would be exhausting for Jeff. I know the physical therapy is working, although at times I think that just means Jeff maintains his strength. The gain seems to be so slow that I don't see the progress until someone who hasn't seen him in a while gives us a reality check and confirms the improvement. He's still not motivated to exercise or do any extra work that would increase his strength. I have trouble deciding when to tell him to "push on" and when to let it all slide.

Obviously, it's tax season, which equates to my "harvest" time. Brittany has received medical clearance to play slow-pitch softball only. Jeff went with me to Fort Cobb last Saturday to watch the team play in a tournament. I took along the foldout tent/canopy, and we used it for a couple of games to keep Jeff in the shade. He watched the last game from the car. It was a beautiful day, just a little windy. As we've been doing anytime we leave the house, Jeff used the wheelchair. Pushing it through grass was a bit of a workout for me.

Jeff's wound from early November has still not healed and continues to require a fresh dressing every day. My midlife crisis occupational change may be to nursing—probably *not*.

We had a bit of a scare on Tuesday morning, but before I elaborate and tell the whole story, I want you to know that the CT scan that Jeff ended up having showed no bleeding.

Since Britt was out of school for spring break, we were taking the morning quite a bit slower than usual. I was getting everything to the table for Jeff to have a bowl of cereal for breakfast and told him it was ready and he could head toward the kitchen. As he started toward the kitchen, he either dropped his glass of tea (shouldn't have been trying this juggling act with a walker), or bumped the table with the walker and knocked it over. After the tea spilt, he tried to bend over and pick up the glass and ice. He lost his balance and fell backward. On his way down, he hit the coffee table with his head. I think I might have been there before he hit. I saw the fall coming, and it seemed to be in slow motion. As soon as he hit the floor, he reached for his head with both hands. When he pulled his hands away, they were both covered in blood, so I grabbed the back of his head where I thought the blood was and put pressure on it and hollered at Britt to bring me some towels to use to catch the blood and put pressure on his head. There was enough blood I had Brittany call the Hydro first responders. Their response time had to be a record of some kind. Later we found out that one of the guys was just a few miles away at one of their farms (what a blessing that God put him there at that time!), and he got a head start (no pun intended).

I have to take a short pause for a public service announcement now: Hydro has a fantastic, all-volunteer fire department and first responder unit. These men leave their jobs in town, put their other responsibilities on hold, drop everything else to help their friends, neighbors, and fellow townspeople when they get an emergency call. A lot of these men are second- and third-generation businessmen. They join the ever-growing list of people God has used to help our family. A side note to ponder: how many of the men and women who are often given the title "heroes" would continue to do their jobs if they were not paid? Your generosity with your time is something that isn't taken lightly. Thank you!

Okay, back to the point. The first responders found that the cut was on the top of Jeff's head, not on the back where I was putting pressure. (Hidden blessing: Very rarely do I miss giving Jeff his medication on time. I have tried to be very diligent about his medications, but I had missed Jeff's Coumadin pill the night before, which left his blood a little thicker than it would have been if all the pills had been taken as directed.) An ambulance from Weatherford also arrived but really didn't need to do anything. The bleeding had stopped pretty quickly. Jeff stayed alert the whole time. The men helped get Jeff up off the floor and into his chair. When the first responders left, we believed that was the end of the story, but....

After Britt called the first responders, but before they arrived, one of the therapists called; she wanted to check and make sure that we were home and tell us she was on her way. At that time, I was sure we would be headed to the ER to get stitches of some kind, so I explained the situation and cancelled the session. After she notified the home health office, they notified the doctor's office, and we heard from the home health nurse that Lauren wanted Jeff to have a CT scan. Because he's taking the blood thinner Coumadin and had the bump to the head, it's customary to have a CT scan to determine if there is internal bleeding. So… off to the ER? Not so quick. Jeff refused to go. I know that since we were in the ER waiting room for five hours last time he was there; he just didn't want to go. Before he could argue too long, one of the men from our church arrived to drop off some papers. His timing—or more accurately, God's timing—was perfect. I didn't have to take all the heat for forcing Jeff to go to the ER. Only a couple hours on this trip and the results were good: less swelling than the last scan and no indication of any bleeding.

Just as his physical strength is an outward gauge of his physical progress, his inability to maintain his focus and hold his thoughts together long enough to carry on a conversation is a constant reminder of the damage done and the long road of recovery ahead. Occasionally, he's able to grasp all the words and convey his thoughts. Many times, though, we are left guessing what he wanted to say—a very tiring task for all involved. To the visitor, this speech aphasia is easy to write off as a one-time issue. We have all had times when we can't find the right word we want to say. With Jeff, though, it's almost a constant hurdle with every conversation.

This morning, just before dawn, we had very dear friends show up to spray our yard for weeds. No wind and an absolutely perfect morning for the task. The sausage biscuits we shared for breakfast after they finished were a very futile attempt at saying "Thanks." Again, our unwritten list grows as God continues to use others to be His hands and feet to provide for our family.

People often ask me personally, how am I holding up, how am I doing? To be honest (and I have tried to be), the only way I know to describe how I am is to say "I'm tired, both physically and mentally." I know when I'm at my weakest, God's provision for me is the most visible. The little Sunday school song "Jesus Loves Me" says it pretty well: "They are weak, but he is strong." I need to remember daily that regardless of my age, size, or even my own parental status, I'm nonetheless one of God's "little ones." I'm welcome to climb in the lap of my Heavenly Father and daily find rest.

> "Come to me, all you who are weary and burdened, and I will give you rest. Take my yoke upon you and learn from me, for I am gentle and humble in heart, and you will find rest for your souls. For my yoke is easy and my burden is light."

> Matthew 11:28–30 (NIV)

According to *my* schedule of plans for *my* life, I have Jeff scheduled for more independence and clear thinking very soon. But I still trust that according to God's plan for our lives, there is a reason, or maybe even multiple reasons, for this precise combination of challenges, and that *His* timing and *His* plans are absolutely perfect.

As always, thanks for the prayer.

Maple Lawn Manor

03/23/11 (Wednesday), 1:16PM-Karen

Once again, we're in the ER.

This morning, just before eight, Jeff had a couple seizures back-to-back at home, which required an ambulance trip to Weatherford. Currently, he's still in the ER, but I expect this setback to cause yet another hospital stay. They have done the usual things: pulled blood, ran an EKG, and took chest X-rays and CT scans. No results yet.

The best way to describe the seizures is to say that he makes a motor sound similar to a groan and then loses consciousness. After that passes, he regains eye control but doesn't speak. Right now he responds to his name by opening his eyes briefly, only to see who is speaking, and then he drifts off to sleep again, but he hasn't said anything yet. After some of the seizures, it has taken several days for things to reset, so to speak.

The ER doctor said that the CT did not show anything new, so that is a good report. Jeff seems to be having some mini seizures now.

Thank you for your continued prayers. You are lifting our concerns to God, and that is more effective than even the most diligent doctors.

03/23/11 (Wednesday), 10:34PM-Karen

The report from the CT scan was good. They want to keep Jeff overnight to make sure he's stable. The ER doctor increased his Keppra (antiseizure) med starting tomorrow morning. Jeff's brother Randy came and stayed for a while this afternoon and evening. That allowed me to spend a few hours in my office. Thanks for checking on Jeff.

03/24/11 (Thursday), 9:54PM-Karen

Our Journey Continues: Jeff was released from the hospital today. However, he still needs physical, occupational, and speech therapy similar to what he was receiving at home. The seizure and required med changes have no doubt set him back. Even before this last round of seizures, Jeff's constant need for care was challenging my physical abilities. Clearly stated, Jeff needs more care than I can provide by myself at home. When Jeff was released from Weatherford Regional, he was moved to Maple Lawn Manor in Hydro.

This facility comes highly recommended, and many of the long-term employees are local people who have a history of truly caring for the residents. Location, location, location may be the number one factor in sales, but when finding a nursing facility to move a family member into, their care should be very high on the priority list. We looked at Maple Lawn in January. At that time, most parties involved believed that the additional therapy at Jim Thorpe was what Jeff needed more than location. Now the wound care is our priority, but Jeff also needs the other therapies. I do believe this is a good decision in Jeff's ongoing care.

Although it seems things are moving fast, this has not been a quick decision. Brittany and I have prayerfully contemplated this decision for some time and believe this is a good decision. I wanted to schedule a visit with Lauren about our options but didn't make the time—most likely procrastination. Once again, God's timing is perfect, and I know he has already prepared Brittany and me for this time.

Please pray for a peaceful transition from the hospital to the nursing home and for God to continue to use this situation to draw others closer to Him. Pray that God will provide ample peace for each of us as we move forward as we believe God directs us.

Jeff's in a "swing bed" similar to the nursing situation at Jim Thorpe in January. He should be able to get all the therapy and extra nursing that I haven't been able to provide.

After dropping off Jeff's wheelchair and walker and a few other personal items, I went to Brittany's softball game. Today was her first time to start in a high school game. I thought she did great, but I might be a little biased.

Once again, as I close another update, I'm reminded of what has become our family's favorite verse: Jeremiah 29:11 (NIV): *"For I know the plans I have for you," declares the Lord. "Plans to protect you and not to harm you, plans to give you hope and a future."*

Karen Remembers:
God's Preparation

When Brittany was a toddler, we often joked she had more friends that lived at the nursing home than she had her own age. Jeff's grandfather, Val Krehbiel, was a resident of Maple Lawn Manor when Brittany was born. Several years later, Jeff's greatuncle was a resident. Grandma Fern often took Britt with her when she went for visits. I believe even then God was preparing Brittany for the events that would lie ahead.

03/29/11 (Tuesday), 11:13PM-Karen

Maple Lawn has reached an agreement with our insurance company for Jeff's care, including his medications, nursing, physical therapy, occupational therapy, and speech therapy. There is no other way to describe it than to say that the first few days were rough. Jeff kept asking, "How long do I have to stay here?" Hopefully, we have made a few cosmetic changes that will make his room a little more like home, and maybe a little more cheery. On Saturday, Jeff's dad and a couple of our farm employees delivered the "sleep-infested" La-Z-boy, and on Saturday evening, Brittany and I took a few Oklahoma State decorations for the walls and a few pictures.

Today Jeff was far more alert than he had been at any time since his seizures last Wednesday. I don't know what to attribute that to: if it's because he's getting some clarity back after the seizures or if he has readjusted to the different medicine times/ routines. It was good to ask questions and actually get answers. We'll take the improvement as a blessing. They have a new wound care routine for Jeff that should keep his wound cleaner and promote healing. They have added vitamin C and zinc to his daily meds list in a specific effort to promote wound healing. They are using a different packing medium that basically melts, leaving the medication in the wound.

They are trying to keep Jeff rotated every couple hours, but he's stubborn and just wants to lie on his back. He isn't getting out of bed much at all, and hasn't even wanted to sit in his recliner. When I encourage him to sit in his chair or get out of bed and use the walker, he gets defensive and just wants me to leave him alone.

They bring all of his meals to his room, and he doesn't seem to have any desire to get up and move—at least no desire yet. He left the room, via wheelchair, yesterday to get a shower, but that absolutely wore him out. It's discouraging to see Jeff's physical ability decrease, because of lack of physical activity. The nursing home administrator told me that therapy evaluations would start today, and shortly after that, they will start his sessions: two sessions for each therapy type per week, which is what he had with home health before his seizures last week.

On a personal note: Brittany got her driver's permit today. She and I are both excited. Now, even though I will have to be in the car with her, at least I'm not the only one that can drive.

Thanks for checking on Jeff, and I will try to keep you posted every few days.

Please pray that God will provide good, clear guidance I can follow as I seek to make good decisions for our family, our businesses, and, of course, Jeff's care. I know that God has a plan, bigger than I can comprehend. I want to make choices that conform to that greater plan. Above all, I want to be a good steward of the things, talents, and gifts (blessings) God has given me. In other words, it's all God's, and I want to be a good trustee...(See Matthew 25:15–20: *the parable of the Talents.*)

04/03/11 (Sunday), 11:10PM-Karen

I have been to the Manor to visit Jeff at least a little while each day. It's hard to juggle activities and schedule downtime to just sit and watch TV with him. He's definitely more alert the last few days than a week ago. He has trouble carrying on a conversation. Aphasia, as it's called, is trouble in word selection. You almost have to know what he wants to say before he speaks. I noticed this evening that Jeff wanted to discuss something about church, but he used the words *sheep* and *equipment* instead. Brittany saw the connection he wanted to make and was able to guess the correct words and repeat back to him what she thought he wanted to say. Sometimes that process works; sometimes what we guess isn't what he wants to say and causes him to further lose his train of thought.

He isn't getting out of bed much, and he's losing any strength he had in his legs. I wish he could make the connection between physical activity and strength for things he wants to do. I may have to look into a TV that only runs when you peddle a bike. Sounds like the answer to an overweight society, doesn't it? It would work similar to a hand crank radio. Maybe that can be my first million.

We have tried to take a few OSU items along so that he can have something fun on his walls. I'm not sure if that is really for his benefit or ours.

Jeff saw the physical therapist on Wednesday to evaluate his PT (physical therapy) needs. I happened to be there when she was trying to get Jeff to sit up on the edge of the bed for part of the evaluation. He wanted no part of that. He told her she could try another day, but he wasn't going to do that on that day. Jeff has always been a little stubborn, but it seems to be even more pronounced lately. If he doesn't want to do it, he won't. That strong personality that was attractive twenty years ago isn't near as attractive when it seems to be working against his healing.

For now, I continue to trust that God has a purpose in this set of obstacles. We continue to pray for Jeff's healing and that he could be free of the speech limitations that hinder his ability to carry on a meaningful conversation, while, hopefully, allowing God whatever room He needs to work in this situation to bring honor and glory unto Himself. What an awesome God we serve, able to do abundantly more than we can ask or think (Ephesians 3:20–21). And believe me, I'm asking and thinking plenty. I know the peace God's giving during Jeff's illness is more valuable than a lifetime of perfect health without His guidance and peace.

This road that we are traveling seems to have lots of twists and turns. I feel a relief physically from allowing others to provide the physical care for Jeff. But still, I feel drawn to spend time with Jeff at the Manor—a precious commodity right now. Please pray that Jeff will be patient with us when we aren't able to be with him and that when we are with him, our time together can be enjoyable for each of us.

I took Jeff his cell phone this week, and he seems to be able to answer it, and even returned a call this morning when he missed a call from his brother. He often gets his remote to the TV, his nurse call button, and the remote to operate his bed confused. Sometimes he calls the nurse when he really just wants to change the channel. Sometimes he raises the bed when he wants to call the nurse. So I have been reluctant to add his cell phone to the mix. Hopefully, he'll be able to use the phone well enough to answer when people call him.

Seeing negative change is emotionally hard. I remember the brilliant man I married (I might be biased). He could fix anything, design irrigation systems, discuss politics and agricultural issues, was a problem solver on several boards, could fix my computer, and was interested in Brittany's sports and school activities— and that was all before lunch on any given day. To see him now struggling with expressing his thoughts in even the simplest of conversations is hard. Having God carry us is invaluable. As I've said before, on many occasions, I don't know how anyone would be able to do this without God's help. Our faith in Christ Jesus allows us to see an eternal aspect to these trials that those with Christ cannot understand.

Please continue to pray we'll be bold to share our faith, our story, and our hope with others who cross our paths.

Thanks for checking on us and thanks especially for the many, many prayers you offer on our behalf.

> Now unto him that is able to do exceeding abundantly
> above all that we ask or think, according to the power that

worketh in us, Unto him be glory in the church by Christ
Jesus throughout all ages, world without end. Amen.

Ephesians 3:20–21(KJV)

04/17/11 (Sunday), 11:22PM-Karen

Whew! We survived tax season! I apologize for the two-week gap
in updates. Please be patient with me—no news on CarePages can
probably be interpreted as good news or, at a minimum, that things are
relatively the same. You're so faithful to read and check on us, and pray.
I feel like I take advantage of you when I don't post.

Jeff's getting physical and occupational therapy. I don't think he's
getting any speech therapy. I will try to follow up on that this week. He
seems more alert and participates in conversations a little more than he
did a couple weeks ago.

Big news this week for Jeff's dad: On Wednesday, he was presented
with the Oklahoma Governor's Award for distinction in agriculture and
inducted into the Oklahoma Agricultural Hall of Fame! He's only the
fourteenth individual to receive this honor. We're very proud. Jeff had
schemed with his dad and was interested in attending the ceremony. I
was left to be the bad guy and object to his leaving the Manor for such a
big outing. I know he wanted to go; I wasn't sure that Jeff could endure
the physical demands of the trip.

You would think that was enough excitement for one day, but
Wednesday evening, the Oklahoma Wheat Commissioners came to
Hydro to the Manor and presented the Krehbiel family with their
highest award—the Staff of Life award. What an honor!

Britt's ball team is still playing slow-pitch softball and won their
district. Now their districts aren't scheduled until this coming week,
but the other two teams don't have enough players, so Hinton wins by
default and moves on in playoffs. More regularseason games this week
in place of tournament play. Their team is pretty good this year, and I
think they are looking forward to the challenges ahead.

Saturday, Brittany and I drove to Kremlin and saw my family. All of my immediate family and their spouses were there, except Jeff. It was fun to get to do something besides taxes for a change.

Thanks for all your prayers. I ask that you pray for Jeff's motivation to improve and for him to want to be up and moving around on a regular basis—not just when physical therapy comes by.

This week, I seem to be getting a lot of comments concerning my perceived strength. That is a big compliment, but I need to set the record straight: It isn't me that's strong—I'm just a weak little lamb. On my own, I would be devoured by the wolves that surround us. It's my Lord, the Shepherd (Psalm 23) who is my source of strength. Again, songs from my childhood are a comfort. The song "Jesus Loves Me," while widely accepted as a children's song, has great truth for adults too: "They are weak, but He is strong."

Pray that we can be faithful to witness to those God puts in our path.

04/23/11 (Saturday), 7:40PM-Karen

On Tuesday, when I went to visit, Jeff's occupational therapist came. Part of Jeff's therapy is to use his own strength to get himself to the therapy room. So she talked him through putting on pants, putting on his shoes, standing up, and getting in his wheelchair; and then he used his hands and feet to maneuver down the halls. It was good to see him making progress in the area of physical strength. I see glimmers of his old personality, and they are so very welcomed after such a long stretch without them. His speech continues to cause frustration for most of us. He starts a lot of conversations but isn't always able to finish them. When I go by after he's had a full day, the aphasia seems to be even worse. Often I catch myself offering the words I think he's searching for. I'm not sure if that's the right thing to do. If I would hold off on giving him the words, would we be better off in the long run? Would his mind eventually forge pathways to the missing words? Or would that be mean—to make him hunt for words I could guess? Maybe that's another area on which to focus prayer.

Jeff has had several visitors this week and is able to enjoy the short visits with friends and family. Thanks for the cards, calls, and especially the prayers.

04/28/11 (Thursday), 9:12PM-Karen

Jeff had an appointment with Lauren Binder yesterday. Instead of the hassle of getting Jeff to her office, she made a "Manor call." It kind of reminded me of all those episodes of *Little House on the Prairie* where they send for Doc Baker, and he would hitch up the surrey and make a house call. I'm certain Lauren's trip didn't involve livestock, but once again, her thoughtfulness and caring spirit are apparent. I'm reminded of how blessed we are to have her overseeing Jeff's care. It's fun to live in the suburbs of what my Uncle Jimmie might call a one-horse town.

Lauren said she definitely sees that Jeff has made progress but that he still has a long way to go. His blood work looks good, and his INR level is where they want it to stay. She said she had a pretty good conversation, but at least twice, he was midsentence and couldn't find the word needed to finish a sentence. She said his spirits seemed good, and he told her about what was going on with Britt and me. Some of his facts were not correct in the story he told her. It was kind of like playing telephone where you pass a secret around a circle and then compare the gossiped story with what was told to start the game. What she told me he said was nowhere near the original story I told him last Friday. At least his inaccurate story was humorous.

Jeff's scheduled for an oncologist appointment in OKC next Friday to have labs drawn and then see a new physician's assistant. I expressed a little concern with seeing a new PA after nineteen months into this journey. I was assured that Dr. Keefer was working that day and would be able to pop in to see Jeff. I asked about whether Jeff was due for another MRI. They want to see him first and then make the decision on when to have an MRI. Initially, I planned to take Jeff to that appointment, but Lauren strongly encouraged me to let the Maple Lawn staff take care of Jeff's transportation.

God keeps putting in our path people who ask about Jeff; each one is an opportunity to share our story of God's provision

and care. We are so blessed to have such a wonderful support crew (that includes each of you) continually holding us up in prayer. It's been a few months since I reminded everyone that this is not something I see as survivable without Christ. The peace that's ours by accepting Christ as the sacrifice for our sins allows us to accept each day as a blessing from God and then use the opportunity to reach others with the Good News. (I still need help in that area. It sounds good in theory, but my actions don't always follow through to witness.)

> But sanctify the Lord God in your hearts: and be ready always to give an answer to every man that asketh you a reason of the hope that is in you with meekness and fear:
>
> 1 Peter 3:15 (KJV)

05/04/11 (Wednesday), 11:18PM-Karen

Oh, how I miss the good ole days when Jeff was the farmer and irrigation specialist, and I was the accountant. All businesses have their quirks and ours is no different. Owning your own businesses are, as the TV character Monk would put it, "a blessing…and a curse." In the economic times our country is experiencing, I'm thankful that we are able to make payroll each week and pay the mortgages.

Jeff's still interested in activity, but his energy level and physical ability dictate that his actual involvement is almost nonexistent. I know there are literally hundreds of people lifting us in prayer. I know prayers are being answered because we are surviving. However, "thrive" always seems to be just beyond grasp.

My conservative personality traits—the ones that made accounting look good as a career, the traits that push for order, balance, planning, and advance notice—those traits are being challenged by the unknowns of farming: drought, production variables, yield, the flexibility of when harvest will start, and how to plan harvest around fixed commitments. I'm definitely out of my comfort zone.

Imagine with me: A player says, "Put me in, Coach!" He's anxious to play and gets in the game, only to realize that not only did the rules change, but he's been traded to another franchise to play a totally different sport. As I continue to learn the aspects of the businesses that Jeff had always handled, I feel a little bit like that player. And regardless of my skill level at my old sport, I constantly battle the legitimacy of my rapid promotion to start for the new team. Some of this conflict is external, and some is internal. Just as quality athletes often excel in multiple sports because the basic athletic skill set is the same, I have no doubt basic business skills will be adaptable from managing an accounting business to managing a farm. However, I know there will still be a lot to learn.

Please pray I will quickly grasp the concepts needed to be a good steward of the farms and irrigation business that God has entrusted to us and that with God's guidance, our businesses will "thrive" in spite of the challenges in our path.

Brittany's softball team found out last Thursday that they are the Oklahoma Class 4A Softball Academic State Champions. Their softball team had the highest grade point average of all the 4A softball teams in the state. Way to go, Lady Comets! The team went to watch the games. I slid in this afternoon in time to watch their presentation.

On Saturday, the Hinton FFA Agricultural Communications Team competed in the State FFA contests in Stillwater. Individually, Brittany placed ninth out of about seventy participants. As a team, they placed third in the state. This week, she found out that the first two teams actually tied for first and that the Hinton team was only one point away from their scores. So third it is! Way to go, Ag Comm Team! This was Britt's first year to compete in Ag Communications, so we are still learning. She's improving her skills, and I'm learning the things moms should know. The contests involve editing articles, providing critique for judged photos and logos, as well as a written test.

Sunday morning, Britt played the offertory at church. She played a medley of "Fill My Cup, Lord" based on John 4:9–13 and "It's

Beginning to Rain." The central theme of both songs is allowing God to provide for our needs and a willingness to accept His provision. Once again, I see such pain and honesty in writers' lives to be able to compose songs and hymns. I have found myself humming both of the choruses.

Jeff's gaining endurance. He still has a long way to go. He's out of bed for thirty minutes in the morning, thirty minutes in the afternoon for therapy, and about thirty minutes for showers on Mondays, Wednesdays, and Fridays. Strength and endurance are things you have to use up completely before you can get more. Pray he'll want to do more activity so he'll improve his stamina and agility. Jeff goes to OKC for an appointment with Dr. Keefer's office on Friday. I plan to take him, but we will have someone from the Manor traveling with us to help me with logistics.

Pray God will grant wisdom to Jeff's medical team, that they will accurately assess his progress and the treatment he needs or doesn't need at this point.

Jeff's dad celebrated his eightieth birthday on Tuesday. Happy birthday, Wayne. Hope you have a great year ahead.

GALL BLADDER TROUBLE

05/08/11 (Sunday), 12:15PM-Karen

Jeff's in the ER this morning with abdominal pain that started Thursday evening.

When I went to get Jeff on Friday morning, the staff at the Manor said he wasn't feeling well, that he was complaining of a pain below his ribs on his right side. He had refused both occupational and physical therapies. So there was some question as to whether he should make the scheduled appointment. After weighing the pros and cons of the matter with the director of nursing and the administrator, a member of the Manor staff and I did take Jeff to OKC so that he could have his appointment with Dr. Keefer's PA.

They really just pulled blood work and caught up their records with current meds and what has changed since he was there in February. They reasoned away his abdominal pain as gas but ordered a urine sample to check for infection. Jeff was pretty lethargic all day, dozing when he could, and he didn't want to eat and wasn't watching TV (that should have been a major red flag). He ran a little fever on Friday, but it seemed to go down and stay down with Tylenol.

All the blood results were within the "normal" range. Sometimes it's nice to be normal. Jeff's scheduled to have an MRI on May 24 and then see Dr. Keefer in about a month.

Each week a different church in town has the morning service at Maple Lawn. This was our church's week to be in charge. Britt and I went early so that I could help Jeff get dressed and down the hall to the commons area for the service. When I started down the hall to Jeff's room, a member of the staff stopped me to tell me that Jeff was still having pain. I went on down to Jeff's room. He and I visited a little, and he didn't think he felt up to going to the church service. All of a sudden, he started having sharp pains in his upper abdomen. The nurse called Dr. Stutzman and she said to get him to the ER. I brought him in my car. They are still in the assessment stage of the process. They have given him pain meds (I think this is the first time he has asked for drugs since this journey began.) They have drawn blood and are working on an x-ray and a CT scan.

Please pray the doctor and experts can determine the cause of Jeff's pain.

05/09/11 (Monday), 11:42AM-Karen

I spoke with Dr. Jackson, Lauren Binder, and the anesthesiologist. Surgery was scheduled for this morning but has been postponed until tomorrow morning. Since December, Jeff's been taking Coumadin to regulate the clotting time of his blood. Today's INR level was too high (over 3), meaning that Jeff's blood would take too long to clot. According to Dr. Jackson, they will give him FFP (fresh frozen plasma) to shorten the clot time and lower the risk of uncontrolled bleeding during the surgery. The FFP is a blood product and, as such comes with some risks.

They will try to complete the surgery laproscopically to minimize Jeff's recovery time and discomfort.

Jeff's getting IV antibiotics and pain meds today, and he's on a clear liquid diet until after surgery.

Thanks for keeping up with Jeff.

05/10/11 (Tuesday), 9:54AM-Karen

Surgery has been cancelled. This morning's INR test shows Jeff's blood is still too thin for surgery. IRN was still 2.1. Dr. Jackson said Jeff's improving while on the IV antibiotic. Although he believes the gall bladder will eventually have to come out, he doesn't want to subject Jeff to a surgery if it can safely be avoided—for now.

Jeff will stay in the hospital today to continue the antibiotics and liquid diet.

I was reminded yesterday of 1 Thessalonians 5:18, which discusses giving thanks in everything. One person posted on CarePages yesterday that the postponed surgery would allow more time to pray. Apparently, I still have a ways to go to automatically give thanks. Too often, my first response is selfish— frustration with loss of *my* time, annoyance with changed plans, uncertainty about tomorrow's plans...and I have to get past that to a point where I can find things to be thankful for. When I make a conscious effort, I *can* see the blessings of time, quality healthcare, insurance, friends, church family, prayer warriors, and give thanks.

> In every thing give thanks: for this is the will of God in
> Christ Jesus concerning you.
>
> 1 Thessalonians 5:18 (KJV)

05/12/11 (Thursday), 10:31PM-Karen

Jeff's settled back in at Maple Lawn. He called me this morning and said they were releasing him. After I confirmed with the hospital and the nursing home, I served as taxi driver to get Jeff from the hospital back to the Manor. He wanted real food, and after I confirmed he could have a regular diet, we made a side trip through Sonic. Don't tell anyone, though, because after we got him to the Manor, the nurse read the discharge paperwork that we had been carrying with us. Turns out, Jeff's on a low-fat diet.

I'm certain the Super Sonic with Cheese is *not* on the low-fat menu. Jeff said it tasted really good. At least I didn't knowingly go against the doctor's orders.

Jeff's still on antibiotics and seems to be comfortable. He has some pain, but it seems to be manageable. Based on an ultrasound of Jeff's abdomen, Dr. Jackson believes he's still seeing progress from the antibiotic, so he wants to hold off on surgery for now. He seemed to expect gall bladder surgery at some point (and so do I, except for divine intervention), but not this week.

Thanks for the many prayers offered for our family. God still seems to be answering. What a blessing that given Jeff's weakened state, he isn't facing recovery from another surgery right now.

05/16/11 (Monday), 4:03PM-Karen

Jeff's headed back to ER with severe abdominal pain and rectal bleeding. Maple Lawn called me when the decision was made to take him to the ER. I left home right away and beat them to the ER. I will know more when he gets here.

05/16/11 (Monday), 8:06PM-Karen

Jeff was released from the ER and is back at the Manor. They gave him a prescription for pain, and we are to follow up with Lauren Binder and/or Dr. Jackson tomorrow about the gall bladder. The bleeding had stopped by the time he was examined. The ER doctor believes the bleeding was from internal hemorrhoids that were a prior issue.

05/24/11 (Tuesday), 12:18AM-Karen

Jeff's still experiencing pain in his abdomen that still appears to be an irritated gall bladder. Because the pain flares up when he moves around, his participation in occupational and physical therapy has not been possible since his initial ER visit for his gall bladder on Mother's Day (May 8). Insurance coverage of Jeff's care at Maple Lawn has been conditional on his receiving that therapy. Because he hasn't had therapy, the insurance company gave us a May 9 cutoff of their payment for his care. I found out at 3:45 p.m. that same day. While the insurance representative seemed to agree that Jeff isn't strong enough to come home, she seemed adamant that because he wasn't well enough to participate in therapy, the insurance would no longer cover the costs of his care at the Manor. A couple of phone calls later, they agreed to cover his nursing care until this Tuesday (May 24) to allow Jeff to again see Dr. Jackson about the gall bladder and allow us more time to formulate a plan. Susan Dowman is our contact with the liaison group assigned by our insurance company shortly after Jeff was first diagnosed with cancer. She calls every two or three weeks to catch up on Jeff's situation and has offered suggestions and provided information from time to time. Susan was out of her office Thursday and Friday, but I was able to speak with her today. She was able to help facilitate a little longer time period for us to work on a plan for Jeff's care. Our new time frame is to have a plan for Jeff's care in place by Tuesday, May 31. So this week, the doctors, Maple Lawn, the Krehbiels, and the therapy staff will work on reevaluating Jeff's care. I hope they will be able to provide therapy for Jeff that won't irritate his gall bladder but will still meet the insurance requirements.

Also today, Jeff had an appointment with Dr. Jackson, the surgeon dealing with the gall bladder issue. He seems to be concerned that two weeks out, Jeff still has pain. He also seems concerned that surgery would carry some additional risks. Even laparoscopic surgery (if possible), would set Jeff back considerably in strength and recovery. He wanted to visit with our primary care physician (Lauren Binder, PA) today, and I expect to hear from Lauren and/or Dr. Jackson possibly tomorrow.

Jeff's MRI at Mercy is still scheduled for tomorrow morning, May 24. Because we need all available information to formulate a treatment plan for Jeff, I have asked for a phone update on the MRI as soon as the results are available—possibly as early as tomorrow afternoon.

These challenges with the insurance company are the first we've had, and I fully expect the bugs will be worked out and we'll be able to continue Jeff's care at the Manor. Again, I'm reminded of how blessed we are our insurance policy has covered all of Jeff's care to this point. Our only expenses have been our annual family deductible and our travel expenses. That's certainly a blessing worthy of thanks.

Today's humming has included the following:

Many things about tomorrow, I don't seem to understand
But I know who holds tomorrow
And I know he holds my hand.

I have no idea how or when I learned this song. "I Know Who Holds Tomorrow"[7] has powerful words—probably from a writer who experienced pain, sorrow, and uncertainty. Funny how God can turn circumstances for His glory!

05/27/11 (Friday), 10:02PM-Karen

After a day of challenges yesterday, it was decided to try giving Jeff pain meds on a scheduled basis in an attempt to allow him to finish his therapy sessions. I received a call from the Maple Lawn administrator late this afternoon: Jeff finished both of the therapy sessions and his shower today! We are definitely thankful for the good news.

SEIZURES, VENTILATOR, AND NEW GROWTH

05/29/11 (Sunday), 6:12AM-Karen

Once again, Jeff's in the ER for seizures. The night nurse for Maple Lawn called about 10:00 p.m.Saturday with information that Jeff had a seizure similar to those he has had in the past. Dr. Stutzman had been notified, and she had prescribed something to be used if he had another seizure. The nurse said he did speak to her after the seizure, which was reassuring. Britt and I headed to the Manor to see for ourselves.

When we arrived, Jeff was in the middle of a second seizure. Dr. Stutzman was again notified, and an ambulance was called. The seizure, or to my untrained eye, a series of seizures, lasted over an hour.

Early in that time frame, they inserted a breathing tube and transported Jeff to the local ER in Weatherford. Once he seemed to be coming out of the seizure and stable, and after what seemed like a few rounds of sedatives, they tried to remove the breathing tube. When they did, his oxygen level dropped. They transported Jeff to Mercy in OKC, where he'll be on a ventilator until Sunday or maybe Monday when they will test again to see if he can keep his oxygen level up while breathing on his own. I know God is in control. To the creator of the universe, there aren't any surprises, nor does he operate in panic mode. As a Christian, I believe that God micromanages and choreographs (if we let Him) each detail of our lives to equip us for the tasks that are in our path. I know He'll walk with us each step of the way.

Prayer is always welcome.

05/29/11 (Sunday), 9:51AM-Karen

Once at Mercy, we learned of the MRI results from May 24, Tuesday. There appears to be either new growth of the cancer or necrosis buildup again. The lobes of his brain have shifted a little more toward the right side. The doctor says the necrosis possibility is unlikely given the time distance from cancer treatment.

For now, the most pressing issue is the breathing tube and whether Jeff can be weaned off the tube today, tomorrow, or Tuesday.

05/29/11 (Sunday), 8:15PM-Karen

Jeff's still on the ventilator. He's getting 50 percent oxygen, and his O2 saturation is staying in the high 90s. When they start weaning him off, they will decrease the oxygen percentage and want to see Jeff maintain the high O2 saturation percentages. Update before I post: they just dropped the oxygen to 45 percent, and saturation is staying in the high 90. That is progress—slow, but progress.

Jeff had a CT scan this morning that shows there isn't any bleeding in his brain and that is a blessing.

Our primary care, Lauren Binder, took several mobile calls during the night and has called several times today to check on us. We are blessed that God has provided such a caring individual to help.

Randy will stay with Jeff in ICU tonight. Since I was up all night and have only slept intermittently during the day, I can go home and get some sleep.

05/29/11 (Sunday), 9:45PM-Karen

After resting quietly for most of the day, Jeff has had another seizure, lasting about twenty minutes.

05/30/11 (Monday), 2:45PM-Karen

Jeff seemed to rest well Sunday afternoon, but about nine last night, he had a seizure that lasted about twenty minutes. Then he rested during the night but has had three seizures this morning. The neurologist was by this morning, and he saw Dr. Grode (I think he's the internist) last night. Most of the doctors have seen Jeff before. The familiar faces are comforting.

The PICC line nurse was here this morning to place a line. The same lady, Carolyn, remembers Jeff from both Christmases. I wish Jeff could talk so he could harass her back this time. As she worked, we remembered the snowstorms the last two Christmases. Since Jeff's first diagnosis, she has placed four PICC lines. We spoke of snowstorms and tornadoes and spending holidays in the hospital. She has a relative's family of five living with her because they lost their home in last week's tornadoes. We don't have to look far to find someone affected by personal circumstances that cause stress and hardship. Jeff, Britt, and I don't have that market cornered on conflict—far from it. We have peace, and that makes us blessed. Her last comment was "Next time, let's meet at WalMart." I'm all for seeing familiar faces somewhere other than the hospital.

They have added a second antiseizure med in an effort to control Jeff's seizures—Cerebrex.

They are still hopeful to be able to wean Jeff from the ventilator soon. They want the seizures under control first.

05/31/11 (Tuesday), 1:02PM-Karen

Jeff's still in ICU at Mercy. He's still on the ventilator, and the respiratory therapists want to stair step him off of that soon. That would be fine with us, the sooner the better. I don't like the onesided conversations very well.

According to the neurologist, Dr. Mikawa, Jeff's Keppra (antiseizure) prescription was not entered correctly when he was admitted. It was recorded to be 500 mg twice a day. It should be 1500 mg twice a day. He had me confirm the dosage with Maple Lawn yesterday or the day before, so I don't believe that Jeff went very long with the incorrect dosage, but that may explain a few of the seizures. It would not explain what triggered the initial seizure while he was still at the Manor, but any of the seizures could easily be the result of the increased pressure in his brain that is reflected on the MRI. No blame, but glad he's now on the proper dosage.

Dr. Bova, the oncologist substituting for Dr. Keefer over the weekend, said that she has increased his steroid dosage to 4 mg four times a day. Prior to the ER visit, I believe he was on a total of 4 mg daily. The steroid Decadron will reduce the swelling/ pressure on his brain. We are waiting to visit with Dr. Keefer to get more case specific information about the MRI results and their interpretation for planning future treatment.

I continue to be thankful for our connection to Lauren Binder. Her personal experiences and medical knowledge, combined with her willingness to remain involved in Jeff's care, add tremendously to my mental comfort with the situation. However, I still give God the credit for placing her in our lives. The same could be said for each of our prayer warriors—I know God has hand-selected each one to be a part of our lives.

> In everything give thanks for this is the will of God in Christ Jesus concerning you.
>
> 1 Thessalonians 5:18 (KJV)

06/01/11 (Wednesday), 8:23AM-Karen

Dr. Keefer came by late afternoon. He reviewed the MRI results with Jeff's brother, Randy, and me. He pulled up the February MRI and compared it with the MRI from last year. He's confident that the new area of enhancement is new growth. It appears that the cancer is now growing on the right side of Jeff's brain. Until now, all the activity was on the left side. Dr. Keefer wanted Jeff's original surgeon, Dr. Reynolds, to review the MRI and give us the medical probability of debulking the growth using surgery. Within fifteen minutes after Dr. Keefer left Jeff's room, Dr. Reynolds called my cell phone. That conversation didn't yield anything new, but it was reassuring to have another set of trained eyes review the situation. Dr. Keefer did discuss briefly the possibility of a chemo treatment.

But the priority at this time is still to get Jeff off the ventilator. He hasn't had any seizures since Monday morning.

Early this afternoon, Jeff took advantage of an unrestrained hand and removed the nasal tube that was used for giving him some of his meds prior to yesterday. The good news is no harm done, and it won't have to be repositioned.

Please pray for wisdom for the medical personnel and for our family. It looks like we may face some tough decisions ahead.

06/01/11 (Wednesday), 6:39PM-Karen

Earlier today, they adjusted Jeff's air intake level down to 40 percent oxygen and 60 percent room air, and his oxygen saturation stayed in the high 90s. That's good news.

More recently, Dr. Adler from respiratory therapy came by about four this afternoon. After a general once-over, he gave orders to put Jeff on what he called "flow-by." This was to test how he would do on his own. He failed this test, but they have plans to try again in the morning. Dr. Adler also said that the size of the tube really isn't adequate for Jeff. Without pressure of the ventilation machine, it would be similar to breathing through a straw. So they hooked the ventilator back up. They want to run a scope down the breathing tube tomorrow morning to get a look at his lungs before they completely remove the ventilator.

Jeff has had a lot of mucus that seems to clog the ventilation tube from time to time, so this afternoon (after Dr. Adler was here), they started some breathing therapy/treatment that should reduce the mucus.

Once again, like so many times before, I'm reminded we are *"fearfully and wonderfully made."*

Thanks for checking on us, and especially, thanks for the prayers.

> I will praise thee; for I am fearfully and wonderfully made: marvellous are thy works; and that my soul knoweth right well.
>
> Psalm 139:14 (KJV)

On a lighter note:

It's quicker and causes less stress to actually take the car to the gas station to refuel than to phone a friend and have them deliver the gas to you. Don't ask me how I know!

06/02/11 (Thursday), 10:35AM-Karen

Early morning, they took another chest x-ray. About six thirty, they took Jeff for a CT scan. Dr. Adler ran a scope down the breathing tube about eight thirty. They gave Jeff Valium for that procedure, and he's sleeping now.

They have changed Jeff from a Coumadin blood thinner to Lovenox. The Coumadin had a longer reverse time, sometimes taking five days to reverse out of the body. Lovenox can be reversed in a few hours if needed, so it's a safer choice for now.

The scope showed some puss/mucus, but none in the bronchial tubes; and Dr. Adler suctioned some of that out. The x-ray showed some blood clots that have redeveloped in Jeff's lungs. Dr. Adler said there were enough there to bring a healthy person to the ER.

The plan now is to test Jeff's breathing again after he wakes up from the meds they gave him for the scope procedure. So for now we wait. Everyone anticipates taking Jeff off the ventilator today.

06/02/11 (Thursday), 2:34PM-Karen

The flow-by test went well. Jeff was on wall oxygen for an hour and a half, and his numbers stayed up, so Dr. Adler made the decision to pull the breathing tube and disconnect the ventilator. This is great news!

06/02/11 (Friday), 4:48PM-Karen

Jeff's resting. His brother Randy and I have alternated night sifts. He said that a speech pathologist came by this morning and worked with Jeff a while. She had him try to eat/drink a variety of juices and soft fruit. However, Dr. Adler said he wasn't quite ready to have him on foods. So for now, Jeff's nutrition is all via IV. He was able to have ice chips, but they made him cough, so they were taken away. I suspect we will see a doctor or two yet this evening.

Harvest is well under way. For the first year since Jeff and I have been married, this year is the first that Jeff hasn't been right in the middle of the activity. I appreciate all the ladies who are feeding my harvest meals and for a good group of employees that are taking up the slack. Wayne has been so willing to oversee a lot of the day-to-day operations of the farming and the irrigation work since Jeff has been sick. Not growing up on a farm, I have a lot to learn to keep both the farm and the irrigation businesses running smoothly. Until I can, it's good to have Wayne's help.

06/05/11 (Sunday), 11:28PM-Karen

Jeff's voice is getting stronger, but he's still pretty raspy most of the time. He was moved from ICU to the intermediate care wing. Dr. Adler came by earlier this afternoon and indicated that he wants the speech pathologist to give Jeff another eating evaluation before they let him eat and drink anything. For now Jeff receives all his nutrition through the IV. The concern seems to be that the vocal cords also deflect food away from the lungs.

I hope we can meet with Dr. Keefer tomorrow and get a professional opinion about what treatment/care Jeff needs. Jeff's next scheduled appointment with Keefer is a week away on Monday, 6/13. [no change]

Please pray that the specialists will have wisdom as they provide insight into Jeff's medical needs.

06/07/11 (Tuesday), 9:59PM-Karen

Our pastor volunteered to stay last night at the hospital with Jeff. When I arrived today, he mentioned that someone had mentioned the possibility that Jeff may be released tomorrow to go back to Maple Lawn. Dr. Lee, the admitting doctor, came by this afternoon. He also thought that tomorrow might be the day. I spoke with the case manager here at Mercy as well as the administrator at Maple Lawn. Hopefully, the transition will be smooth.

Jeff has been very sleepy today, and his thoughts have been more scrambled than yesterday. He has had a very hard time carrying on a conversation this afternoon. I don't know what would account for the difference from yesterday.

Jeff's still receiving some nutrition through the IV, but is also eating well. Jeff saw a physical therapist this morning. They tried to get him out of bed for a while. Another week in a hospital bed has obviously taken a toll on Jeff's strength.

I look forward to having Jeff closer to home. It would solve several time issues on my part. We should be able to finish cutting wheat by Thursday.

Thanks for checking on us. I'm continually humbled by the number of you who invest your time in our lives to pray for and encourage us. We don't know what is ahead, but no question about it—we aren't alone. I'm continually reminded of God's provision for our lives, and in turn, I'm thankful.

06/08/11 (Wednesday), 7:49PM-Karen

Jeff was released from Mercy early afternoon. I took him in my vehicle from OKC back to Hydro. He's very weak. The orderlies had to literally pick him up and put him in the wheelchair and then pick him up and place him in the car. Physical therapy will have to be a priority. On the way back to Maple Lawn, I took a detour and drove past our farm where we are harvesting wheat. I think he was glad to drive by, but he was also ready to get back to the Manor.

> Rejoice in the Lord always. I will say it again: Rejoice!
> Let your gentleness be evident to all. The Lord is near.
> Do not be anxious about anything, but in everything,
> by prayer and petition, with thanksgiving, present
> your requests to God. And the peace of God, which

transcends all understanding, will guard your hearts and your minds in Christ Jesus.

Philippians 4:4–7 (KJV)

06/13/11 (Monday), 9:25AM-Karen

Change of plans: Jeff's doctor's appointment for today was cancelled and rescheduled for two weeks out. I have contacted the office and requested a conference type of appointment. That is scheduled for Wednesday at one thirty. Hopefully, this will be a time to get answers to some questions that we have concerning the treatment plan. Jeff should be restarting physical therapy today. He's extremely weak, and I expect some resistance to the motivational part of the therapy. He has had several guests over the weekend, and I have visited with some of them after they were there. My best description is that he has good hours and bad hours. Some people say he carried on a pretty good conversation with them, and some say he was tired. I think his medications play into how he feels and how well he can communicate what he wants to say. I'm developing a list of questions for Dr. Keefer to address on Wednesday. Pray that the time will be valuable as a planning tool. I believe a plan will prove beneficial for us, the nursing home, and our health insurance. Tentatively, I believe Jeff will start Temodar in a couple of weeks. I'm sure they want Jeff to gain strength back after his hospital stay before starting the chemo.

Whew! What a week. With generous help from an area farmer, we finished cutting our wheat on Friday, literally as the rain came. Jeff's nephew from Tulsa worked for us during harvest, as well as a couple of area guys. Brittany got to drive the combine a little this year, not near as much as she wanted, but she got to cut a little on our home place Jeff and I bought just days before he was diagnosed in 2009. She commented on how bittersweet that moment was. It was something Jeff would have treasured with her. Several dear ladies from church brought meals to our workers while we were at the hospital. That was a tremendous help. I missed the time in the kitchen but am very thankful others were able and willing to take my chores so that I could focus on Jeff and my accounting work.

Friday Brittany called and said, "Mom, three combines and a grain cart just pulled in the field to help us cut. She was speechless—that doesn't happen much. We had been talking about how tired she was and how she wanted to hibernate after harvest. For another family to give up their day-after-harvest catch-up-on-everything-that-got-put-off-day to come help us,

all I can say is "what a blessing." I know this family, and I know they did it because God sent them. We have had several offers of people wanting to help. Each offer is given with the same sincere desire to help, and whether accepted or declined, the same feeling of being blessed remains.

After lunch, I wanted to go by the field for a short time. As I was leaving the field, I noticed that the ditch was on fire. A quick call to notify the fire department, and the men were there to put out the fire. A couple of them only had to leave the comfort of their farm equipment in our field to help. We have no idea how a fire started. It was in the ditch in the corner of the field—away from all the combines. A flurry of activity for the last day of harvest, but no one was hurt, and no property was lost. Having been on the receiving end of both the volunteer first responders and the volunteer fire department in the last year, I know firsthand how valuable an asset they are to our community. In a competition, I would put them up against any paid department. Truly, these men are only in it because it helps their neighbors.

Sunday, my parents came back through Hydro on their way home from a family reunion/anniversary party of sorts and showed up at church. I got to sit between my mother and my mother-in-law. That will be a day to treasure. I don't know that I have ever done that before. Both sets of parents have been in the same church building many times, but I haven't been on the same pew with both before. My family is so blessed because of the Christian heritage our families have passed on to us.

I get to help with a KidSing class before Sunday school. Yesterday, as we sang the old familiar songs, I couldn't help but think, *Maybe all I needed to know I may have learned in Sunday school.* My sister Janice was in the first ever kindergarten class at Granite. She likes the saying "All I ever needed to know I learned in kindergarten." This is an adaptation of that. The simple songs like "The Wise Man" teaches us that when we build on Christ, even though storms come, what we have built on Him will stand. Everything else is just sand. Yesterday, we sang "I am a Christian." Knowing that we will "live eternally" gives us perspective when the storms of life come. The song "The B-I-B- L-E" says we "stand alone on the Word of God." Wow, such deep concepts in simple words. "I stand alone" could really be a scary thing, but when it's on the Word of God, that removes all fear. "I Have a Wonderful Treasure" was a new song to me when I started helping with KidSing. The other lady helping had learned it as a child, but it was new to me. The line "We will travel together, my Bible and I" prompted a question of "How can we travel with our Bible, if we don't physically take it with us everywhere?" What's the answer? We carry it in our hearts. All those memorized verses that we learn as kids tend to be remembered when we are adults facing storms. What a blessing, what a comfort.

Again, you have my sincere thanks for all the prayers on our behalf.

06/17/11 (Friday) 1:39AM-Karen

Maple Lawn called on Tuesday. They were concerned that Jeff wasn't strong enough to make the trip in my vehicle to Oklahoma City to see Dr. Keefer. In fact, they were concerned that he wasn't strong enough to make that trip at all. It was taking two and sometimes three workers to move him in and out of bed. They are considering using a lift to help move Jeff around. Since the visit was scheduled as a conference and not an exam or testing, they let me keep the conference appointment even though Jeff wasn't able to go. I wanted to get an overview of what treatment he was recommending and a timeline of when it would start, what form it would be in, would he need to travel to OKC for the treatments, or for testing the day he started treatments.

Keefer summarized the available chemo drugs and their side effects: Temodar (caused the decrease in Jeff's white blood cell count and put him in the hospital for twenty-one days in December 2009) and Avastin (side effects include blood issues

that Jeff's already battling—pulmonary embolisms and deep vein thrombosis). He stated he generally doesn't prescribe chemo for patients confined to bed and as immobile as Jeff. Keefer said in Jeff's already-weakened state, the side effects of chemo would be even more exaggerated. He isn't recommending any chemo treatment. If Jeff gains mobility, Keefer will address treatment options at that time. As I got up to leave, Dr. Keefer said he wished he had better news and gave me a hug. Keefer has no plans for further MRIs or followup visits.

Jeff still receives physical and occupational therapy five days a week at Maple Lawn. Dr. Keefer said that was probably good because it would keep his joints from hurting. To my knowledge, his therapy sessions are limited to what can be accomplished while Jeff's in bed—mainly arm and leg exercises. He's taking two antiseizure drugs, Dilantin and Keppra. The combination seems to be controlling the seizures. He's taking 8 mg of Dexamethasone, the steroid to control inflammation, irritation, and pressure that the tumor causes. He doesn't seem to be in any pain. That is a definite blessing!

For the conversations I have with Jeff, it seems to work best if I ask yes-or-no type questions. If Jeff has to formulate questions to maintain a conversation, his aphasia causes a lot of road blocks. It almost seems like I have to know what he wants to ask so that I can interpret what he says. I do think he has times when he can think clearer than others. Sometimes it just comes out wrong, and sometimes he can't find the words at all.

> Let us therefore come boldly unto the throne of grace, that we may obtain mercy, and find grace to help in time of need.
>
> Hebrews 4:16 (KJV)

Thank you to each of you who continue to pray for our guidance, strength, and encouragement. I know that the guidance, strength, and encouragement we receive are a direct result of those prayers.

HOSPICE

06/22/11 (Wednesday), 10:06PM-Karen

Since my last update that no treatment is scheduled, Lauren recommended, and we have contacted and started, hospice care in addition to the regular care of the nursing home. Monday was his last day of physical therapy. All parties involved were reluctant to vouch for any improvement from the therapy, and it seemed to be a point of argument and frustration.

Today the hospice company brought a different bed. Jeff says it's about six inches longer than the old one. This should be more comfortable and keep his feet from being scrunched at the end of the bed. I don't know if it's longer or not. I haven't pulled out the stainless steel, hundred-foot, locking measuring tape to find out; it just looks longer. They also brought a lift, which should help with maneuvering Jeff in and out of bed; paraphernalia for oxygen, should it become necessary; and a heavier duty wheelchair. The people with the hospice seem very nice, and they came highly recommended. For now, they will function in addition to the wonderful care Jeff's already getting.

Our past pastor (that's like past president or past chairman) and his wife drove down from Kansas to visit Jeff yesterday. Jeff enjoyed their visit and time of prayer.

Jeff's dad celebrated his eightieth birthday on Saturday. His actual date of birth was May 3, but conflicts with school and other commitments made it necessary to postpone the party a little over a month. It was good to see the relatives I already knew and to meet a few for the first time. Of course many took advantage of the opportunity to stop by and see Jeff. Often that is a hard visit to make.

Brittany is driving a tractor this year for the first time. She's a huge fan of autosteer. I know it's something Jeff would have enjoyed with her. I see pride in his expression when he hears her stories about the farm.

I'm not always at the Manor when Jeff gets his meals, but again today, Jeff wanted to pray and offer thanks for his food before he ate. The same food that he fusses about because it doesn't taste just right or fit what he thinks he would rather have. But he's still thankful.

I know that the Creator of the universe is still in charge. I know that *"all things work together for good to them that love the Lord, to those that are the called according to His purpose"* (Romans 8:28 KJV). Just because I see no earthly point to some things or some circumstances doesn't mean God can't/won't use it for good. For now, that will have to be enough. I choose to trust God to make better decisions about my future than I could if I was given that power. I know that He'll guide my footsteps as I choose to follow Him (Psalm 119:133). The challenge seems to be focusing on Him, not my circumstances.

Thanks for the prayers. God's still providing answers and blessings as a direct result of those prayers.

> Order my steps in thy word: and let not any iniquity have dominion over me.
>
> Psalm 119:133 (KJV)

06/27/11 (Monday), 11:18AM-Karen

Things seem to be about the same with Jeff. He has days where he can visit pretty well with visitors and some days when he just seems tired. Almost always, he recognizes people and can carry on decent conversations. But often he thinks of something he wants to say, starts the sentence, and then cannot find the words to convey his thoughts. If it's obvious what he was commenting on, whoever he's talking to can sometimes get him back on track by offering what they think is the word that he is trying to say. Sometimes that works; sometimes it doesn't.

I've noticed some of his mannerisms seem to be a little "off" at times. I notice some things I had never seen him do before. Yesterday, he put sour cream on his hot roll and then topped it off with grape jelly. Jeff usually turned down sour cream for just about everything except green beans. Maybe I shouldn't knock it until I've tried it—sour cream and grape jelly on bread might be a tasty dessert.

I don't think most visitors notice these quirks. Often they comment they think he's doing better. Maybe because Brittany and I are closer to the situation, we are able to see the subtle changes more clearly.

I received a CarePages notice this morning that David Mogg died yesterday evening. David (and his wife Donna) had been battling the same cancer that Jeff has; and often, Donna's updates about David seemed to parallel my own thoughts and observations about Jeff. My thoughts and prayers are with the Mogg family during this time.

07/03/11 (Sunday), 8:36AM-Karen

A quick post before church: Overall this week, Jeff has had several enjoyable visits with friends, and his attitude seems good.

However, Tuesday when I was there, Jeff absolutely blew up at one of the nurses who came in to help him. Those of you who know Jeff personally will understand how much of a shock this was for me. He might get upset with those he loves, those he's around on a day-to-day basis, but he rarely raises his voice, and never with a stranger. I was absolutely caught off guard. I tried to defend the nurse; after all, it wasn't her fault; she was just doing her job. Later, he seemed calmer, but still missed the whole point that the nurse was just doing her job.

Brittany spent four days this week as a counselor at church camp. She came home totally exhausted, but I have no doubt that she'll never regret the time she invested in the kids. It's a small church camp. She said there were seventeen campers starting the week. One had to leave early, and one went home with a high temperature. Out of the fifteen left, several made decisions to follow Christ at camp in prior years. At least one made a decision this year, and they were able to sow some seeds of God's Word that we're promised *"will not return unto Him void.*" Next week, she's directing our Bible school. I'm so proud of her summer choices.

I'm constantly reminded that I'm not on this path alone. It's such a comfort to know that you're praying. Be assured, God's answering your prayers, providing for our needs each day.

> So shall my word be that goeth forth out of my mouth:
> it shall not return unto me void, but it shall accomplish
> that which I please, and it shall prosper in the thing
> whereto I sent it.

Isaiah 55:11 (KJV)

07/09/11 (Saturday), 12:18AM-Karen

Jeff seems to be settled. I asked him the other day if he gets bored just lying in bed and watching TV. He promptly replied, "No." I think he enjoys having visitors and hearing what they are doing. His memory is good; he just has trouble with word selection. He does well in chitchat, but major conversations where he has to put a lot of effort into choosing words to form sentences reveals the aphasia problems that have been present since the first surgery. He doesn't get too upset by the problem; he just loses the thought. Often he gets distracted by other things in the room. We have learned that if we really need or want him to focus, the TV needs to be turned off.

Whew, we have had another busy week. Britt volunteered to be the director for our Bible school. She really got the word out about dates and times. She put a lot of effort into decorations for the front of the church, organized the workers, made a schedule of where classes would be, and had leaders lined up to get them between locations. Tuesday, the first day, we only had six students. We gained two on Wednesday and held the number at eight or nine the last two nights. We are holding on to the promise that God's word won't return unto Him void (Isaiah 55:11) and that wherever two or more are gathered in His name…He is present (Matthew 18:20). I trust that seeds of the Word are being planted in the precious kids. Although some of them are definitely rowdy, still they are precious.

Some days, this path seems very long; other days aren't too bad. God continues to sustain us—one day at a time, and sometimes an hour at a time. Thanks for the many ways you each have a part in that sustenance. Knowing we have so many friends who are praying for our family is truly a blessing. I don't know what God has planned for any of us, but I know he knows how things will work together for *good* (Romans 8:28), how things will work together for *better*, and how things will work together for the *best* overall result. After all, he's not willing that even one should perish (Matthew 18:14), and I know he's constantly pulling out all the stops to make sure that each individual is given every possible opportunity to trust Him as their personal Savior. I have to trust that somehow, in His unfathomable wisdom, if we allow ourselves to be led by the Holy Spirit, our situation and circumstances will be knit together with the situations and circumstances of other believers, who are also being led by the Spirit, and the result will be *"all things work together for good"* as Romans 8 speaks about.

Maybe our journey will have some impact on reaching others with the message that Jesus loves them enough to die in their place, or maybe we can help encourage other believers on their journeys.

> For where two or three are gathered together in my name, there am I in the midst of them.
>
> Matthew 18:20 (KJV)

> So shall my word be that goeth forth out of my mouth: it shall not return unto me void, but it shall accomplish that which I please, and it shall prosper in the thing whereto I sent it.
>
> Isaiah 55:11 (KJV)

And we know that all things work together for good to them that love God, to them who are the called according to his purpose.

Romans 8:28 (KJV)

Even so it is not the will of your Father which is in heaven, that one of these little ones should perish

Matthew 18:14 (KJV)

07/18/11 (Monday), 5:42PM-Karen

While Brittany and I were at Yukon for a dental appointment this morning, I received a call from the hospice nurse at the nursing home in Hydro telling me that Jeff was experiencing some problems. He had received his shower and was using the bathroom when he became unresponsive. When I got to the nursing home, I was told Jeff had experienced another seizure. After regaining consciousness, he has been responding to voices, but he hasn't regained his ability to speak. He has been eating well, so we believe his speech will return with time. Of course, Jeff has been having difficulty finding the word with which to carry on normal conversations, so we anticipate that will take quite a bit of time.

07/19/11 (Tuesday), 2:54AM-Karen

Monday morning at about nine thirty, Christy, the director of nursing at Maple Lawn, called to tell me that Jeff's color had changed. He was kind of gray, and he wasn't responsive. She said that the hospice aide was there helping the staff aide give Jeff a shower when he became nonresponsive. Brittany and I were in Yukon at the dentist when she called, and we left between appointments to come back to Hydro. The hospice nurse said he responded to her tickling his feet, and when we would speak to him, he would open his eyes and look at us; but just as quickly, he would close them and go back to sleep. She probably stayed an hour and a half, and his vital signs were good the whole time. Based on my limited medical knowledge but extensive history with the patient, I believe the incident was a seizure (only one) because the symptoms are almost identical to those he has had following other seizures.

Jeff didn't eat his lunch and rested all afternoon and evening. He took some medications without having them crushed (some of the first meds after the seizure were crushed to make sure he could swallow them), and he held his glass by himself to get a drink of water. Late afternoon, he reached for the nurse call button on his own. I helped him with supper; he ate two sausage links and some pudding.

When I left about seven this evening, he was still resting and had really not spoken all day. He did make some grumblings that were interpretable, but they were not very clear. Mid-afternoon, we had to hold things up to see which item got the reaction to figure out what he was trying to tell us. This evening, a friend stopped by, and his report was that he got Jeff to chuckle a couple of times, which is definitely a good sign.

Every time Jeff has changes in his abilities or we learn more of his diagnosis or skill level, I'm reminded that we are *"fearfully and wonderfully made."* The complexity of the human mind *still* baffles the medical community.

> I will praise thee; for I am fearfully and wonderfully made: marvellous are thy works; and that my soul knoweth right well.
>
> Ps 139:14 (KJV)

07/21/11 (Thursday), 11:34AM–Karen

The last couple of days, Jeff's speech has been rebounding from Monday's seizure. Last night we watched part of *Ratatouille*. I believe Jeff was able to enjoy the humor of the animated movie about a rat that can cook. He's still struggling with word selections. For the most part, he's cooperative to find the replacement or help us play charades to find the missing words.

July 21, 1990. We stood in front of family and friends, and in the presence of God, we vowed to share our forevers including the "better or worse" and "in sickness and in health." Today we celebrate twenty-one years. As young twenty-something kids with stars in our eyes, that was a relatively easy promise. We only envisioned the "better" and expected the best of "health." In fact, people of all ages make that promise easily. What doesn't come as easily are the years that follow. Marriage is a challenge. Actually, for us, the "sickness" part has not been our worst days. It's when you're both healthy and both have stubborn streaks that make rough days. Having an outside enemy—in our current case, cancer—it's easier to unite and focus against a foe.

I've been blessed. I've enjoyed the security of knowing Jeff was faithful. I was never given a reason to doubt his love, and I knew he only wanted the best for me. That's only my side, but I know that even though he can't express himself today, he's felt the same way.

I don't know if this will be our last anniversary. If I listen to the council of medical "experts," that's my only conclusion. But as a Christian, praise God! I'm not bound simply by the laws of the physical world. I know I serve an awesome God. Ephesians 3:20 tells me that God is able to do immeasurably more than I can ask or think. Believe you me, I'm asking (and so are many of you). I'm planning out ways that God can get glory out of this trial. But that makes it "my plan," not "His plan."

God loves us, not just enough to heal us, but enough to die for us—literally. And if he loves me enough to die in my place, then he also loves others enough to die for them (John 3:16). As his servant, if he sees a way that others can know how much he loves them by using my trials to His glory, then so be it. I choose to trust God enough to allow him to chose the path for our lives that works best in His plan, and if total healing is not in Jeff's future, then I can know that this trial, this round of "worse" and "sickness" I vowed to be faithful through will be a witness of how much God loves me and how faithful he is to never leave us nor forsake us. (Hebrews 13:5, Jeremiah 29:11, Matthew 28:20)

It's no wonder marriage between a man and a woman is a picture of how Christ loves his chosen, those who have chosen Him—His bride, The Church.

> For God so loved the world, that he gave his only begotten Son, that whosoever believeth in him should not perish, but have everlasting life.

> John 3:16 (KJV)

> For he hath said, I will never leave thee, nor forsake thee.

> Hebrews 13:5b (KJV)

> And, lo, I am with you alway, even unto the end of the world. Amen.

> Matthew 28:20 (KJV)

07/27/11 (Thursday), 1:03AM–Karen

On Tuesday, when I got to the Manor, Jeff was lying in bed and was on his side. He looked up and told me he didn't feel good. He couldn't put words to what "felt" bad, just that he didn't feel good.

I noticed more aphasia. Jeff starts to say even the simplest of sentences and stumbles over the words. I noticed a dramatic increase in this last night and was hoping/praying that it was just because he was tired; however, there wasn't any change tonight.

I continue to waver between prayers that focus solely on Jeff's healing and prayers of submission to God's "bigger" plan. I would certainly love to see Jeff home and whole again. I have no control over the outcome, except by way of prayer; and if prayer alone would heal Jeff, no doubt, he would never have had to have his first surgery. So obviously, I'm not in control. I continue to trust that God's plan is the best. He'll carry us through no matter the outcome (Deuteronomy 31:8,

Joshua 1:5). I will praise him if Jeff's healed. Wow, how great would a miracle of that proportion be! I know Christ has not changed (Hebrews 13:8). I believe He's still able and still willing to grant miracles in the context of verifying His authority over the physical so that "the world may know" (John 14:31, 17:23) and understand His authority over the spiritual realm. But it's my intention to choose to praise God even if Jeff's physical healing isn't the best option under His plan to reach the most people and have the most positive impact on others with the message of the gospel—that believers have a future (Jeremiah 29:11) that even death can't destroy and a peace that's beyond description (Philippians 4:7).

Continue to pray with me for a miracle! Pray for continued peace for all our family and the boldness (Acts 4:29) to reach those for whom God's "better" plan is choreographed to reach (Romans 8:28).

Thanks so much for your time and energy to "checkonjeff" and to reach out to our family. We are truly blessed that so many of you are concerned for us.

> The Lord himself goes before you and will be with you;
>
> he will never leave you nor forsake you. Do not be afraid; do not be discouraged.
>
> Deuteronomy 31:8 (NIV)
>
> No one will be able to stand up against you all the days of your life. As I was with Moses, so I will be with you; I will never leave you nor forsake you.
>
> Joshua 1:5 (NIV)
>
> Jesus Christ is the same yesterday and today and forever.
>
> Hebrews 13:8 (KJV)

But the world must learn that I love the Father and that I do exactly what my Father has commanded me.

> John 14:31(NIV)

May they be brought to complete unity to let the world know that you sent me and have loved them even as you have loved me.

> John 17:23 (NIV)

And the peace of God, which transcends all understanding, will guard your hearts and your minds in Christ Jesus.

> Philippians 4:7 (NIV)

Now, Lord, consider their threats and enable your servants to speak your word with great boldness.

> Acts 4:29 (NIV)

And we know that in all things God works for the good of those who love him, who have been called according to his purpose.

> Romans 8:28 (NIV)

07/28/11 (Thursday), 5:22PM–Karen

I know I posted last night, but I want to quickly share the following: Today Britt and I popped in on Jeff midafternoon. After visiting a while, with Jeff struggling with every sentence, Britt left the room, and two of the nursing staff were in the room with Jeff and me. He was trying to tell me something, and we were both working pretty hard at figuring it out. I tried the old standard Twenty Questions to try and narrow down what he wanted. I never did figure out what specific item he was trying to tell me about. He worked at it a while and then finally gave up on what he wanted to tell me, and out of frustration, he said loud and clear, "What I need is a miracle." To which I immediately replied, "Yes, you do!" It was a very special moment to share—a sad moment to know he realizes that without a miracle, he has little hope, but a comforting moment knowing that he knows where his hope lies.

Thanks for your prayers.

08/09/11 (Tuesday), 9:39 AM–Karen

I'm noticing more changes in Jeff's speech. He used to have one wrong word in a sentence. Guessing what the correct word should be wasn't too challenging. For the last week or two, he's had a couple words in a sentence that were wrong. As time progresses, more and more of his sentences are jumbled. Tonight, I resorted to guessing at what he wanted, based solely on "how" he said things, not on what words he used. He reached and pressed the call button to have staff come help him. He tried to tell them what he wanted but then finally said, "You tell them" when they asked what he wanted/needed. Most of the time, I'm not concerned about his physical safety. He's receiving good care, and he's coherent enough not to try to get out of bed on his own. It's his inability to express his thoughts that has me questioning if I'm spending enough time with him at the Manor. Would I be able to help the nurses "guess" what he needs? I do know he doesn't like to be fussed over, so I suppose as long as he is safe, I shouldn't be there constantly, which is good. I probably don't have the energy for it anyway.

Brittany will start back to school this week—a sophomore if you can believe that! Their first softball game will be tomorrow. Hundred-degree days don't really qualify as prime weather for softball. We keep praying for cooler weather, and rain. We received a light sprinkle this evening, and for that we are very thankful. Sounds like areas east of us received some damaging winds with their rain. It's so dry here that I resorted to watering the lawn to keep it from crunching under our feet. We normally don't water our lawn—it just makes the grass grow, and we have enough farm work without extra mowing requirements. I watered a ring right around the house as extra fire insurance. You can't be too careful while in a burn ban.

I had a doctor's appointment last Thursday. I have been having some pretty severe pain in my right knee. I was sent for an MRI and got the results back today—torn ACL. I have an appointment scheduled with a specialist on the nineteenth. I'm not sure what kind of recovery time I will need. I have a growing list of questions to ask about the treatment and recovery.

My sister Janice and I took her grandbaby to a family reunion on Saturday afternoon. Brittany had a softball game in Hinton (Varsity against Alumni), so she wasn't able to go on Saturday. We came back home late, stopped by the Manor to peek in on Jeff, and then came home for the night. Janice's husband Larry and Brittany went to the reunion with us after church on Sunday.

As always, it's great to catch up with family. I'm blessed with a wonderful batch of kin.

I continue to enjoy the sermons I receive from the old hymns and often wake with a song on my mind. One I've thought about several times lately is "Precious Lord, Take My Hand." Here's a couple lines to get the song stuck in your mind for a while.

Thro' the storm, thro' the night
Lead me on to the light
Take my hand precious Lord, lead me home

The idea is to follow where we are led—that's assuming we have chosen *whom* to follow. I believe, by design as a human, I will function at my highest efficiency when I choose to allow the Holy Spirit to guide my decisions. By choosing to change my "control" system from manual, where I make the choices myself (my will), to a much better option of yielding to the will of my Heavenly Father, I switch to a more efficient setting for every area of my life. Submitting to God's will is a daily, almost moment-by-moment choice that we make to be used in His will.

This choice is different from the choice to accept Christ's death as the substitute payment for the debt our sin creates (Romans 6:23). I believe that is a one-time choice (John 3:16). But to daily choose to follow the leading of the Holy Spirit allows Him to control my actions and my decisions, and that is when I become a willing part of His plan.

And in case you didn't know, by not choosing, we remain set to what is almost the factory default setting of Sin Only (John 3:18). Not that God created us to run in Sin Only mode. We are created with a choice. Without the constant supervision of the Holy Spirit, we will choose sin, our own will over God's plan, every time.

So how does that tie in with an update on Jeff? My constant struggle these days is to yield to God's plan. Obviously, my plan would involve an awesome miracle of God that would allow Jeff to come home and resume his role as father, husband, brother, brotherin-law, son, friend— all the roles he has held. How great would that be! But I have to continually remind myself that only God knows what is best. I keep asking for the miracle and reminding myself that should the miracle not come, that doesn't mean God doesn't love me—just that there is a better way to accomplish even the minutest details of the bigger plan (Romans 8:28). It's tough to yield our will to God's will. Not so much in theory, but in action, it's hard to give up the feeble control we have and allow God to use us in His plan. I have to trust that we, the Krehbiel family, have been placed in our situation because it has purpose in His plan. From that trust and submission to His will comes great peace. What a blessing. I hope that in your own circumstances, in your own daily walk with God, each of you is able to experience that peace that is beyond human comprehension (Philippians 4:7).

Once again, thanks for checking on Jeff and for allowing me an outlet for the emotional and spiritual therapy I receive from writing these updates.

> For the wages of sin is death; but the gift of God is eternal life through Jesus Christ our Lord.
>
> Romans 6:23 (KJV)

For God so loved the world, that he gave his only begotten Son, that whosoever believeth in him should not perish, but have everlasting life.

John 3:16 (KJV)

He that believeth on him is not condemned: but he that believeth not is condemned already, because he hath not believed in the name of the only begotten Son of God.

John 3:18 (KJV)

And we know that in all things God works for the good of those who love him, who have been called according to his purpose.

Romans 8:28 (NIV)

And the peace of God, which transcends all understanding, will guard your hearts and your minds in Christ Jesus.

Philippians 4:7 (NIV)

08/17/11 (Wednesday), 12:14AM–Karen

Jeff continues to struggle with speech issues. Today he wasn't able to even answer simple yes-or-no questions. In fact, he isn't speaking much at all. He seems to be very sleepy and opens his eyes only briefly when you speak directly to him. I have had trouble holding his attention with conversation of any kind. He seems to drift back to sleep pretty quickly. I spoke with Lauren today. She had been to the Manor to see Jeff on Friday. She noted that Jeff had difficulty using a fork and some trouble getting choked while he ate. She has added orders to have someone from the Manor help him with his meals. I have noticed that he definitely eats better if I help him. I know that it must be hard from Jeff's point of view to need help feeding himself. Jeff doesn't seem to have any interest in what is on TV. I have noticed that it seems to stay on whatever channel it was on when I left. Jeff has always been a channel surfer, and this seems to be an obvious deterioration of his abilities.

Last week, I mentioned that I injured my knee. At that time, I was still able to walk on it, but I had an appointment to see a specialist. Last Tuesday, I stepped up into the Tahoe after the softball game and heard and felt a loud pop in my knee. Immediately, I was unable to put any weight on that leg. I sort of collapsed into the driver's seat. I contemplated getting Brittany to drive me home but decided I would drive myself as opposed to maneuvering myself to the passenger seat. When I got home, I asked her to help me walk in, but since any pressure on that knee sent me straight into orbit, I ended up using a wheelchair for the next two days. Fortunately, the doctor's office was able to schedule an appointment for last Thursday. He gave me a shot in my knee to calm down the inflammation. By the next morning, I was able to put pressure on the knee and walk on it without too much pain. He has ordered a knee brace for me to use, and the plan is to use physical therapy to strengthen the muscles around my knee enough to compensate for the lack of an ACL. Apparently, the ACL was torn several years ago, and I've lived without it just fine. The pop that I heard was a bone-on-bone sound that caused inflammation. I expect to gain strength back [regain the strength] in my knee and avoid having surgery.

Brittany has started school—she's officially a sophomore! Her softball team has practice or games most afternoons, and that keeps us busy. I have been going to see Jeff at some point each day. I try to get her into town to see him every couple of days. The logistics of coming home from softball games via the Manor is sometimes a challenge. It makes me sad thinking about the short time available to spend with Jeff. I guess our lives were always hectic. We often saw each other only a few minutes or an hour or two each day. The difference was/is that before, we could talk to Jeff on the phone anytime we wanted. Now we have to be physically in his room at the Manor to get to see him and talk to him. And now he's unable to talk back.

Please keep praying God will work out a miracle for us. I remember the words of encouragement Jesus gave to Jairus concerning his faith in the face of the death of his daughter. Jesus told him, *"Be not afraid, only believe"* (Mark 5:36, KJV). I know that Jesus is the same yesterday, today, and forever (Hebrews 13:8) and that His ability to perform miracles has not changed. As an adopted child of the King (Ephesians 1:5), I'm granted the privilege of "boldly" approaching the throne room (Hebrews 4:16). I simply come to His throne and ask my Heavenly Father for a miracle in the same way I would ask my earthly father for a favor. What earthly father wouldn't give me a miracle if it was within his power? I know then that should the miracle not come, it's because God has a reason not to grant the miracle, a reason that is beyond my comprehension.

So for now, I continue to ask. Thank you for your prayers of petition on our behalf (Luke 18:1–5)

Since Brittany was little, I have shared the duties of a Kidsing program on Sunday mornings. We have tried to teach the children the good ole Sunday school songs that have stood the test of time. Sunday as the kids sang "The Wise Man," I couldn't help but think of how true those words are.

> The wise man built his house upon the Rock, The wise man built his house upon the Rock, The wise man built his house upon the Rock, And the rains came tumbling down.
> The rains came down and the floods came up, The rains came down and the floods came up, The rains came down and the floods came up, And the house on the Rock stood firm.

Just about every time we sing that song, Karla, the other teacher, will emphasize what the "Rock" and the "sand" represent. As the kids sang, I couldn't help but think that the rains—the trials, the tribulations, the challenges—come no matter where we build our houses (our lives), whether on the Rock of Jesus Christ or on the sand, which is anything other than the Rock. The end results of facing the challenges with or without Christ are the difference in crumbling beneath the challenge or standing strong in strength that only a foundation in Christ can give. I can't help but think how blessed I am to be raised in a Christian home, where I was encouraged to build on the Rock, and how equally blessed I've been to marry into Jeff's family, where he was also given access to quality building materials and exposed to the only solid foundation on which to build his life—Jesus Christ. I know that people from all walks of life have faced the challenges that cancer brings. We certainly aren't the first to face them, and by no means do I claim to be an expert. I simply continue to repeat the message that "this is not something you want to face without Christ" and try to give Him the credit for propping me up so consistently.

I continue to be humbled by the number of people that pray for our family. Thank you!

Jesus Christ is the same yesterday and today and forever.

Hebrews 13:8 (KJV)

In love he predestined us to be adopted as his sons through Jesus Christ, in accordance with his pleasure and will.

Ephesians 1:4b-5 (NIV)

Let us therefore come boldly unto the throne of grace, that we may obtain mercy, and find grace to help in time of need.

Hebrews 4:16 (KJV)

And he spake a parable unto them to this end, that men ought always to pray, and not to faint; Saying, "There was in a city a judge, which feared not God, neither regarded man: And there was a widow in that city;

and she came unto him, saying, Avenge me of mine adversary. And he would not for a while: but afterward he said within himself, Though I fear not God, nor regard man; Yet because this widow troubleth me, I will avenge her, lest by her continual coming she weary me."

Luke 18:1–5 (KJV)

08/17/11 (Wednesday), 11:16PM–Karen

We stopped by to see Jeff after Bible study this evening. He was sleeping so soundly I couldn't even get him to wake up and look at us. When I would speak kind of loud, he would open his eyes, but just drifted back to sleep quickly. I spoke with his dad on the way home, and he said that Jeff refused help to eat this evening but ate some on his own. From that report, it's possible that we caught him after some medication had taken effect, or he was just extremely tired. Either way, he was resting quietly when we left.

I have plans to pop in earlier in the day and see if he's more alert at a different time.

Thanks for all your prayers.

08/24/11 (Wednesday), 9:48AM–Karen

Last Thursday, after the staff had given Jeff his shower, he had another seizure. They said it took five of them to get him back to bed. They said this was a minor episode, that's all I know. As we have seen before, there is a period of time after a seizure when Jeff isn't alert and seems to be resting. Those symptoms were there before the seizure, so I'm not sure how much of the decrease in alertness over the past week can be attributed to the seizure and how much is a result of tumor growth.

On good days, Jeff has a period of time, maybe an hour or two, when he's somewhat alert. He eats some of his meal when someone else feeds him and can drink some liquid, again, if someone helps. He has trouble swallowing. Sometimes he needs to be reminded to swallow, and other times, it seems swallowing is painful. Sometimes he doesn't get liquids swallowed quick enough, and they choke him or drip back out of his mouth. His eyes can track movement in his room, and he focuses on faces, although in the last week, I wonder if he has actually recognized me at all.

On bad days, he's so sleepy that he can't hold his eyes open. Even when pestered, he falls right back to sleep. I continue to speak to Jeff even though he isn't able to respond. Mostly, I just clean and straighten his room as an outlet for extra energy and eventually resort to watching TV—usually something I think he would enjoy watching, usually sports, but often the history channel or the food network.

The changes in Jeff are hard to watch, hard to experience. If they are hard for me, then I know they are hard for others as well.

As an adult, it's hard to watch the changes in Jeff. I know they are even harder to watch when it's your dad. For Brittany, at fifteen, with the majority of her life ahead of her, losing her father's daily influence and thinking of all the events of her life that he'll miss is extremely tough. Already, she has had to adjust to not having Dad at her ball games, at church, in the car with us, or at the kitchen table at suppertime.

It's in those moments that I begin to question God: "What kind of a life does Jeff have? If you aren't going to heal him, then why does he have to go through this?" I question, and then I always come back to "Who am I to question the wisdom of God?" The Psalms often start with that tone and somehow end up in praise to the creator and sustainer of all life (Psalm 13). I too find myself following my questions with praise for who God is and thankfulness for the blessings he has poured upon us. Who are we that he would die for us? Who am I to question God's will for Jeff? I eventually come around to praise.

I have often written about different hymns that have been a blessing. I am thankful for the contribution to worship the hymn writers have made. I believe many were "inspired." With that in mind, it's no wonder that they have such profound insight into the nature of God. It came out of their personal understanding of God's provision for their lives. Often the treasures are in the second, third, or fourth verses. The song "Have Faith in God"[8] is like that. The third verse says, "Have faith in God in your pain and your sorrow, His heart is touched with your grief and despair; Cast all your cares and your burdens upon Him, and leave them there, oh leave them there." That last line has been a pointed finger shaking in my face scolding me. "Leave them there, oh, leave them there." Often we give our burdens to God, only to take them back again when we say "Amen."

Keep up the prayers. My human strength was used up early. Now everything that is done, all the strength that seems to appear out of nowhere, is an answer to prayer—your prayers. God continues to provide strength in just the right portion at just the right time. Thank you for your prayers for all of our family.

Cast all your anxiety on him because he cares for you.

1 Peter 5:7 (NIV)

"Have faith in God," Jesus answered.

Mark 11:22 (KJV)

Take my yoke upon you, and learn of me; for I am meek and lowly in heart: and ye shall find rest unto your souls. For my yoke is easy, and my burden is light.

Matthew 11:29-30 (KJV)

How long, O Lord? Will you forget me forever?

How long will you hide your face from me? How long must I wrestle with my thoughts And every day have sorrow in my heart? How long will my enemy triumph over me? Look on me and answer, O Lord my God. Give light to my eyes, or I will sleep in death; My enemy will say, "I have overcome him," And my foes will rejoice when I fall. But I trust in your unfailing love;

My heart rejoices in your salvation.
I will sing to the Lord, For he has been good to me.

Psalm 13 (NIV)

08/30/11 (Tuesday), 2:43AM–Karen

What a busy weekend! Bible study Wednesday evening, Brittany was sick on Thursday and missed most of the day of school, so she also missed the first game of a softball tournament Thursday afternoon and the first night of the Hinton Fair Thursday evening. Friday, Brittany was able to go back to school, and my niece from Nashville came to visit. We were waiting for Brittany to finish softball practice when I received a call from Allen Entz, chief of the Hydro volunteer fire department. Allen asked if I had been notified. I answered no and immediately assumed they were having a fund-raiser, so I waited for the details. His next words were "Wayne and Fern are okay, but they have been in an accident." He said he stopped in to check on them and that their injuries didn't appear life threatening. He was sure they would need someone with them if only to give them a ride home. When I got there, Wayne and Fern were already getting CT scans and x-rays. Wayne's nose was broken in a few places.. His vital signs were good, and he was released. Randy came from Tulsa to take him home and stay with him Friday night. Fern's blood pressure and all vital signs were good Friday evening, until she would stand up, and then her blood pressure would drop. I stayed Friday night with her at the hospital. When the reports didn't indicate anything internal that was causing blood loss, they were left to assume that Fern's extensive bruising has pulled blood from her system and left her low on blood. They gave her two units of blood and kept her another night. My in-laws are now home. Sore and bruised, but home. We are definitely thankful that they're okay. Having seen the pictures of the pickup they were in, and considering the fact that neither of them was wearing their seatbelt, we are blessed that they are still alive.

Saturday morning, I left the hospital and came home to cook breakfast and visit with my niece before she left. Then Brittany had to leave for the softball tournament, and I left to go visit Jeff. With all the ER activity, I had missed seeing Jeff on Friday.

Our softball team played five games on Saturday—starting and ending with games against Hobart. We lost by one point in a sudden-death situation that ended about midnight. We placed second. After church Sunday, we had lunch with cousins and then went home with the intention of taking a nap. Instead, we just goofed off for a couple hours. (And didn't even feel guilty!) Then we went to the Manor to see Jeff, then to a church business meeting and back home.

As for Jeff, he seems to have recovered somewhat from last week's seizure. My understanding is that even a 100 percent recovery from a seizure would only restore Jeff back to the place he was the day before the seizure. I don't believe he has had 100 percent recovery from that last seizure. He's eating some and wants to hold the glass to control his own liquid intake. He uses his left hand almost exclusively. I believe he knew who I was this evening.

I teach the junior high class, and Sunday's lesson was on the invalid man at the pool near Bethesda (John 5). We discussed the man's healing, the fact that Jesus created the physical world (John 1:1) and has authority over the physical world. We discussed working on the Sabbath and how that was a conflict with Jewish law, and how the Jewish leaders were threatened by Jesus and how that eventually led to his arrest. By name, I went around the room and asked the students, "Does Jesus love you as much as Jesus loved the invalid that he healed?" Repeatedly, the students answered, "Yes!" In retrospect, maybe I was asking myself, *Does Jesus love me as much as he loves that man at Bethesda?* The obvious answer that even the fifth-graders know is "Yes." Jesus loves me as much as he loved the man by the pool at Bethesda. So what determines whether the answer to our prayer is yes or no? Sometimes the answer to prayer requests has to be no; otherwise, there would be some 100-, 200-, or even 300-year-old people around. So sometimes, even when Jesus loves us enough to heal us, the answer has to be no. Daily, I have to choose to leave Jeff's care to God and trust that in His wisdom, from his vantage point, he alone knows best. But how awesome would it be if Jeff's healing could get a "Yes"? Would we write his healing off as a delayed medical breakthrough, or would God get the glory? Would knowing someone with a miraculous healing spur us on to reach others? Would our faith be strengthened? I feel a little like the man in Mark 9:23–24 (KJV), who replied, "Lord, I believe; help thou mine unbelief."

Today, among other regular Monday tasks, I spoke with the insurance company about the wrecked pickup, the insurance agent about a crop insurance claim, and with the dealership about a replacement pickup for the farm. I have often picked out and purchased my own vehicles (with Jeff's blessing, of course), so I'm not afraid of the process. But I haven't ever purchased a vehicle for Krehbiel Farms. That was always Jeff's job (with my blessing, of course), but now it's my responsibility. I'm possessive of my new farm responsibilities; they are something I'm very sentimental about. Making big decisions without Jeff feels awkward, like I'm betraying him or going behind his back to do things because I am not able to get his blessing on the matter. Jeff's simply unable to give that needed feedback.

This afternoon Britt had a softball game at home. Then she and I went out to eat (since I forgot to start anything in the Crock-Pot) and then I went to the Manor to see Jeff.

Wayne bought a cake last week at the Hydro Fair Cake Auction, only the cake he bought wasn't actually there, it was to be made at a later date. For convenience, the German Chocolate cake was delivered today to Jeff at the nursing home. The plan was I could pick it up there and bring it to Wayne and Fern.

I cut Jeff a piece of cake and got him a glass of milk. While I fed him cake, I remembered out loud some of the memories I had of Jeff bidding and buying cakes for Southwest Center Pivots and then sharing the cake at Sunday school the next morning along with a gallon of Braum's milk. Jeff seemed to share the memory with me although he wasn't able to add anything to my one-sided conversation. When I got home and retold the cake story to Brittany, she added that we always forgot to bring the partial jug of milk home after church. We either had to make a trip back to church to get it or do without milk the next morning. A bittersweet memory served with a glass of milk.

Thanks for all the prayers. Keep Wayne and Fern in your prayers as well. Please pray that we can remember the good times and not just the cancer.

> Jesus said unto him, "If thou canst believe, all things are possible to him that believeth." And straightway the father of the child cried out, and said with tears, "Lord, I believe; help thou mine unbelief."
>
> Mark 9:23–24 (KJV)

Transition from Earthly to Eternal

09/05/11 (Monday), 11:13PM-Karen

About six this evening, the nursing home called and left me a message to call them. When I called back, they told me Jeff was having another seizure. I was already headed into town to see Jeff when I got the message. When I arrived, Jeff was still seizing. It was more physical than his seizures in the past, they were unable to give his evening meds that were all oral. They called the hospice to come assess his condition and oversee getting a prescription for something to relax Jeff and/or stop the seizures.

Currently, his pulse is fluctuating between the 80s and the high 150s. They have him on oxygen, and that seems to be keeping his oxygen saturation level stabilized at a good level. They have given Jeff a Valium, and they expect that to allow Jeff to rest.

I have returned home for the evening, but I will check in on Jeff tomorrow morning, and I know that the staff at the Manor will keep a close watch on Jeff during the night. I will update again when I know more.

Thanks for all the prayers.

09/06/11 (Tuesday), 5:44PM–Karen

About nine forty-five this morning, Jeff passed from this feeble life into a wonderful place prepared for him by God Himself (John 14:3). Although our human nature is saddened by the loss of a husband, a father, a brother, a son, we are able to rejoice in spirit that this day, Jeff is present with Christ (2 Corinthians 5:8).

We are confident, I say, and willing rather to be absent from the body, and to be present with the Lord.

2 Corinthians 5:8 (KJV)

"Let not your heart be troubled: ye believe in God, believe also in me. In my Father's house are many mansions: if it were not so, I would have told you. I go to prepare a place for you. And if I go and prepare a place for you, I will come again, and receive you unto myself; that where I am, there ye may be also. And whither I go ye know, and the way ye know." Thomas saith unto him, "Lord, we know not whither thou goest; and how can we know the way?" Jesus saith unto him, "I am the way, the truth, and the life: no man cometh unto the Father, but by me. If ye had known me, ye should have known my Father also: and from henceforth ye know him, and have seen him."

John 14:1–7 (KJV)

Thank you for your prayers for our family during this time.

Things I Remember

Brittany Remembers: The Funeral

There are many things I remember about the day of my dad's funeral. There are many things I don't. I don't remember the time I got up that morning, but I remember my first thought. *I'm fifteen years old, and today, I'm going to bury my father.* I don't remember getting ready, but I remember what I wore. I remember I made sure I had on the necklace Dad brought me from Egypt. I don't remember much about the funeral dinner. I remember I drove my pickup, the one Daddy taught me how to drive. I remember pushing the clutch in and knowing he would have been so proud of me. I don't really remember going back home and getting in the family car to go to the funeral, but I remember the ride into town in the family car. I remember the fear in my grandpa's voice during that ride as he wondered if our family farm and business would survive. God has blessed, and will continue to bless, our businesses. I know that for a fact.

My memories of arriving at the gym are blurred. I remember walking through the tunnel that leads to the floor and realizing this was no pregame walk. During my years of playing sports at Hinton Public Schools, I have many times run onto that very court to cheering hometown fans. That day, however, the gym was filled with different fans. That day the people in the stands were there to celebrate a victory. They had been with our family every step of the way, keeping up with our journey, reading the CarePages updates, etc. The people there that day had been cheering and praying us on from the very beginning. They had watched the two-year game unfold. They had seen the tough breaks and wonderful moments of triumph. They were there for the fifth-quarter celebration. As I walked onto the floor, before I could stop myself from looking around, I saw my softball team. They were all standing together, many with tears running down their faces. It was all too easy for them to see themselves in my shoes. In the blink of an eye, it could have been their mom, their dad. I remember laughing and crying all at the same time during the slideshow. Those pictures helped play back multitudes of memories that are now truly priceless. I remember standing in my high school gym singing "When We All Get to Heaven" with the promise "what a day of rejoicing that will be!" I remember walking out of the gym and greeting hundreds of people who came to celebrate my daddy's life.

I remember the drive to the cemetery. I remember seeing a group of about fifty people who were chopping weeds in a field slowly remove their hats, pause their work, and bow their heads at the passing line of cars. That was a small gesture that has touched my life forever. I remember seeing the mile-long line of dust that filled the air. I remember seeing OSU flags on every fence post surrounding the cemetery. Truly humbling. I remember the sting of my tears falling at the realization of the end of my father's earthly life. Though I will see him in eternity, I will always miss him.

When we got back home after the funeral and were getting food together for supper, someone asked if they could open a new package of something since the old was out of date. I replied, "Definitely. Life's too short." As I was growing up, we always used the phrase "Life's too short for brown bananas." As time went on, it was shortened to "Life's too short." When I said those words that day, everyone in the kitchen turned and looked at me.

Though I will never know the thoughts that went through their minds, I know what went through mine. "Life is short, but this isn't the end. Life will go on." Though my father's life was much shorter than what we would have planned, he lived every single second God intended. He did every task God laid out for him to do. Though to some the final score of the game would show he lost and cancer was victorious, I know scores aren't always a good representation of a team. You have to play the game to the best of your abilities and know that with God on our side, He will take care of the score.

I press toward the mark for the prize of the high calling of God in Christ Jesus. Philippians 3:14 (KJV)

—Brittany Krehbiel (2012, age sixteen)

322

Hope on the Horizon

09/20/11 (Tuesday), 9:50AM-Karen

You have been informed of just about every event in our lives for the past two years. I feel it's appropriate to catch you up on our lives since the last update with information about Jeff on the evening of September 5.

Tuesday morning, I had plans to be in Weatherford at a client's office for the day. I was planning to stop by the nursing home before I went to Weatherford. That was going to work out well. I could zip back and forth to check on Jeff as I wanted and get some work done while he was resting. As I was finishing getting ready, I got a call from Maple Lawn saying that Jeff was having another seizure, and this one seemed more physical than the one the night before. I told them I was about five minutes from leaving anyway and would be there as soon as I could. When I arrived, Jeff was still seizing, but the physical part of the seizure seemed to be over. The head of nursing reviewed with me the signs of active dying that I should expect to see over a period of time. She wanted to make sure I was aware what could happen so that it wouldn't alarm me when/if it did happen. Although I knew there was no possible way for her to know how much time Jeff had left, I asked anyway. She said sometimes a sign will be apparent and then go away. She didn't give me any guideline for time, only said that it could be days, weeks, or even longer—there was no way to know. Once Jeff was calm again, I thought about Brittany and was going to go get her from school so that she could be with me. While we were talking, the active signs seemed to progress. The director of nursing thought I should stay. So I called Brittany's piano teacher and asked her to get Brittany from school and bring her to Hydro so she could be with me.

Although I'm sure more time passed than I was aware of, the signs she reviewed with me seemed to be showing up one right after the other, just as she had told me. Within a few minutes, Jeff's breathing had slowed, and in a few minutes more, it had stopped. It was as though Jeff just stopped breathing and was gone. I received word from a nurse shortly afterward that Brittany and Marsha (piano teacher) were there, and I went to meet her at the door to Jeff's room and tell her that her daddy was gone. There was a sadness that came in that moment—really, it's more a human selfishness that causes the sadness that we no longer have Jeff, husband and father, to share our lives.

I'm thankful Jeff's passing was peaceful. Even at the end, he wasn't in pain. That was definitely answered prayer. Brain cancer could have been a very painful foe. Other than when Jeff was recovering from a surgery or in the hospital, I can only remember four or maybe five times in the last two years that he asked for or accepted pain medicine when it was offered, including Tylenol.

Then on Wednesday morning, September 7, 2011, the day after my husband of twenty-one years died, the sun came up— again. As it has since creation, the earth continues to turn, the sun appears on the horizon, and life moves forward (Genesis 8:22). We still remember, but life will go on—with or without us. It might be easier to sit down and let life pass us by, but then what earthly good would we be to our Heavenly Father if we stopped living because Jeff was called to Heaven before we were?

During the time Jeff and I shared together, he traveled quite a bit. Some trips were more "road trips." He might call me in the middle of the day and tell me he was on his way to Hastings, Nebraska, for parts, and that he would be back tomorrow. Sometimes the trips were planned well in advance and required airline tickets and hotel reservations. At least two of Jeff's trips required a passport and almost a year's worth of planning and scheduling. For his last trip—an intricately planned home going with a spontaneous start—Jeff made arrangements with his maker to completely plan the trip over thirty-two years ago. At the age of fifteen, Jeff accepted Jesus Christ as his personal savior. That acceptance put Jeff's name in the Lamb's Book of Life (Revelation 21:27), and from that point on, Jeff had a reservation to go to heaven.

Although Jeff never knew when the trip would take place, God always knew that Jeff's departure date would be September 6, 2011.

On January 1, 1976, I also placed a reservation for my trip of a lifetime. For Brittany, her name was placed on the passenger list on April 21, 2003. Just like everyone else in the Book, we don't know when we get to go. For now, I like to think of it like Jeff has gone to DC or to South America, and we get to go too, just not now. For Christians, that's how real heaven should be.

Should our pending transport to heaven be so real that we don't grieve? Certainly not. We are still human and somewhat selfish in nature. We want our loved ones with us, or at least, we want to be able to talk to them. Even when Jeff would go to Hastings overnight, I would miss him. Most of our married life, we had cell phones, so I could talk to him anytime I wanted, wherever he was—even when he was in Africa! This last trip, however, is different. There are no cell phones in heaven. I'm pretty sure that is part of the whole Keeping Heaven Perfect plan. If cell phones were there, the coverage issues would cause heaven not to be so heavenly, so I rationalize, there are no cell phones in heaven. I grieve for the companionship that is gone. But I lean on the promise that *"blessed are they that mourn, for they shall be comforted"* (Matthew 5:4, KJV).

Throughout Jeff's battle, we have been gently surrounded by an overwhelming peace. That unexplainable peace continues. For that, we are truly blessed—and thankful. Thank you for your prayers for our family as we transition into the part of our lives where Jeff won't have an audible, visible presence. Sure, we have the history with Jeff to allow us to remember what he would have said, done, or wanted done, but speed dial is no longer an option.

I received a notice in the mail from our health insurance company last week. Apparently, a year of our health insurance premiums for Britt and me will be paid as a survivor benefit to our existing health insurance policy. They automatically issued new cards in my name for the one-year policy, identical coverage to what we had and refunded a prorated portion of September's premium for Jeff that was not used. This was such a huge, unexpected blessing!

Thank you for your continued prayers. God continues to provide peace—what wonderful peace!

> While the earth remaineth, seedtime and harvest, and cold and heat, and summer and winter, and day and night shall not cease.

> Genesis 8:22 (KJV)

> Blessed are they that mourn: for they shall be comforted.

> Matthew 5:4 (KJV)

> Nothing impure will ever enter it, nor will anyone who does what is shameful or deceitful, but only those whose names are written in the Lamb's book of life.

> Revelation 21:27 (NIV)

10/08/11 (Saturday), 12:11PM-Karen

One of Jeff's responsibilities for our church was maintaining the cemetery plot records. When a church member died, he would go to the cemetery and carefully measure and mark the boundaries of the plot. Sometimes the graves were dug by a crew that the funeral home had contacted; sometimes the graves were hand dug, and several times, our hired men used our backhoe to dig the graves. When it was time to dig Jeff's grave, I knew it would be something our hired men would want to do themselves. On the afternoon before Jeff's funeral, a couple of church trustees and our hired men met at our church cemetery, about a mile west of our home, to measure and dig Jeff's grave.

Several times, I went to hold the other end of the tape measure for Jeff when he measured off plots. He wanted it to be perfect. If it was off a little, the next plots would be off even more; and before you know it, the tombstones would not be in a straight line. To know you've done your best is something that creates an unexpressed, internal pride that I don't have words to explain. There is honor and pride in a job done well—even in digging a grave.

Several of these men have since told me that there was no moisture until they had dug past the five-foot depth. Now that comment may seem crude or rude to some of you, but if you know that I have heard comments of that nature in our home on numerous occasions, it really was something I wanted to know. "How was the moisture of the soil?" It's kind of a drought monitor of sorts. Jeff would say, "When So-and-So died, there wasn't any moisture until about three feet." All that said, our soil is dry. We have been in this drought situation for over two years.

But there is hope on the horizon. This morning, there are rain clouds in the west, and we are once again prayerful that God will send rain on our land.

I find it somewhat interesting that Jeff's cancer battle has been during a drought. Both were situations that outsiders would view as sad, discouraging, and a time to throw up our hands and quit. But as Christians, we have a hope that the world, without Christ, won't understand. We have known that both the rain and the physical healing could come only at God's command. There is a reason that Jeff's physical healing didn't come on earth. I may never know what the reason was, but that doesn't change my trust that there is a reason, and my submission to God's will for our lives. As for the drought? Again, I don't know why. I trust that there is a reason and know that God will sustain us *through* the dry valley as well.

During Jeff's cancer battle, we were not alone. God, through the Holy Spirit, has sustained us. He has given us an ever-present help in our times of need (Hebrews 4:16) and a lasting peace that surpasses human understanding (Philippians 4:7). As Christians, that indescribable peace I have written about on several occasions is just one attribute of the Holy Spirit in our lives. Galatians 5:22–23 lists peace as fruit of the Holy Spirit. As Christians, we have a hope that is literally uncrushable—the promise of eternal life. No matter how dry the *"valley of the shadow of death"* (Psalm 23 NIV), no matter how lonesome the journey without Jeff, no matter how long we wait for rain, I know I don't walk alone. God will walk with me and provide the funding, the materials, the mental stability that I need as His servant to do the tasks he sets before me.

As real as the rain clouds are in the west, heaven is a valid promise on the horizon. I dare not wallow in grief. I press on. There is work yet to be done for my master today.

> Let us then approach the throne of grace with confidence, so that we may receive mercy and find grace to help us in our time of need.
>
> Hebrews 4:16 (NIV)

> And the peace of God, which passeth all understanding, shall keep your hearts and minds through Christ Jesus.
>
> Philippians 4:7 (KJV)

> But the fruit of the Spirit is love, joy, peace, patience, kindness, goodness, faithfulness, gentleness and selfcontrol. Against such things there is no law.
>
> Galatians 5:22–24 (NIV)

> The Lord will guide you always;
>
> he will satisfy your needs in a sun-scorched land and will strengthen your frame.
>
> You will be like a well-watered garden, like a spring whose waters never fail.
>
> Isaiah 58:11 (NIV)

> To be continued eternally…

ENDNOTES

1   "checkonjeff" was the name of our patient site on CarePages.

2   10-20-10 is an agricultural fertilizer with a breakdown of 10% Nitrogen, 20% Phosphorous 10% Potassium and 50% inert matter. This was Jeff's wit in prime form.

3   Stanphill, *I Know Who Holds Tomorrow.*

4   See note 3 above.

5   Jean Bradford, *Lord I Need You, Again Today.*

6   Tim James, and Doug Johnson, *Love Like Crazy.*

7   See note 3 above.

8   B.B. McKinney, *Have Faith in God.*

As a leader in the wheat industry, Jeff was often called upon to give interviews for radio and newspaper. This photo taken on "Jeff's Place" during one such interview captures Jeff checking the quality of the grain in the wheat head in the middle of a field just prior to harvest.

Jeff and Karen's Wedding July 21, 1990

A 1985 graduate of Oklahoma State University, Jeff had
a lifelong passion for OSU football. Taken in December
2008, this photo reflects Jeff's pride in his Cowboys!

Brittany and Jeff in Union Station, Washington D.C. Spring 2009

Jeff and his Dad, Wayne with the sheep herd. Jeff was the fourth generation to farm family land. Jeff's great grandfather purchased the family's first land in Oklahoma by trading a team of horses and a wagon loaded with corn for 160 acres of farmland.

Jeff and Karen in Bricktown during Oklahoma Farm Bureau Annual Convention in Oklahoma City, December 2004. Once opposed to wearing any necktie at all, Jeff eventually developed quite a collection of ties that he wore to board meetings and to church.

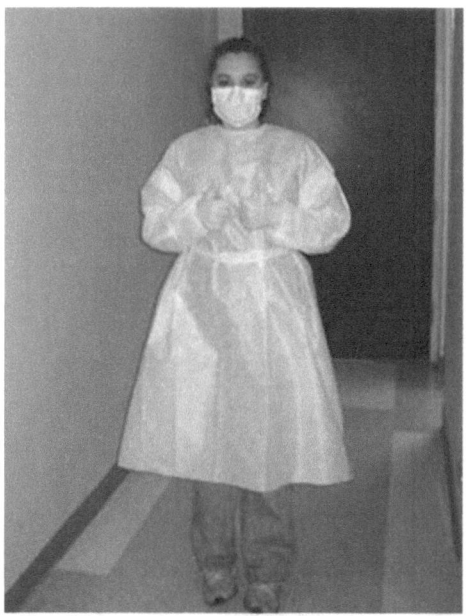

Brittany wearing the gown, gloves and mask required to
visit Dad December 4, 2009. During the Christmas 2009
hospital stay, Jeff's white blood count stood literally at zero for
multiple days, severely compromising his immune system.

Brittany's 15th birthday party in September 2010 was
the last of her birthday's Jeff would celebrate. Ironically,
the steroids prescribed to reduce the swelling in Jeff's
brain caused swelling in his face and neck.

Jeff visiting progress of new dam construction on "Jeff's Place"
on the way home from his first surgery September 2009

Jeff the morning of his last hunting trip November 28, 2009

The Krehbiel Family on the steps of the Capitol,
Washington D.C Spring 2009

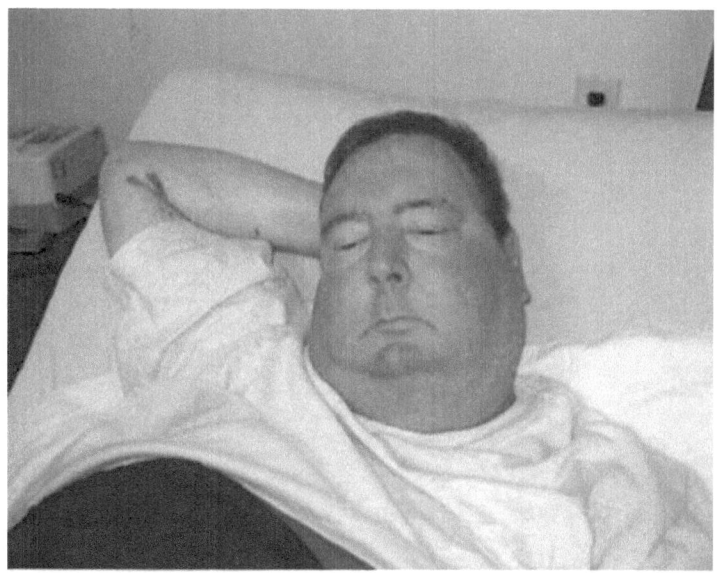

Jeff at Maple Lawn Manor in April 2011. Although Jeff never lost all his hair, it slowly changed from grey to jet black.

Jeff and Brittany enjoying a cold Bedlam Baseball Game between OSU and OU at the Bricktown Ballpark in Oklahoma City, May 2004

Karen and Brittany Krehbiel Christmas 2011

Early after Jeff's diagnosis, Brittany voiced concern that
her dad might not live to see her graduate from eighth
grade. This photo reflects a major milestone.

Jeff and "His Girls" at Red Rock Canyon a few miles from
the family home, July 2007. Jeff often asked readers to pray
for his wife and daughter referring to them as "my girls".

Jeff was proud to serve the wheat industry as an Oklahoma
Wheat Commissioner. Here he was serving fresh cinnamon
rolls 2006 at Septemberfest, an annual agricultural promotion
on the lawn of the Oklahoma Governor's Mansion.

In addition to farming, the family sells and installs T-L brand irrigation systems. This photo used as the family's Christmas card for 2000 showcases the family's love of agriculture.

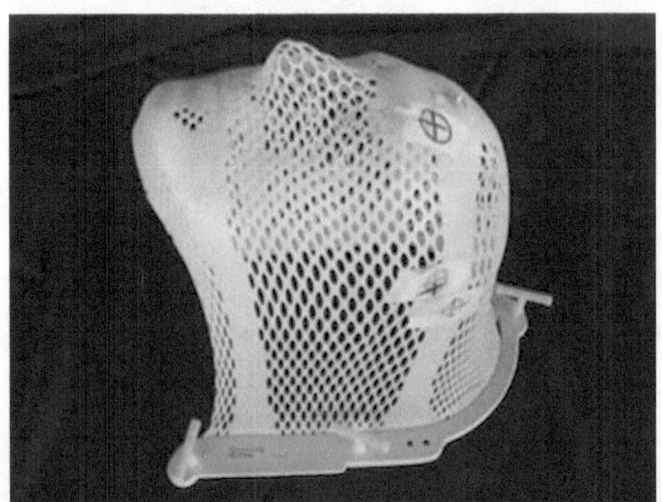

Prior to radiation treatment, Jeff was fitted with a mesh plastic facial harness that would be placed over his head and bolted to the treatment table for each radiation session to ensure the precision of the radiation placement. This mask became quite tight as Jeff gained facial mass due to steroid prescriptions.

www.ingramcontent.com/pod-product-compliance
Lightning Source LLC
Chambersburg PA
CBHW021702120626
46545CB00004B/1358